THE BOOK OF
HOMERSFIELD

SOUVENIR of HOMERSFIELD

XMAS
GREETINGS
from
HOMERSFIELD
Sweet thoughts and kindest wishes
Are the burden of my lay
May they all be ever with you,
Guide and cheer you on
your way.

KEN PALMER

HALSGROVE

First published in Great Britain in 2007

British Library Cataloguing-in-Publication Data.
A CIP record for this title is available from the British Library.

ISBN 97818 4114 629 4

HALSGROVE

Halsgrove House
Rylands Industrial Estate
Bagley Road, Wellington
Somerset TA21 9PZ
T: 01823 653777
F: 01823 216796
Email: sales@halsgrove.com
Website: www.halsgrove.com

Printed in Great Britain by CPI Antony Rowe Ltd., Wiltshire

For Mum and Dad
In memory of childhood holidays

Foreword

Being asked to write a foreword to this book about Homersfield has given me great pleasure and brought back many memories.

It was a great surprise when a letter arrived for my mother from her sister, who lived in London, telling us that she was hoping to buy a cottage in Suffolk. 'Going back to our roots', was my mother's comment, as my grandparents and great-grandparents had farmed in and around Peasenhall and Heveningham. Although I had never been to Suffolk, I had always felt I knew its people and traditions because of the stories my grandfather had told me as a child.

My first view of Homersfield was from a small branch line railway carriage in the early summer of 1952. My mother and I had come from our home in south Essex via Liverpool Street Station to Ipswich, where we changed to get to Tivetshall and then to the two-carriage train which stopped at each station. At every stop, villagers left and joined us, very often having been to market, so that there were coops of chickens and hutches of rabbits, dogs of every size, enormous baskets of fruit and vegetables, delicious looking cakes and pies and much chatter. It seemed everyone knew everyone else, but we were greeted with politeness, if a little warily.

My Auntie Annie Welton met us on the platform of Homersfield Station and we all walked across the bridge over the River Waveney, flanked by young reeds, past the Black Swan and towards the village green. Everything seemed so peaceful and pretty.

The green was quite small, triangular in shape, with three beautiful mature trees, signposts to St Cross straight ahead, and Flixton and Bungay to the left. As is usual, the houses and cottages, some of which were thatched, were gathered around the green, along with the traditional almshouses and small general store-cum-Post Office and a telephone box. Further along was the Mill House, and at the top of an incline the quite large church and graveyard. The village had obviously been a thriving farming community at one time, a part of the large Flixton estate.

My auntie's thatched cottage was opposite the green, with the garden running right down to the river. It was to be named 'Plumtree Cottage' because of its similarity to her mother's childhood home, Plumtree Farm, in Heveningham. Everything was delightful, and since, in subsequent years, I have made visits to Homersfield with my husband and daughters, the village is very special to us, with many happy memories.

Brenda Meachen
March 2003

Village Green, Homersfield.   No. 3360.

A postcard sent by Annie Welton to a friend, c.1954.

4

CONTENTS

Foreword   4

Acknowledgements   6

Introduction   7

Chapter 1   Once Upon A Time...   11

Chapter 2   Foreigners   17

Chapter 3   Domesday is Coming   25

Chapter 4   Church Matters   31

Chapter 5   From Pillar to Post   47

Chapter 6   Christmas Day in the Workhouse   55

Chapter 7   The Big House   61

Chapter 8   The Best Days of Our Lives   73

Chapter 9   Only Two Things in Life are Certain...   83

Chapter 10 The Three Rs   91

Chapter 11 A Victorian Perambulation   109

Chapter 12 Acts of God   127

Chapter 13 The Swinging Sixties   135

Chapter 14 The Twentieth Century and Beyond   151

Sources   157

Subscribers   159

Acknowledgements

In a book such as this, there are necessarily many acknowledgements that need to be made. First and foremost, I must thank Halsgrove for giving me the opportunity of fulfilling a dream; also, Mrs Brenda Meachen, niece of the late Annie Welton, who kindly wrote the foreword and supplied many photos. I owe thanks also to all those who were willing for me to photograph their pictures and documents over the years. Some deserve a special mention: Frank Honeywood, the Bungay Recorder, who allowed me to copy many photographs from his huge archive; Charmian Smy, daughter of the late Rosalys Skene, some of whose priceless photographs were a mandatory inclusion; Harry Bedborough, proprietor of the village shop in the latter half of the 1960s; Leighten Ball, formerly of the Black Swan; Glen Earl, who has an excellent selection of local views; also Lady Darell, who kindly allowed me to photograph her personal collection. Mrs Mary Rackham, daughter of the late Mrs Adlington of Alburgh, kindly gave permission to use some of her mother's photographs. I would also like to thank Mrs Hilda Rowe and Ms Diane Poppy for providing information and photographs relating to the Poppy family of Heath Farm. Mr and Mrs Les Riches entertained me with stories, equipped me with useful information from more modern times and put names to many faces.

Erik Goldstein kindly gave permission to use material from his book on the arms once owned by the Adair family at Flixton Hall.

The photos, figures and some of the text used in connection with the Roman face mask, Roman kiln, and individuals appearing in the court held in Homersfield Church are reproduced, with kind permission, from the *Proceedings of the Suffolk Institute of Archaeology*, specific details of which are listed in the Sources.

Thanks are extended to Mr John Fairclough and Mr Michael Hardy, who gave permission to use material in their book *Thornham and the Waveney Valley*; the latter I must similarly thank in relation to the book *Village Appraisal with Stories Relating to Life in Wortwell* (again, details are listed in the Sources).

The Homersfield and Limbourne Domesday entries have been reproduced from *Domesday Book: Suffolk* (Chichester 1986), general editor John Morris, volume editor Alex Rumble, by kind permission of the publisher, Phillimore & Co. Ltd, Shopwyke Manor Barn, Chichester, Sussex, PO20 2BG, www.phillimore.co.uk.

I must thank Norfolk Record Office for their assistance and for allowing me to quote text and include photos of some documents.

In carrying out much of the research, staff at the Suffolk Record Office in Lowestoft have been consistently helpful in relation to endless trips to the strongroom, with my questions and requests for help, and have suffered my deranged sense of humour with amazing grace and few or no visible signs of stress (or distress).

Last, and by no means least, I must thank Sue Harris, who suggested many corrections and improvements to the text the whole time this work was in preparation, and who helped with the selection of photographs and proof-read the final text. She also accompanied me on virtually every excursion while compiling this book; without her help, it would have been a lot longer in the making and a great deal less enjoyable.

To anyone I have inadvertently omitted to mention, I offer my sincere apologies and equally sincere thanks.

Every effort has been made to ascertain copyright ownership of material used. For any infringement of said copyright, which is entirely accidental and unintentional, the author sincerely apologises.

Notes

Capitalisation and spellings have been retained when quoting from original documents. Additions of my own within quoted text are in square brackets, e.g. '[no longer applicable]'.

Until 1752 the calendar year did not run from 1 January to 31 December as it does now, but from 25 March (Lady Day) to 24 March, and a date falling between 1 January and 24 March would (by our present calendar), have taken place a year later than actually recorded. Where relevant, these dates are shown, for example, as 25 February 1725/26.

Our currency for hundreds of years prior to decimalisation in 1971 was in the form £1 = 20s. (shillings) = 240d. (pence). A guinea was 21s.

Land measurements in older documents are often expressed in acres, roods and perches. An acre is 4,840 square yards; there are four roods to an acre, and 40 perches to a rood. A perch was defined as a square $5\frac{1}{2}$yds in length and breadth, or $30\frac{1}{4}$ square yards.

Those villages dedicated to a saint refer to South Elmham unless otherwise indicated. Abbreviations included are as follows: NRO (Norfolk Record Office), SRO(L) (Suffolk Record Office (Lowestoft)).

Introduction

I first came to Homersfield with my parents and paternal grandparents in the summer of 1964. I was ten years old, it was my first ever holiday and I had been looking forward to it for weeks and weeks. Dad worked with a lady who had a friend that let her cottage to family and friends. Advertising was all done by word of mouth, and when the cottage was occupied, she stayed in a green caravan half way down the garden. I knew the cottage was very old, thatched, and had a river at the bottom of the garden. I was keen on fishing then, and had been reading in the *Angling Times* about large catches from the Waveney in weeks preceding the holiday. It sounded perfect. It was.

As we age, we wear out, and our recollections of times past are not exempted from this unwelcome fact of life. Time progressively distorts our distant memories, but to this day I can remember, as though it were yesterday, dad driving into the village for the first time on a very hot summer's Saturday afternoon, past the white walls of an attractive semi-circular group of thatched almshouses, and on towards the green, where he spotted our accommodation for the following week. As we pulled up outside the house, Miss Welton was standing in her front garden, talking to her neighbour. Upon seeing her new guests arrive she bade a goodbye to Mrs Calver, and, as is customary in this part of England, welcomed us into her cottage via the back door. Upon entering, we passed through a tiny lobby into the kitchen, where she had placed a plate of neatly arranged fairy cakes on a small table. She made us a pot of tea, chatted to us for a while and then walked down the path to her caravan, leaving us to enjoy our holiday. I remember too, standing in the doorway between the kitchen and the sitting-room, looking at all the dark beams. It was the first time I had ever been inside a really old house, and even at that very young age, I fell in love with it instantly. The rest of the house had a similar impact on me, the weather all that week was what an English summer should be, and as well as having trips out to villages and towns

The author with Annie Welton and Tessa at the bottom of her garden, taken by the author's father in 1967.

that were new to all of us, I, dad, and granddad caught over 300 fish during the week. It was with some reluctance that I left the cottage the following Saturday morning to return home, but we returned each year, sometimes more than once. In all, we came to the cottage 15 times, sometimes for a week or a long weekend, and on one occasion, for two weeks. As well as my parents and I, all four grandparents and an aunt came with us over the years. It was with

Greenview and Plumtree Cottage in the summer of 1967.
(PHOTO TAKEN BY THE AUTHOR'S FATHER.)

much sadness that we came to the cottage in 1970 knowing it was for the last time. Miss Welton was getting older, the village shop had closed and her cousin's husband in Bungay had died, leaving her his house in Bridge Street. Reluctantly, she decided to sell her little cottage in Homersfield and move to the town. In so doing, our holidays in the country came to an end. For me, the impact these holidays had on me was such that anywhere else afterwards just wasn't the same. After a holiday here, it always took me several weeks to get back into my normal routine of going to school, homework, exams., my newspaper round and other such things of everyday life then.

We never forgot the village and our holidays, and would come back to Homersfield every now and then when my parents and I had a day out, stopping to talk to Bunny at the garage opposite the Black Swan, where dad used to park his car when we came to stay in the cottage. Time marches on much too quickly, and much water flowed under Homersfield Bridge as well as under mine during the next two decades or so after we last came to stay. After I had bought my first home, I then moved to Norfolk, to an old thatched house that was once three cottages. I moved again twice during the next few years, ending up in another thatched house in the west of Suffolk. Now and then I would drive over to Homersfield, hoping I would see a 'For Sale' board in the front garden of the cottage I adored. I never did. But after I'd been to the village, I would always go to Bungay and buy the *Beccles and Bungay Journal* from Martin's

Miss Annie Welton (centre) with the author's paternal grandparents and parents, 1967.

A view of the green, taken by the author's grandfather in the summer of 1968.

Annie Welton's old home, 1990.

newsagents, hoping I would see an estate agent advertising the cottage for sale. One day, I did.

The cottage is my fifth home and is intended to be the last before one of the two things in life that are certain takes effect and I go to rest in the churchyard 100 yards away. Dad said he always thought I wouldn't settle anywhere until I'd bought it. I never dreamt I would. Wanting it and actually buying it are two very different things that don't very often coincide; it is a remarkable story and to put it mildly, I have been exceedingly lucky.

Most of us have some regrets in our short lives, and I confess I am not devoid of that common human characteristic. My one regret where Homersfield is concerned is that I was not able to bring Miss Welton back to see her cottage before she embarked on her final journey from Bungay to Homersfield churchyard. I was a mere 15 months too late in a life which had lasted nearly 89½ years.

The enormous impact that she, the cottage and this village had on my young life meant that during the period when I stayed at the cottage, I had already decided I would like to write its history someday and hopefully have it published. I collected information for many years before I had the opportunity of coming to live here, and amassed a large repository of documents, photographs and the odd film or two. But realistically I always thought it would be just a dream.

A mailing sent to some parish council clerks in East Anglia initially brought Halsgrove to my attention. I will be eternally grateful to this company that has done much in recent years to publicise local history, but primarily of course, for giving me the chance of fulfilling the dream.

It became ominously apparent, after only a short time spent conducting serious research for this book, that the main problem would not be what to include, but rather what to omit. On reflection, I am not sure which qualifies as the less desirable of the two, but I veer towards the latter. That short period of time enabled me to accumulate enough material for several more books, and I would estimate that a further 15–20 years' work lies ahead of me before my research is complete, at which point, God willing, I will be in a position to publish a complete history of Homersfield.

In writing this book, I have chosen a selection of topics which I hope will be of interest to the majority of those who are likely to read it, and if they derive only a very small percentage of the pleasure I have had researching it, then it will have been entirely worthwhile.

Ken Palmer
Homersfield, March 2007

Agricultural labourers at Flixton, c.1910.
(REPRODUCED BY KIND PERMISSION OF GLEN EARL.)

A delightful group of children pose for the camera, with the Post Office and Waveney House behind, c.1912. The small building with the sloping roof housed the mail cart.

The Dove, c.1910. Although not strictly in Homersfield, for many years it was referred to as such.

Homersfield railway station, c.1925.

The Black Swan, seen from near the bridge, c.1913.

A rather muddy corner of Church Lane, with a field behind the thatched cottage, c.1905.

Two newly built houses (Swan Cottages) with the police house (No. 68) in the background, c.1905.

CHAPTER 1

Once Upon A Time...

ROCKS AND STUFF

Suffolk As We Know It

The soil which would become known as the Land of the South Folk looked very different half a million years ago. Britain was a long way from becoming an island and at that time formed a peninsula jutting out of Europe. A massive river, flowing over the majority of Suffolk from the London area, had developed continually over a long period of time. A few tens of thousands of years later, the river was enveloped and virtually the whole area covered by a huge sheet of ice, hundreds of yards thick. The ice-sheet crawled forward over clay and silt containing flint and chalk, smoothing and flattening the land beneath, resulting in the generally level appearance of Suffolk and Norfolk today. The thick glacial sediment underlying these soils is called 'Lowestoft till', or boulder clay. As the sheet melted, the resulting huge volume of water ran in fast-flowing torrents which created channels and carried silt in their paths. Larger materials were dragged by the flowing water and, together with huge quantities of sand and small stones, were deposited at random, forming large areas of gravel over a period of time. The channels developed into valleys as more and more water flowed through them, eroding the land continuously. One such channel was responsible for creating the Waveney Valley. The river, now quite sluggish, is immensely different from when it first flowed. Thousands of years of natural weather patterns have modified the terrain still further since the end of the last ice age, producing the landscape we see now.

There have been several cold periods, or ice ages, in Britain's history. In the intervening warm periods, plants and trees populated the landscape. Coniferous forests once covered Suffolk and, as deposits of decomposing matter improved the soil quality, the conifers were gradually superseded by other species, such as lime and oak. The more open vistas which appeared as the soil was gradually drained of its nutrients were sustained through the next cold period The most recent period of intense cold descended on Britain around 24,000 years ago and lasted for about 9,000 years; we are currently enjoying one of the intervening warmer periods.

The sea level was around 65 yards below its current level during the last ice age, and man could walk from Suffolk to Denmark or Holland. As the ice age ended and it became warmer, so the sea level rose correspondingly, until, about 8,000–9,000 years ago, Britain became an island, possibly not for the first time. Though the coastline extended a little into what is now the sea, Suffolk's basic form could then be seen.

Rocks

In Suffolk, chalk, a relatively soft material, is the main rock to be found below ground. A mass of calcareous material at the bottom of the sea was responsible for its formation between 70 and 100 million years ago. Changes in the earth deep underground resulted in the chalk being raised from the sea, and flint was created from the remains of sponges and minute sea creatures. Lumps of flint, regularly found within the chalk, can be seen everywhere in Suffolk soil in the form of nodules and rounded stones, the latter the product of natural erosion.

Most of Suffolk is covered with deposits from ancient ice ages. When the ice sheets disappeared they left a generally flat plain with occasional hollows and, as the temperature gradually rose, these filled and became lakes. Deposits from one such lake have been found locally at South Elmham. One glacier travelled from central England and brought large quantities of chalk and clay. The debris from this ice sheet (the Lowestoft till), has a greyish or brownish hue with pieces of chalk embedded in it. Within or beneath this clay can also be found gravel deposits which, above the current valley bottom, are indicators of ancient plains.

Soil local to Homersfield has generally been produced from the boulder clay deposits left by the receding ice sheets. These loamy, nutrient-rich deposits cover much of the county.

Dem Bones, Dem Bones...

Life forms existed for around 3,800 million years before man appeared. Backboned animals appeared about 230 million years ago. In prehistoric times large animals were prolific throughout Britain, and the leopards, lions and hyenas at that time were virtually indistinguishable from those living today. Other animals were much larger than their living descendants – the straight-tusked elephant stood 12ft at the shoulder. The mammoth, hippopotamus and giant deer lived here, as did two species of rhinoceros, elk, auroch (an extinct type of cattle), bears, wolves and the sabre-toothed cat, among many others. Some lived here during warm periods and moved south once the temperature began to drop, their place being taken by others capable of surviving the cold. Many were extinct before man appeared.

A small proportion of animal bones have survived the passing of time – how well depending on the material in which they are embedded. Those in acidic soil often leave nothing more than a dark stain in the surrounding soil, while others are incredibly well preserved.

Many ancient bones and other fossils, dating from hundreds of thousands of years ago, have been found in Homersfield, many in the gravel pit next to the church or in the commercially run pits which have operated for some years in what was once part of Flixton Hall park. Huge quantities of sand and gravel were taken from Homersfield during the Second World War for use in constructing local airfields, and many fossils of now extinct animals were found by workmen during the course of extractions. Many more finds occurred in the 1950s and 1960s. Bones that have been unearthed include part of the jaw and skull of a woolly rhinoceros (*Coelodonta antiquus*), rib and limb bones from a species of elephant (*Elephas*), vertebrae from a rhinoceros (*Rhinoceros antiquitatis*), the pelvis and leg bones of a species of horse (*Equus ferus*), antler fragments from a reindeer (*Rangifer tarandus*), bison or auroch bones and the complete skull of a giant deer (*Megaloceros giganteus*). Tusks from the woolly mammoth (*Mammuthus primigenius*) have been uncovered, as have teeth from several animals, including horse (*Equus caballus*), rhinoceros and woolly mammoth. The larger mammoth molars can weigh over a stone!

THE DAWN OF CIVILISATION

Palaeolithic/Old Stone Age (c.500,000–10,000BC)

Earlier species of man, using crude stone tools and weapons, are known to have lived in parts of Africa two and a half million years ago. He was there for a very long time, spreading outward over one and a half million years to reach the warm northern hemisphere of Europe. As far as is currently known, *Homo heidelbergensis*, a predecessor of modern man, set foot in Britain half a million years ago (in Sussex), although there is little evidence of him having been in Suffolk, most of which was then covered by the ancient river known today as the Thames. It was to be a further 150,000 years before he appeared here.

The people who lived here spent their lives hunting and gathering food. There was plenty of the latter to be found in our region, particularly along the river valleys and in woodlands, and the animals which roamed here in warm and cold periods which

supplied a large and varied diet. As well as huge numbers of game birds, several animals now extinct in Britain or globally were hunted; the long list includes mammoth, the woolly rhinoceros, the straight-tusked elephant, bison, horse, bear, lion, hippopotamus, hyena, monkey, wolf, red deer, pig, otter, beaver and even the tiny vole. They also ate fish and were adept at catching them. The non-meat part of their diet, generally found in woods, comprised fruits, nuts and some plant roots.

The large hand-axes used by these people, often symmetrical, heavy and pointed, were used for cutting up birds, fish and animals. Many worked flints of the Palaeolithic period have been found, mostly in river gravels. A number found on one site at Hoxne in 1797 included hand-axes which were at the very edge of an ancient lake. Hand-axes found in Homersfield include one found in a gravel pit in 1962 by Wing Commander Franklin, then landlord of the Black Swan. People in this area were making axes up to nine inches long, ideal both for cutting up carcases and for working wood. These people had other flint tools – scrapers were used to extract the very last scraps of meat from animal hides. Little was wasted of any slaughtered animal, bones were used to make needles and other implements, while the skins were used for making clothing and, possibly, shelters – there were no ready-made caves to move into!

In the Old Stone Age the species of trees which grew here changed with the alternating cold and warm periods. The oak, yew and elm which grew here in warm times were replaced by pine and birch when temperatures plummeted.

From around 200,000 years ago, during a cold phase, it is thought, most of those living here moved a long way south to escape the unbearable temperatures. After 150,000 years, during which time the land was largely the kingdom of the animals, man eventually returned. Modern man, *Homo sapiens*, appeared in Europe about 35,000 years ago and, roughly 21,000 years later, there was human settlement in this area once again.

Mesolithic/Middle Stone Age (c.10,000–5,000BC)

The Middle Stone Age commenced at the end of the last glaciation and continued existence ceased to depend on constant hunting and gathering. By the beginning of this period, the Lowestoft till had arrived, the river valleys were much as they are now and there was an abundance of birch, pine and willow trees. Some of the animals once hunted, including the woolly rhinoceros and the mammoth, were now extinct, and the climate had improved sufficiently to attract deer and horses to Britain. Where there are animals, there is food, and groups of migrants from Europe, particularly from Denmark and Germany, hunted together.

However, from around 9,000BC the population was subjected to another very cold period of about 700 years. Towards the end of it the temperature started rising and there is evidence for human occupation in Suffolk. Hunting implements have been found, including barbed antlers and bones, some with tips hardened by fire. Men made long blades from flint, along with scrapers and other tools for working antlers and bones. Sites in the Waveney Valley have yielded discarded flint slivers. As the climate warmed, dense oak, lime, hazel and elm woodland appeared, and reindeer, grouse and hare were to be seen here. Over a significant period, these animals were superseded by aurochs, giant elk, wild pigs, badgers and cats, among others. Attracted by the increased warmth, more animals roamed here than in the preceding cold phase. The sea level rose and, c.6,500BC, Britain became an island. Although this restricted animal movement it also reduced the hunting grounds, seriously impacting on communities. Reindeer became extinct here and red deer became an important component of the local diet.

A new kind of axe, the hafted, or tranchet axe, came into being and new technology in the shape of microliths (very small barbs) was used on hunting spears and arrows, which, no doubt, were often coated with lethal poison. Saws were made by inserting several of these flint barbs into a wood or bone holder. The Homersfield area was certainly inhabited at this time, as evidence of human activity has been found in Flixton, by the river, and also in some South Elmham villages. Post holes have been found, indicating shelter of some kind, and blackened soil shows where fires once burned. In this relatively short period advances in know-how and technology were huge in comparison to the much longer period that had preceded it. It is generally regarded as a time when people were often on the move, hunting and collecting food, though more recent finds have shown evidence of early settlements.

Neolithic/New Stone Age (c.5,000–2,350BC)

In the New Stone Age came many changes, most notably the introduction of farming. Neolithic farmers cleared wooded areas with fire and polished flint axe-heads (some have been found along the Waveney Valley), which were used to cut timber for housing made of wood, daub and thatch. The undergrowth was burned and the soil broken up with wooden ploughs for the growing of such crops as emmer wheat, barley, einkorn and some vegetables. Fields were probably enclosed for keeping goats, cattle and sheep, with the surviving woodland housing pigs. The nutrient-rich soil, further enriched with potash from fire ash, would have produced excellent crops for several years before it was drained of goodness. Understandably, the first farmers did

not understand that you get back what you put in, and consequently would simply have moved to another site once crops started to be less prolific.

Hunting with bows and arrows, with leaf-shaped flint arrowheads, supplied additional food, typically red and roe deer, the antlers of which provided further material for tools. High-quality flint scrapers were used for cleaning animal skins to use as clothing. Animal bones were put to various uses, including as needles and very crude musical pipes. Some tools were also made. The numerous finds in South Elmham of axe-heads, scrapers and arrowheads suggest considerable activity in this area.

Another innovative introduction by Neolithic man was of pottery, used for cooking and storage. The vessels were made using local clay with fragments of flint added to prevent cracking during firing in a simple kiln. Sherds found in the landscape now provide valuable evidence of occupation. Such sites can be dated from the pottery found and are always near water with a clay source nearby. As the clay pots could not withstand high temperatures, cooking was achieved by heating piles of flints and transferring them with crude wooden tongs into pots of water. The water would boil instantly without destroying the vessels, and meat or vegetables were cooked by repetition of the process.

By around 4,000BC buildings of larger proportions were being constructed, including long barrows (most of which have been ploughed out of recognition in relatively modern times) and causewayed enclosures. The exact purpose of the latter is still unknown, although various possiblities are that they were meeting-places, markets, or places where the dead were cremated. Boarded walkways and palisades were also constructed.

Neolithic people in Suffolk traded with those in the north of England; the polished flints used in making hand-axes came from two separate areas, the Lake District and the extreme south-west of England. Flint tools were also being made relatively locally, in the mines at Grimes Graves, Norfolk, during most of the third millenium BC.

A few settlements have been located in Suffolk, each consisting of a number of post-holes and pits. A settlement was normally established in an area close to water but free from flooding. One such site, adjacent to the Waveney, was close to Flixton, where there are indications of a burial site. The burial mounds would have been clearly visible from long distances when first constructed. Another site has been found in quarrying areas in Flixton Park, consisting of a number of pits and post-holes, probably of the late-Neolithic period.

The Bronze Age (c.2,350–800BC)

Another major change took place in man's way of life when metal tools and weapons were introduced.

Bronze-Age axe-heads found in Homersfield.

A Bronze-Age dagger, found near the two axe-heads.

Bronze, an alloy of copper and tin, was the first metal to be used, although flint arrowheads, knives and scrapers were still made for some considerable time. Around the same time as bronze was introduced, Beaker ware (drinking vessels of a new kind of pottery), commonly highly decorated with complex patterns, also made an appearance. The discovery of bronze waste indicates that some of these people were skilled and made tools using moulds.

The quantity of artefacts uncovered over the years very much suggests the Waveney Valley was actively farmed along much of its course, and probably much woodland was cleared. During the Bronze Age, as temperatures started to fall and rainfall increased, some farmers may well have switched from growing wheat, barley and flax to rearing pigs, cattle and sheep. It was a time of much trading, and farmers would no doubt have constantly aimed to produce an excess of crops or animals which they could then barter or exchange for other goods.

The fields in the Saints, comprising the four Ilketshalls, the seven South Elmhams, Homersfield, Flixton and a few other villages, run noticeably parallel along an axis intersected by more or less parallel hedging, occasionally bounded by lanes. Other than some fields having been made larger, these have existed in their original form for some considerable time. This pattern is extremely similar to the Bronze Age reaves found on Dartmoor, the principal difference being that field boundaries there are stone walls rather than ditches and/or hedging. Whilst there is continuing debate among archaeologists as to the precise age of these fields, it is nevertheless possible that they date back to this period.

Bronze Age settlements are seldom found, but it appears that, while roundhouses were built, they may not have been lived in all year round. Animals may have been grazed on damp meadows in the summer months and the people lived on drier land in the wet winters.

In Suffolk have been found round barrow burial mounds dating from the early years of the Bronze Age, those which have been destroyed showing up as ring-ditch crop marks. Barrows are associated with areas of lighter soil, and the claylands found in the vicinity of Homersfield mean that there have been virtually no barrow finds in the region, although ring-ditches have been located at nearby Flixton and Mendham. Those barrows which have been excavated reveal either the bones or ashes of a variable number of burials, from one to a dozen or more.

In later times, burial customs changed and cemeteries came into being – sites level with the ground rather than raised and containing cremations (small depressions or pits with inverted pots under which can be found the ashes). So far such cemeteries have been found in the south-west of Suffolk only, while in other parts of the county cremated bones in pottery urns have been found, typically, near water.

Bronze Age man, whose lifespan was typically less than half that experienced today, certainly lived in Homersfield, as artefacts dating from the period have been found in the parish. On the outskirts of the village were found axes and a dagger, together with an arrowhead and a partial spearhead. Beaker pottery has been unearthed near the site of the Roman pottery kiln.

The Iron Age (c.800BC to AD43)

The introduction of iron 1,000 years ago heralded a new era of technology in Britain. The changeover from the Bronze Age to the Iron Age was gradual and, unlike other eras, there was no clear point when

A view towards the bridge from the green, c.1903.

A tranquil river view, with the rear of the mill at centre right, c.1905.

A very smart gentleman in boating attire (although lacking a lady companion) on the river near Mendham Lane, c.1905.

An almost complete view of Homersfield Bridge, with the village centre in the background, c.1935.

Homersfield Bridge about 35 years after its construction, with the village centre in the background.

one ended and the other began. There was the widespread manufacture of tools and weapons, now from iron in preference to bronze, the use of which quickly declined. The same patterns of settlement, which tended to be on lighter soils, continued, but also now included the claylands that covered much of Suffolk. The people lived in roundhouses, like their predecessors, with their fields close by. From the beginning of the Iron Age, increasing quantities of land were farmed and there is evidence of pits being used for the storage of cereals. Flour was produced by grinding wheat in mills operated manually. Fields were regularly improved by the scattering of all kinds of domestic waste, including human and animal dung and surplus vegetable matter.

Water has always been an important factor in deciding where to settle or graze animals, and in areas devoid of natural rivers, streams and ponds, rabbits were prevalent in the landscape. It was during this period that drove roads first came into being. Through their repeated use they evolved into accepted routes for moving animals from one grazing to another or for taking them to and from market.

Towards the end of the Iron Age, fields were cultivated for the first time with wheeled ploughs pulled by teams of several oxen, brought from overseas in around 100BC by the same Belgic tribes who introduced the potter's wheel and gold and silver coinage.

The Iron Age is, possibly, the time when people first grouped themselves together in significant numbers, and these groups of people, known as tribes or kingdoms, populated most of Britain and adopted what is known as a Celtic culture. No doubt these tribes were nameless, but names were bestowed upon them by the Romans more than 2,000 years ago, names which are still in use today. Norfolk and north Suffolk were inhabited by the Iceni – druids originally from Gaul. At least two dozen small silver coins, minted by this tribe from around 40BC, have been found in Homersfield, as has a gold coin of Cunobelinus, king of the Trinovantes,

15

The gravel pit in 1970. Fossilised bones were found here before it become a lake.

Dating from c.1905, the occupants of the early motor car (a Model Ford 'T') are no doubt inside the Black Swan
(REPRODUCED BY KIND PERMISSION OF LEIGHTEN BALL.)

A very early photograph of Homersfield Mill.
(REPRODUCED BY KIND PERMISSION OF CHARMIAN SMY.)

A wonderful image of Homersfield Mill, c.1905.
(REPRODUCED BY KIND PERMISSION OF GLEN EARL).

An early photo of Heath Cottage and the road towards Flixton. (REPRODUCED BY KIND PERMISSION OF CHARMIAN SMY.)

The Post Office, c.1913. The people in the garden are almost certainly Mrs Ellen ('Nellie') Borrett and her daughter.

the tribe that occupied the southern half of Suffolk and Essex. The Iceni coins bear the names of their leaders or distinctive patterns, and the clay moulds used in creating the dies for such coins have been found in the Waveney Valley. Iron Age jewellery has been found locally, much of it bronze but some gold items such as torcs, and fragments of Iron Age pottery have been found in local fields.

Several Iron Age sites in Homersfield provide evidence that fields were being fertilised with waste

matter. Other sites have been found in Mendham, Flixton and South Elmham, some of which continued into the Roman occupation. The indications are that this region was intensively farmed some considerable time before the arrival of the invaders from Rome. More recent discoveries have shown that there were trading centres at Scole and Needham.

✦ CHAPTER 2 ✦

Foreigners

ROMANS

Though Roman armies invaded Britain in 55 and 54BC, their military campaigns were interrupted by wars elsewhere in their empire, and they were obliged to return home. Nearly 100 years passed before the Romans invaded again in AD43, and many were killed during the lengthy fighting. Much of Britain consequently found itself under Roman rule. The Iceni, however, resisted, and continued to govern their kingdom of Norfolk and north Suffolk for a little while longer. It was eventually incorporated into the Roman Empire after the Iceni queen, Boudicca (Boadicea), failed in her attempt to overthrow the invaders in a huge battle in AD60. The Romans stayed for nearly 400 years.

Soon after the conquest, the Romans set about building a system of major highways. These are the best conserved remains extant from the Roman occupation. Some of the roads are still in use today, while other, minor, roads are partially visible or have become lost under the landscape. Many now follow a parish boundary or run alongside hedging. These highways were built not for the benefit of the locals, but for the Roman army, and sometimes cut through ancient roads used by the local inhabitants. We know two of these roads locally as the A140, running through Long Stratton, and the A144, running from Bungay to Halesworth, known as Stone Street.

This is the time in our history when changes in the kinds of settlement are noticed, the time when towns first came into being. The bigger settlements were focal points of trade and industry rather than what we today consider typical Roman towns, with rigid systems of parallel streets and substantial buildings. These settlements are fairly regularly distributed in Suffolk and must have been used as trade centres or markets by those living within a radius of a few miles. Villas, with their mosaic floors made up of tens of thousands of individually painted small, square ceramic pieces (tesserae), painted walls, heated rooms and so on, tend to be found in towns and are quite scarce in the eastern half of the county. However, towns aside, most of the Roman sites in Suffolk relate to individual farms, commonly found throughout the county and particularly concentrated along the river valleys, with others a little higher up along the sides. The remainder of the dwellings were homes for individual families of the labouring or peasant classes. Unexplained is the fact that many sites were abandoned during the third and fourth

Top and above: *The obverses and reverses of three Roman coins found in the village.* From left to right: *a double centenionalis of Magnentius (AD350-353), a silver denarius of Pertinax (AD193) and an as or dupondius of Hadrian (AD117-138).*

centuries. Several settlement sites have been found in South Elmham and surrounding villages.

The Romano–British economy was dominated by agriculture. When the Romans arrived, they found the land already divided up into fields, with little scope or need to impose any of their own methods. Crops were of prime importance and any surplus fed the Roman Army or could be sold at a local market, along with livestock and wool. As the population in eastern England increased, requiring more and more food, so most of the landscape became cultivated.

Coins bearing the heads of Roman emperors started to circulate freely and were in use for a few hundred years. Made of bronze, silver, or gold, examples of these have been found in Homersfield over the years.

Another very important constituent of the economy was pottery, an abundance of evidence of which has turned up over the years. It was manufactured in Homersfield and also at Mendham, the clay

The Homersfield kiln from the side.
(REPRODUCED WITH KIND PERMISSION FROM THE PROCEEDINGS OF THE SUFFOLK INSTITUTE OF ARCHAEOLOGY, VOL. 28, PLATE 24, 1960.)

The Homersfield kiln from above.
(REPRODUCED WITH KIND PERMISSION FROM THE PROCEEDINGS OF THE SUFFOLK INSTITUTE OF ARCHAEOLOGY, VOL. 28, PLATE 23, 1960.)

The gravel pit, where many Roman artefacts have been found, in 1988.

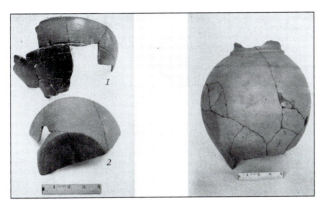

A bowl, dish and waster found in Homersfield pit.
(REPRODUCED WITH KIND PERMISSION FROM THE *PROCEEDINGS OF THE SUFFOLK INSTITUTE OF ARCHAEOLOGY*, VOL. 28, PLATE 25, 1960.)

(A) Sherd of mortarium with stamp.

Some stamped sherds.
(REPRODUCED WITH KIND PERMISSION FROM THE *PROCEEDINGS OF THE SUFFOLK INSTITUTE OF ARCHAEOLOGY*, VOL. 28, PLATE 27, 1960.)

Various pottery sherds from the pit.
(REPRODUCED WITH KIND PERMISSION FROM THE *PROCEEDINGS OF THE SUFFOLK INSTITUTE OF ARCHAEOLOGY*, VOL. 28, PLATE 26, 1960.)

being especially well suited at both sites for firing in kilns, and was made extensively from the second century onwards until the early years of the fifth century. Kilns have been found at many of the trading centres and also in rural locations in Suffolk. One such kiln was found in a gravel pit in Homersfield in February 1959, having been built in a pit in the sand. Approximately 4½ft in diameter and just over 2ft in depth, in places it was 9ins thick. In it were found pottery sherds, the shells of oysters (a Roman delicacy) and animal bones, mostly of sheep. It has been dated to a period in the earlier part of the second half of the second century AD. Although just one largely intact kiln was found, the remains of several others were found nearby.

Analysis of pottery fragments found in the Homersfield gravel pit show it to contain a small amount of mica, as is common in the Suffolk area. Many household wares were manufactured here. Almost half of the pottery remains are of dishes, a third are jars and the remainder mostly bowls. Many are decorated with either parallel or wavy lines, possibly made with part of a red deer antler, also found at the site. There are pieces of smooth grey-brown or burnished black bowls, and of coarser grey-brown ones. The dishes have flat, beaded or plain rims. A large pot, a cordoned jar, was also found there; it had been rejected due to faults during firing and was complete save for its top and bottom. Some sherds found nearby, at Flixton, are from Homersfield pots made during the second and third centuries and embellished with stamped patterns.

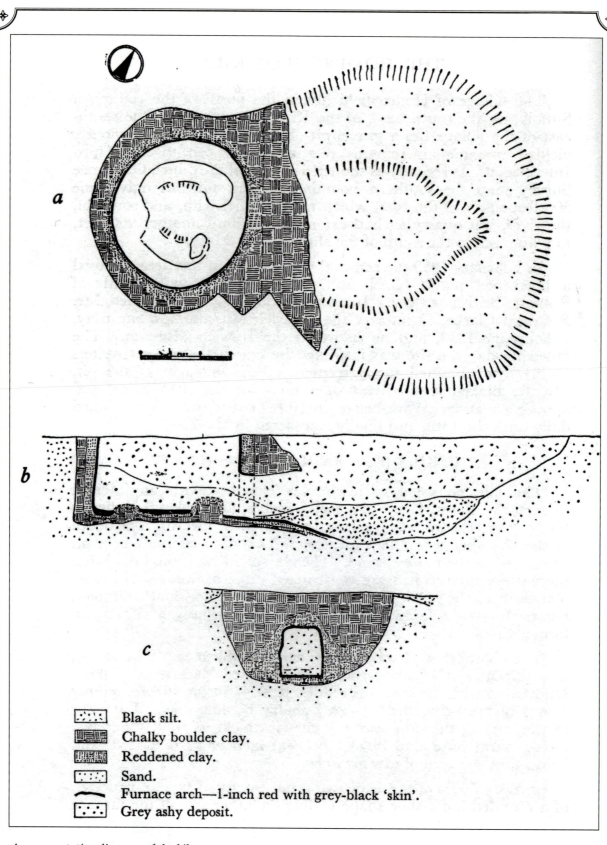

A representative diagram of the kiln.

(REPRODUCED WITH KIND PERMISSION FROM THE PROCEEDINGS OF THE SUFFOLK INSTITUTE OF ARCHAEOLOGY, VOL. 28, FIG. 29, 1960.)

The Roman face-mould, found in the pit.
(REPRODUCED WITH KIND PERMISSION FROM THE PROCEEDINGS OF THE SUFFOLK INSTITUTE OF ARCHAEOLOGY, VOL. 30, FIG. 30, 1965.)

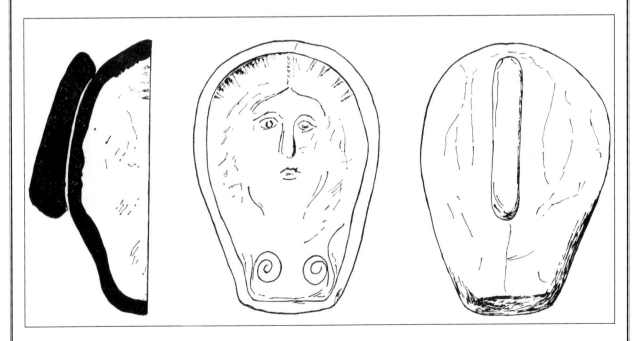

A diagram of the Roman face-mould, including the back.
(REPRODUCED WITH KIND PERMISSION FROM THE PROCEEDINGS OF THE SUFFOLK INSTITUTE OF ARCHAEOLOGY, VOL. 30, FIG. 29, 1965.)

Between Homersfield and St Cross, where the road dips gently downwards and then upwards, it is thought that there was once an active clay pit from which were built the Homersfield kilns and the wares subsequently fired in them. The size of the hollow that we see now gives some indication of significant activity here more than 1,500 years ago.

By its nature, the making of pots devours much wood in heating kilns to the desired temperatures. For this reason it is highly likely that the wooded areas in Homersfield were regularly coppiced and were as carefully and intensively managed as the surrounding fields.

The Homersfield kiln is not the only important Roman item to have been found here. Indeed, of considerably more importance, due to its extreme rarity, is a Roman face-mould, measuring roughly 3 x 2ins, found in 1963 by Mr Leslie Burford, who lived at No. 69 in Homersfield. Only a very few other examples are known. This mould would have been used for the decoration of jugs produced on site and was found in the region of the kiln mentioned above. Hair can be seen represented on the mould, and there is a twisting coil design on each side of the neck, with a handle at the back. Thought to date from around the third century, and therefore later than the kiln, this find indicates pottery production at the site over a considerable period. Almost certainly, production continued until the Romans decided to leave.

During the Roman occupation, Britain was visited by other marauding peoples. The Saxons are recorded as having first come here in AD287, although they had probably visited our shores periodically for many years before. Visits probably became more frequent after this date, eventually resulting in a significant attack 80 years later, in AD367. From this point in time onwards, the invaders penetrated further and further, undermining the Roman presence, and in around AD410, for reasons which are not entirely clear, the Romans left Britain, never to return.

DARK AGES

As this point in our dim and distant past, we enter a period of some 650 years which historians often refer to as the 'Dark Ages', because there are virtually no documents to consult, and the picture of what went on during all those years is only slowly and gradually being built up by archaeologists.

Anglo-Saxons

One view held by some for the drastic change that took place in AD410 is that invading Anglo-Saxons ousted the Romans in a period of violence, but there is little evidence so far of such an event. What took place in eastern Suffolk immediately following AD410

is not clear, but in all probability Anglo-Saxons (Angles, Saxons, Jutes and other Germans), superseded the Romans and gradually took control, claiming the land and the right to govern. There is some evidence of continued settlement along the Waveney Valley, rather than of new areas being cleared and new settlements built on uncultivated soil. The little available evidence tends to suggest that existing settlements and fields were taken over. A fundamental difficulty in reconstructing what took place is that, as Anglo-Saxon communities lived in wooden houses with wooden outbuildings, these have entirely rotted away, leaving nothing, only dark stains in the earth where the supporting posts once stood. Relatively few pieces of pottery have been found, providing some small degree of insight into these peoples' lives.

The average early Anglo-Saxon settlement typically contained a number of houses, with one larger hall and outbuildings for working, housing animals and storing grain or crops. Such settlements would initially have been largely self-sufficient, keeping cattle, sheep, pigs, goats and horses; they grew peas, wheat and barley, and would have supplemented their food by deer hunting and fishing. These people are responsible for the area being known as East Anglia, the eastern land of the Angles.

We may never know how much or how well these immigrants integrated with the British, but no doubt many Britons had new landlords or became slaves. In time, the British and the settlers integrated and the English people resulted from the union. Much valuable information about these people has been ascertained from their cemeteries, which contain few cremations and were predominantly burials, as was their custom. One such cemetery has been found in nearby Flixton. There is a notable difference in the pottery used in these burials from that used in the Roman period; the items found have been made by hand, without the use of a wheel.

Disease decimated the population at least twice during these dark times. In round AD450 came a plague so severe that the living could not bury the dead fast enough, so quickly did they succumb. In another 100 or so years, the plague came again and checked the population increase once more.

The structure of Suffolk towns and villages came about during the seventh century, during which time East Anglia was a powerful kingdom ruled by the Wuffinga family. This was the beginning of a period of great change. At some point during our Anglo-Saxon period, the 'north folk' and the 'south folk' were acknowledged by the division of East Anglia into their county names, Norfolk and Suffolk respectively. It is not known exactly when this took place, but is recognised that it could have been as early as the 630s.

Many Suffolk settlements, deserted after the Romans left, were occupied again during a period of some 200 years from AD650, and by the ninth century the majority of Suffolk's villages were in existence.

The seventh century also saw the reintroduction of Christianity, which had been exterminated when the Romans left. Under the jurisdiction of the Archbishop of Canterbury, the first bishop in Suffolk was Felix, sent from Burgundy by Archbishop Honorious to convert the East Anglian folk. He subsequently established a see (an area under a bishop's jurisdiction) in the 630s at a place known then as Dommoc. This location is now thought likely to be Felixstowe, although Dunwich has been a strong contender in the past. Felix died in AD647 and was subsequently canonised. Probably during the 680s, the diocese was split into two, with bishops at Dommoc and Elmham. As to which Elmham this refers, there is no written evidence to support either. Over the years, opinion has swayed from North Elmham in Norfolk to South Elmham in Suffolk and back again repeatedly. Archaeological evidence has so far been unable positively to settle the matter one way or the other. A modern line of thought sites the second see at South Elmham, with Hoxne and North Elmham becoming sites of the bishop's cathedrals after the Danish invasions of the tenth century.

The population having been converted to Christianity with apparent ease, churches appeared in virtually all villages in Suffolk from towards the end of the seventh century onwards. These early churches being built of timber, they have invariably disappeared without trace. Later, replacement churches of stone, the use of which became widespread, were generally built on the same sites, and of those with visible Anglo-Saxon architecture, only a few can be found in Suffolk.

During the Anglo-Saxon period the parish of Homersfield came into being. Its boundaries will have existed since the early eleventh century at the latest, and quite possibly existed a couple of centuries before then. Parishes founded in earlier Saxon times often took over existing boundaries, either secular or natural, and occasionally of prehistoric origin.

Suffolk was divided for administrative purposes into hundreds, half-hundreds and ferdings (quarter-hundreds) during the tenth century or before. A hundred was a subdivision of a county based on 100 peasant households, and was deemed to require a carucate or four virgates (120 acres) of land to support it. The hundred was the basis for all administrative matters, whether judicial, fiscal or military. Homersfield came within the Wangford hundred (as it still does today), which, like other hundreds, had its own court, controlled by a bailiff and was named after the court meeting-place (in the open air). It was second only to the county court, controlled by a sheriff, which at that time met twice a year, whereas the hundred court met every three weeks.

One of the very earliest administrative areas in Suffolk is the Elmham ferding (also known as a ferthing or farthing), comprising the seven South Elmham villages (of St Cross – or Sancroft, dedicated to St George, St James, St Margaret, St Michael, St Nicholas, St Peter and All Saints), Flixton and Homersfield. Unusually, Homersfield has another, earlier name, that of South Elmham St Mary, and may have had an earlier one before that. These nine parishes are almost certainly associated in some as yet unexplained way with the St Cross Minster, the possible seat of the Elmham bishops.

The origins of the name of the river flowing through Homersfield are lost in depths of obscurity. Though various proposals have been put forward, none appears to provide absolutely conclusive proof. Most of our major rivers have British derivations, those ending in '–ey' being derived from the Old English word for 'river'. 'Waveney' could be derived from a word dating from the Iron Age, 'afon' also meaning 'river'. 'Avona' also appears, and 'Waveney' could be a corruption of it. The Anglo-Saxons called it 'Wahene', or it may originate from the Danish word 'wafenu', meaning 'troubled waters'. It is referred to as 'Wahailey' in the Bishop of London's will, dating from around AD950, and is referred to in a Saxon charter, meaning 'slow' or 'meandering'. Additionally, it could have derived from the words 'wagen' or 'wagian', meaning 'quagmire'. Such references, gleaned from the few precious documents extant from this period, offer a variety of possibilities.

Danes

East Anglia was first seen by the Danes in AD802, but it was only around AD866, when they purloined horses from Suffolk on landing, that they first caused significant trouble, heralding the beginning of more than a century of strife. In AD869 they arrived in significant numbers under the leadership of Inguar and Hubbar, and Viking violence ensued along the Waveney. During these battles, King Edmund, who was later immortalised and canonised as St Edmund, lost his life, and his capital, Thetford, was sacked. Legend has it that Hunberht, Bishop of Elmham, from whom Homersfield may well have taken its name, was killed during the same fighting. The Saxon leader Ulketel (from whom it is thought the four Ilketshall villages acquired their name) was defeated by a Danish commander by the name of Turketel in AD879. It was from this date that they decided to settle, and they totally overran East Anglia, including every village and town as well as the churches. The bishoprics of East Anglia were swept away in the process. Only those communities offering large sums of money as bribes were spared the dubious honour of immediately coming under Danish leadership.

During their attempts to take over the whole country, the Danes constantly came up against local opposition, seriously hindering their progress. Alfred the Great was one of several kings who contributed to the invaders abandoning East Anglia altogether. Guthrum, leader of the Danes, regained the area when he was defeated in Wessex by Alfred, who granted it to the Danes on condition that they be baptised Christians and that they obeyed Alfred's rule during their occupation.

The most common place-name suffix in Suffolk is 'tun' (now spelled 'ton'), followed by 'ham', both of which refer to farmsteads in our county. After these comes 'feld', which we nowadays spell as 'field'. The interpretation of this suffix includes open country, a clearing, a plain, grazing land and plough land, the last of these coming into use by the tenth century. Some places with the suffix 'feld' appear in written documents by the end of the first quarter of the eighth century, indicating early Anglo-Saxon origins. It is likely that Homersfield, however, may have waited a further century before acquiring its current name. As always, topics concerned with the ancient past generate discussions and opinions; there has not been total agreement on how Homersfield obtained its name, although there does appear to be a clear favourite in this instance.

In the Domesday Book, Homersfield is spelled 'Humbresfelda' and most of it was owned by the Bishop of East Anglia. There is general agreement among those who have knowledge of ancient languages and documents that Humbresfelda means 'Hunberht's feld'.

Before the Danes abolished bishops the last was named Hunberht, who is likely to have died at the same time as Edmund, in AD869. The village has other spellings which should be noted here; it appears as 'Humrefeld' and 'Humbresfeld' in a charter or roll of about 1130, now housed in the British Museum. In an instance from 1254, it is spelt 'Humeresfeud' and on the church silver 'Humersfylde'. To this day, locals pronounce the village name 'Hummersfield', phonetically very close to its probable original derivation.

Strange though it may seem, despite much fighting and many battles over a period of nearly 100 years, ending with the throne being occupied by Edward the Confessor after the death of the last Danish king in 1041, the Danish presence is distinguished in very few Suffolk place-names, although evidence of their having been here turns up with increasing frequency.

Pre-Conquest

By now, England had become unified under one crown. Anglo-Saxon society was distinctly aristocratic and the important families here during the eleventh century were mostly descended from those who served kings or principal men. Thegns were those who owed service, especially military service, to their governing earl or bishop, and worked on the king's or bishop's estates as bodyguards and in various other capacities – in fact, they did almost anything. In return for services rendered, thegns were given land or privileges which, in turn, created a noble title that tended to pass to succeeding generations. Earldoms were passed from father to son, subject to the agreement of the king. The concept of lordship in the pre-Conquest years filtered through the ranks from top to bottom and lowly agricultural workers at the foot of the social scale were organised to support the hierarchy above them. This, essentially, was the basis of the feudal system that came into being. The crucial feature of feudalism was the fief, a benefice given to a thegn who had sworn an oath of loyalty. This created a bond between the two parties, as well as a system of land occupancy.

The lord paid his farmers and peasants via leases, lending them land in return for them working it and paying any rents. The land in East Anglia was under the plough constantly. The climate and soil largely dictated the type of crops grown from year to year, and the quality of grassland dictated the type of animals kept.

In Homersfield and many other villages in Suffolk the main crop was corn, used for making bread. Oats and barley were grown for animal food and also used for making ale. Hay was also a valuable food. Pigs, sheep, goats and cows were all kept, as were the working animals – oxen and horses. The natural by-product from all these animals was spread over the fields and renewed the nutrients in the soil, making the land productive year by year. From the milk, the whey was removed and drunk and cheese was made from the milk of both sheep and cows. Sheeps' wool would have been spun in the village. Villagers caught rabbits for food and fur, and some kept bees, honey being a valuable and desirable commodity in times when raw sugar was unavailable. Some of the birds kept for eating are still kept now: chickens, geese, ducks and pheasants, while those now kept less commonly or not at all included swans, herons, coots, pigeon and woodcock.

In Homersfield cottage gardens would have been grown many different kinds of plants for the table, many of them familiar today. As well as herbs, including sage, mint, garlic and parsley, would have been grown lettuce, beet, onions, leeks, shallots, cucumbers and even pumpkins. In addition to this wide variety of plants available 1,000 years ago, seasonal wild fruits were also collected.

CHAPTER 3

Domesday is Coming

THE GREAT SURVEY

Introduction

Nowhere else in the world is there such a comprehensive document of the age as our Domesday Book. Compiled in 1086, when the population was around two million, this exceptional historical record shows a reasonable uniformity of detail over the whole of the surveyed area, and provides a precious insight into how our cities, towns, villages and hamlets looked more than 900 years ago. The book allows us to look back at the social history of England long before the time of its compilation, and at patterns of life which had evolved up to 600 years before. Astonishingly, after the information had been collected, it was written up in less than 12 months by just one man, albeit abridged with details of livestock omitted, on almost 900 pages of yellowish sheepskin

parchment. It was originally known by different names, among others 'The Inquisition' and 'The Great Description of England', as well as 'The Great Survey', but is known today by a name coined in the twelfth century and used ever since – the book of the day of judgement, meaning that the facts contained within it are unalterable: the Domesday Book.

Its Beginnings

King Harold and his Anglo-Saxon army were defeated in 1066 at the Battle of Hastings by Duke William of Normandy, subsequently known as 'The Conqueror' who was crowned king. Then came an event which marked a major change and altered the lives of everyone in England forever, the effects of which are still felt to this day. William confiscated all land from the English nobility, claiming it for his own before dividing it up and granting it to friends and followers, some of whom were his loyal knights.

A delightful view of Homersfield Mill, c.1925.
(REPRODUCED BY KIND PERMISSION OF FRANK HONEYWOOD.)

The back of Homersfield Mill, c.1925.
(REPRODUCED BY KIND PERMISSION OF FRANK HONEYWOOD.)

A few mill wheels, c.1927.
(REPRODUCED BY KIND PERMISSION OF FRANK HONEYWOOD.)

The sad view after the mill had been pulled down, c.1930.
(REPRODUCED BY KIND PERMISSION OF FRANK HONEYWOOD.)

A view of the green, dating from the mid-1930s, when Harry Elsey's name was above the Post Office door.

Homersfield Post Office, c.1937. Note that the name board has now disappeared.

The Black Swan Hotel, advertising a public bar, car park, luncheons and teas etc., c.1935. Interesting to see beer barrels being used as flower pots! The attractive black swan sign was stolen from the premises in the 1990s.

These new lords ousted their Anglo-Saxon counterparts, controlling the manors and leaving the previous incumbents devoid of anything useful. French clergy were installed by William in newly built religious buildings, and the overall effect was to change England completely, demoralising the English population immensely in the process.

Its Reasons for Being

There was more than one reason for the survey taking place. King William, keen to raise money to increase the size of his army, decided that the cost of supporting it should be borne by those under him, by the friends and followers to whom he had granted land. How many troops were the responsibility of any one manor depended on the amount of land held and, in turn, the amount of tax that could be paid on it. William wanted to know who had what land and how much of it they had.

There was also a financial issue. Tax paid in Anglo-Saxon times had been based on the entire value of an estate; in English areas of the country, this was based on the hide, originally considered to be the amount of land required to support one labouring or

peasant household. However, it was a somewhat variable unit of measurement as, although it could be estimated at 120 acres, this depended on the date, the locality and the needs of the government at the time. Danish areas of the country used the carucate, supposedly equal to the hide and calculated as the amount of land that could be ploughed by a team of eight oxen; again, the area varied from region to region. William wanted to know what estates his friends and followers had and who held them.

Additionally, there was a judicial issue. Since 1066, the population had witnessed the totally unfair confiscation and commandeering of land on an unprecedented scale, and written evidence exists of land seizures of this nature often being contested in court. William was keen to put his tyrannical measures on a legal footing, thus dispensing with any further potential problems that might arise.

The Great Survey incorporated all of these things and more. Not only was it a tax inquest, a feudal record and a legal statement, it was more than all those things, for its scope was significantly wider. As well as a detailed description of the country ruled by William since 1066, it also detailed how things were before that time and what had changed, including who had owned what then and who owned it now.

A Misconception

A common misconception is that there was just one Domesday Book. That mentioned so far is actually known as 'Great Domesday Book' or 'Domesday Book Volume I'. There is another, known as 'Little Domesday Book' or 'Domesday Book Volume II', and physically not much smaller than the main volume. It is thought that the contents of this book were not in the main volume because the main work was unfinished when King William died in September 1087. Nevertheless, it is of equal importance. Unlike Great Domesday Book, Little Domesday Book is unabridged and it is fortunate, where Homersfield is concerned, that it is to be found in this book along with the rest of Suffolk, as well as the whole of

Harry Elsey and his daughter at the Post Office, c.1930.

Norfolk and Essex, written up in several different hands. Another, currently less popular theory as to why there are two books, is that when the three eastern counties were written up, they were already so bulky and unwieldy that it was decided to write up the remaining counties omitting the livestock details.

General Notes

Before we look at the Domesday entries for Homersfield in any detail, it will be useful here to give some information not solely, but particularly, concerned with reference to Suffolk as a whole or England in general.

Arrangement of Entries
Domesday Book entries are arranged not under the relevant parish, but under the landowner of the time, followed by the name of the hundred in which the land fell and through which the geld tax was paid. For Homersfield (in Wangford hundred) there were three bishops who held land and, consequently, three separate entries. These were written in Latin, but are not easy to decipher, and scholars have spent significant time unravelling the mysteries and meanings of the many contractions and abbreviations in order to present them in a readable format. Until relatively modern times, there has been no county by county breakdown available for consultation but, thankfully, such a publication has proved a boon for those interested in Domesday Book.

Manors and Vills
A manor, derived from the French word for a dwelling, consisted of an estate belonging to a lord who was often permanently absent, that is to say, he did not live in the manor itself. In such instances, a bailiff was appointed by the lord to live in his manor house. The land around a manor house, which was for the lord's own use and worked by his labouring classes, was called the demesne, and the primary farm on the demesne was usually called the home farm; there are a great many instances of this name still being in use today. The manor was a self-contained economic entity and the various classes of the lord's labourers lived in cottages owned and built by the lord. A manor could encompass one or more vills or, alternatively, a vill could be divided into one or more manors, each of which would have had a manorial house within its boundaries.

Settlements
An important point which must be taken into consideration is that where two villages have very similar names, then often they are not named individually in Domesday Book. One such relevant example concerns the seven South Elmham parishes, none of which is identified individually, although in this instance the aggregate population detailed in the entries certainly indicates that several settlements are represented. Fortunately, Homersfield is referred to as such, rather than by its older name of St Mary South Elmham.

Population
The mass of the population consisted of five classes of people, each representing a different rung on the social ladder. In descending order of hierarchy, these were: freemen, sokemen, villeins, bordars and serfs. The term 'freeman' was not to be taken literally; at a personal level he was a free man, but he could be required to pay rents or carry out duties under his lord's control. A sokeman had the status of a peasant

A view towards the mature tree on the green, c.1930.

Barnfield Cottages, c.1930.

The front of the Black Swan Hotel, c.1930, with an excellent view of the bowling green and its topiary entrance.

but was free to leave his land; he was often able to sell it also. Like a freeman, he would often pay rent or services to his lord, and was required to be present at his lord's court. It is not always easy to distinguish between a freeman and a sokeman, as they appear so similar, but these two classes together represent the free constituent of men living in any one manor. A villein, the highest class of peasant, often held between 30 and 100 acres of land. He was tied to the manor and paid labour services to his lord, but if he absconded and remained absent for a year and one day, then he gained his freedom. Bordars, of lesser importance than villeins, also paid their rent from week to week by working for their lord. Serfs, at the bottom of the social scale, were slaves who had no rights at all and were considered as chattels by their lord, to be treated accordingly. Burgesses, priests and a few others made up the remainder of the inhabitants. The population figures in Domesday Book are taken to represent the heads of households, and take no account of wives, children and anyone else in any one household.

Land Measurement
The unit of measurement for land areas in Suffolk is commonly the carucate, normally considered to be 120 acres, although these are what are known as fiscal acres, one fiscal acre being represented by 1.2 agricultural acres.

Valuations and Geld
In Suffolk, tax charges for payment were amalgamated into larger units for assessment called leets. Not infrequently in our county, measurements are not given for some vills (the forerunners of modern villages) and the assumption, therefore, is that they have been hidden in the assessments of other nearby vills. Typically, a value appears at or near the end of Domesday entries, which tend to be very precise and indicate that a thorough assessment has been carried out. These values are expressed in shillings and pence, whereas in other parts of the country they are stated in terms of hides and carucates. The geld

(direct tax) assessment is denoted in pence per pound and the vill pays a number of pence per pound of geld assessed on the hundred. These assessments vary greatly in terms of the number of acres they represent and therefore cannot be reliably employed at all in calculating the size of vills and manors.

Plough Teams
Domesday entries relate to two kinds of plough teams, those held by people obliged to provide labour services to the lord, and those held in land which belonged to the lord for his own use (his demesne, derived from an old French word meaning right of ownership). The distinction between the two kinds is usually (but not always) made in entries. There doesn't appear to be a constant correlation between the number of acres or carucates ploughed and the number of plough teams used.

Woodland
The amount of woodland present in any manor is not, as one might expect, expressed in acres or fractions thereof, but as the number of pigs that it is capable of supporting. Some woodland was used for the pannage (grazing) of pigs, where they would fatten themselves on autumn acorns before being slaughtered and their meat preserved in salt for winter consumption. When this occurred the lord of

A wonderful picture of three men in a boat! Limbourne Mill, photographed by Benjamin Clarke, c.1900.

Limbourne (or Wortwell) Mill, c.1940.

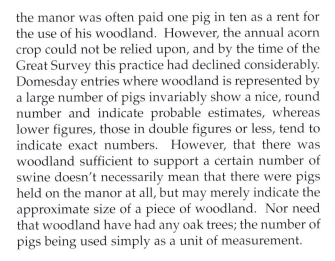

the manor was often paid one pig in ten as a rent for the use of his woodland. However, the annual acorn crop could not be relied upon, and by the time of the Great Survey this practice had declined considerably. Domesday entries where woodland is represented by a large number of pigs invariably show a nice, round number and indicate probable estimates, whereas lower figures, those in double figures or less, tend to indicate exact numbers. However, that there was woodland sufficient to support a certain number of swine doesn't necessarily mean that there were pigs held on the manor at all, but may merely indicate the approximate size of a piece of woodland. Nor need that woodland have had any oak trees; the number of pigs being used simply as a unit of measurement.

Livestock

Domesday figures quoted for the year of the survey and those for 20 years earlier are often markedly different, and the entries give no explanation as to why this might be. Sheep were by far the most common livestock kept in Suffolk, followed by pigs and goats. Strangely, exceedingly few cows are mentioned, although when one thinks of the number of beasts then used to plough fields, there must have been large numbers of them.

Homersfield

The entries below are shown as they appear in the book, translated. Words or parts of words omitted are shown in square parentheses in order to improve the reading.

Entry One

LANDS OF WILLIAM, BISHOP OF THETFORD
WANGFORD Hundred
Bishop AELMER held HOMERSFIELD before 1066; 1 manor at 5 carucates of land. Now Bishop William holds [it].
Always 16 villagers; always 12 smallholders; always 4 slaves.

Then 2 ploughs in lordship, now 3; then 10 men's ploughs, now 5, and 5 could be restored there.
Meadow, 12 acres; woodland, then 600 pigs, now 200; 1 mill.
1 church, 12 acres.
3 horses when he acquired [it] *and now. Always 6 cattle. Always 26 pigs; 200 sheep.*
Value then, with the jurisdiction, £12; now it pays [£]16.
Bishop William has full jurisdiction over the Ferthing of [South] *Elmham, except over Bishop Stigand's men; and Abbot B*[aldwin], *according to the testimony of the Hundred, had a writ from King Edward* [stating] *that he himself ought to have full jurisdiction over St Edmund's land and his men.*

This entry shows that in the time of Edward the Confessor, Bishop Aelmer was the lord of the manor in Homersfield. Although he did not hold all of Homersfield, he did control the vast majority. One of two high-ranked Church people to found Rumburgh Priory, he was the brother of Archbishop Stigand of Canterbury. He was consecrated as the Bishop of Elmham some time after August in the year 1047 and was subsequently unseated from this position in April 1070. The manor comprised an area of around 600 acres, and after King William came to the throne, he granted it to William, Bishop of Thetford. The entry shows that the manor was assessed in 1066 with a value of £12, which 20 years later had increased by a third, to £16.

The lord's home farm had two ploughs in 1066, which had increased by a further plough (together with the necessary additional eight oxen to pull it) in 1086. For working the rest of the land belonging to the manor, there ten ploughs once available were reduced to half that value, although there was scope to reinstate the other half. As can be seen, there was a water-mill in Homersfield over 900 years ago, and no doubt it (or an earlier mill) had been there a good many years before that.

Under both bishops, the numbers of villagers

(villeins), smallholders (bordars) and slaves (serfs) were the same in 1086 as they had been in 1066. The same applies to the numbers of horses, cattle and sheep, but not pigs. The cattle and sheep would have been kept in the 12 acres of meadowland by the river, or other fields on the sloping Waveney Valley sides; no doubt some were also pastured on common land in Homersfield. The woodland referred to was almost certainly on higher land, and, as can be seen from the figures quoted as pannage for pigs, had been reduced by two-thirds between 1066 and 1086. That the reason for this is not mentioned is normal practice in Domesday Book.

Bishop Stigand, mentioned in the last part of this entry, was consecrated Bishop of Winchester in 1047. He shared the see with the Archbishopric of Canterbury from 1052 until he was ousted in 1070. He died in 1072.

Entry Two

THE BISHOP OF THETFORD'S HOLDING
WANGFORD Hundred
1 free man under the patronage of Aelmer held HOMERSFIELD; 40 acres as a manor.
Always 2 smallholders.
Then 2 ploughs, now 1. Meadow, 2 acres.
1 church with 30 acres.
Value then 6s.8d.; now 9[s.] 4d.
Also in the same village, 23 free men; 80 acres. Then 6 ploughs, now 5.
Value then 40s.; now 30[s.].
It has 1 league in length and ½ in width; 20d. in tax.

This entry refers to the second, smaller manor in Homersfield, where an anonymous free man supported by Bishop Aelmer had control over 40 acres of land. In 1066 two bordars worked the demesne land, the same two men possibly still working there 20 years later.

The number of ploughs belonging to the lord of the manor had halved in the 20-year period between the battle in 1066 and the year of the survey. His holding, valued at 6s.8d. in 1066, had increased to 9s.4d. by 1086.

The entry then goes on to describe the rest of the manor, the land other than that belonging to the home farm. There were 23 men working 80 acres with one less plough than they had had before. The value in 1066 of £2 had dropped by a quarter in the ensuing 20 years.

The entry concludes with an indication of size, one league by a half of a league; lastly, a geld payment of 20d. was payable on the vill.

These entries show that there were two manors in Homersfield, one much smaller than the other. There would have been a manorial house in each, with a bailiff residing in the larger manor, representing Bishop Aelmer. The tenant in the smaller manor would probably also have lived in grandeur.

Entry Three

LANDS OF ST EDMUND
In LINBURNE St Edmund's holds 30 acres of land.
Always 5 smallholders.
Always 1 plough.
Meadow, 2 acres; the fifth part of 1 mill.
Value then and always 10s.
Bishop W[illiam] (has) full jurisdiction.
½ church in WORLINGHAM, 5 acres; value 12d.

This entry refers to Limbourne, a lost medieval settlement that never had its own church. It is included here as it is within the parish and has always been regarded as a hamlet of Homersfield. As can be seen, there were five bordars and one plough, both in 1066 and at the time of the survey. The only reference now to this hamlet is found in the mill. Limbourne Mill, also commonly known as Wortwell Mill, was partly owned by the Bishop of St Edmunds. Who owned the remaining four-fifths, we are not told.

Although ploughs are mentioned, as is usually the case in Domesday entries, there is no mention at all of the oxen that were undoubtedly kept to pull them. In these times, a team of eight oxen (the plough team) was used to work the fields. No doubt there were sufficient beasts to keep several ploughs in motion at the same time.

Domesday Book clerks have left behind a myriad of puzzles to unravel, and although only three entries have been presented here, they pose questions that are not easily answered. For example, the measurement presented in the last line of the second entry gives food for thought. A league comprised 12 furlongs, a furlong being one-eighth of a mile. The area concerned is therefore one and a half miles by three-quarters of a mile. This equates to 720 acres, somewhat different from the 40 acres quoted for the manor. Even if this figure includes the land relating to the much larger manor, there is a shortfall of some 80 acres.

CHAPTER 4

Church Matters

The Church plays such an immensely important part in the history of Homersfield and, over the centuries, the scope of topics associated with it would warrant several books of this size alone. In this chapter a flavour is given from a very wide choice available on the ecclesiastical menu.

Church Rule

Ecclesiastically, the whole of Suffolk has been under the direct control of the Archbishop of Canterbury for the last 1,400 years or so, ever since its people were converted to Christianity. The archbishop delegated much of what needed to be done to the lower ranks, his bishops, who in turn delegated it to their archdeacons. These archdeacons took overall responsibility for the clergy, the church buildings and church property. One archdeacon served Suffolk until the second quarter of the twelfth century, when another became necessary due to the division of the county into two archdeaconries. The Archdeaconry of Suffolk now catered for the east side of the county, whilst the new Archdeaconry of Sudbury governed the west.

The archdeaconries were subdivided into deaneries, which started to come into being from the eleventh century onwards. The deanery of South Elmham very probably came into existence during the second half of the thirteenth century; a Norwich taxation list (an evaluation of the value of ecclesiastical property) of 1254 does not mention it, but it appears in an assessment of church property some 37 years later. It comprised the parishes of Homersfield, Flixton, and the seven South Elmham parishes. The South Elmham deanery boundaries correspond to those of the ancient Wangford hundred. The dean's responsibilities were not expressly defined but clearly would have included the well-being of the churches, church property and clergy under his control. All deans became redundant as a result of the sixteenth-century Reformation (the rejection of papal authority and the subsequent founding of Protestant churches), although the deaneries themselves carried on in an administrative capacity.

Parish Registers

In September 1538, King Henry VIII's Vicar-General, Thomas Cromwell, directed that every baptism,

Homersfield Church, c.1930.

Above: *A bill dated 1857 to Homersfield churchwardens for church repairs from James Chappell, whose name appears on a piece of glass in the church tower.*

(REPRODUCED BY KIND PERMISSION OF SUFFOLK RECORD OFFICE, LOWESTOFT BRANCH, REF.: 128/A1/10.)

Above: *John Brock's carpentry bill for putting a new fence around the church in 1775. One item refers to a beer allowance; it was customary to provide workers with beer daily.*

(REPRODUCED BY KIND PERMISSION OF SUFFOLK RECORD OFFICE, LOWESTOFT BRANCH, REF.: 128/A1/13.)

Left: *A bill from Plymouth for Holy Communion wine sent to Thomas Poppy, Heath Farm, in 1901.*

(REPRODUCED BY KIND PERMISSION OF SUFFOLK RECORD OFFICE, LOWESTOFT BRANCH, REF.: 128/A1/15.)

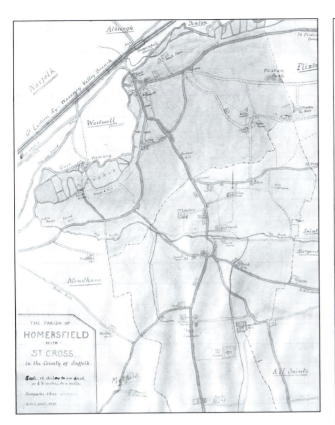

Map of Homersfield and St Cross drawn by Revd William Morley Smith in 1891, photographed in 2007.

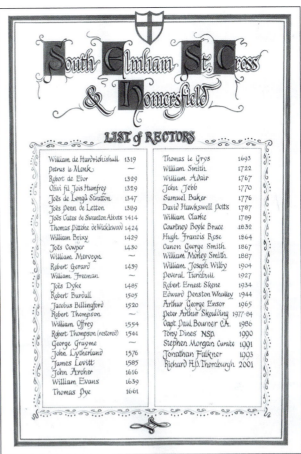

A framed list, photogaphed in 2007, of Homersfield and St Cross rectors.

marriage and burial carried out by a parish priest be recorded in a register. The majority of these records were kept on loose sheets of paper, but a very few parishes used a book for the purpose from the start.

It was ordered that parchment registers were used 60 years later, and stipulated that previous entries were to be copied into the book; however, the precise wording used meant that the records for the first 20 years did not need to be incorporated. Quite often, the loose sheets had been lost, destroyed, affected by damp or were already illegible, and consequently very few registers start from 1538.

The Homersfield parish registers date from 1558 for baptisms, marriages and burials. Hardwicke's Marriage Act of 1753 (which came into force the following year) was designed to prevent clandestine or runaway marriages and basically required that the marriage should take place in the parish church of either the bride or the groom, with banns published beforehand. Homersfield banns date from 1755 and were read out in church for the three consecutive Sundays prior to the marriage. Unfortunately, the Homersfield parish registers appear to be incomplete. There are no baptisms, marriages or burials for the years 1580–83 and no burials from August 1649 to February 1654, nor from May 1742 to February 1761. It seems highly unlikely that there were none during these periods.

The burials between January 1678 and May 1682 comprise 21 souls, all noted in the register as having been buried in wool. Under the Burial in Woollen

Acts of 1666 to 1680, all who died (with the exception of those who died of the plague) were to be buried in shrouds made of wool. Additionally, an affidavit (a statement on oath) had to be sworn before a judge (usually by a relative of the deceased) within eight days of interment confirming that the body had been buried in wool. While the families of those who disobeyed this law were liable for a fine of £5, a great many poor families couldn't afford such a huge sum. However, this was not as great a problem as it might seem, as the fine was commonly overlooked in such instances. The law was repealed in 1814, although it was generally ignored after about 1770. Homersfield registers after May 1682 do not state that the corpses were in woollen shrouds, but very probably the incumbent thought it unnecessary to continually repeat such a detail.

One baptism entry deserves particular mention. An unnamed illegitimate child was baptised on 12 August 1599, the father reputed to be Edward Boothe. The mother was a young woman by the name of Mabell, whose surname is not given, but who resided at the Cock, a public house in Homersfield. The author has come across another reference to this drinking-place in a legal document, dated 1535, describing the facts of a disagreement between Vincent Freeman and Henry Starling over

The parish chest, photographed in 1990.

An interior view of the church, c.1905, complete with hanging oil lamp and plain walls. The organ is the one that is still there today.

money lent for a mortgage on the Cock, the name being a likely indication that there was cock-fighting in medieval Homersfield.

The Parish Chest

The same 1538 directive as began the recording of baptisms, marriages and burials also ordered that the information be kept in a coffer with three locks. Each lock required a different key, one kept by the current incumbent and the others by the two churchwardens. The coffer could therefore be opened only when all three guardians of the keys were present. This coffer, or parish chest, as it has since become more commonly known, was to be provided by the church-wardens at the expense of the parishioners.

The Homersfield coffer had been kept in the church for more than 400 years until it was stolen in the 1990s. It was never recovered. Fortunately, a photograph survives to record its existence.

The Vestry

Secular parochial authority was encouraged by parliamentary Acts, particularly during the sixteenth and seventeenth centuries, resulting in the creation of many vestries. The goings-on at vestry meetings were recorded in vestry books, some of which date from the sixteenth century and cover church repairs, the care of the sick and poor of the parish, schools, charities, police, housing and so on. In order to meet these responsibilities, the meetings included the appointment of churchwardens, overseers of the poor, the surveyor of highways, the parish constable and the sexton. The vestry was also responsible for the annual perambulation around the parish to ensure everyone knew its precise boundaries.

Vestries were empowered to levy rates upon parishioners to fund its parochial duties. The various rates authorised included those for the building or repair of bridges in 1530/31, for poor relief in 1597/98 and for the repair of roads in 1654.

They were also able to levy a rate to pay for the churchwardens' expenses. The various smaller rates were eventually combined and by the eighteenth century were collected with the larger poor rate. These duties, together with those of the churchwardens and overseers, involved considerable outlay, all at the expense of those parishioners able to afford the rates levied upon them.

The vestry was an important body for more than 300 years. Its decline commenced with the handing over of the welfare of the poor in 1834 to Poor Law guardians, while other duties became the responsibility of new civil local authorities. Their remaining duties were taken over by parish councils in 1894 which rendered the vestries defunct.

Meeting minute-books for Homersfield vestry date only from 1865 onwards, and generally do not make for especially riveting reading, recording little more than the appointment of two churchwardens, two overseers and between three and five parish constables each Easter, all of them being the more prominent members of the parish. Names include the Revd George Smith, Charles Smith, Benjamin Clarke, Edward Brock, George Gower, Thomas Poppy and Samuel Gowing, among others.

A special meeting, called by the churchwardens as a result of a requisition by the highways surveyor on 5 August 1869 is of particular interest. A large turnout of the inhabitants of Homersfield assembled in the church vestry to hear that the surveyor had received a notice from Sir Robert Alexander Shafto Adair of Flixton Hall, expressing a desire that certain roads which were partly in Homersfield and partly in Flixton should either be diverted or closed altogether, and new roads substituted. A map was produced showing exactly what Sir Robert had proposed; the proposal was accepted and consent given for the alterations by those present. This meeting clearly represents the beginnings of what became known as the 'New Road', built the following year and now represented on maps by the B1062. The existing road ran past where Homersfield Lodge now stands,

A document detailing a disagreement between Vincent Freeman and Henry Starling. Dated 1679, it refers to the Cock public house in Homersfield.

(REPRODUCED BY KIND PERMISSION OF NORFOLK RECORD OFFICE, REF.: WKC 1/491.)

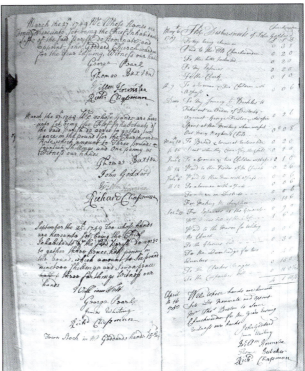

Homersfield churchwardens' accounts book from 1749. Note the signature towards the bottom of both pages of a James Whiting, almost certainly the farmer who provided money for the chapel in Wortwell to be built.

(REPRODUCED BY KIND PERMISSION OF SUFFOLK RECORD OFFICE, LOWESTOFT BRANCH, REF.: 128/E1/2.)

swung inwards towards the hall, bisected the avenue of trees in front of it and exited the grounds where Flixton Lodge was subsequently built. Sir Robert obviously wanted some privacy from everyday passing traffic, and bearing in mind that the majority of (although not all) householders in Homersfield paid him rent, they really had no choice other than to accept his proposals and comply with his wishes.

The Churchwardens

Wardens of the church came into being in medieval times, and either the vestry or the vicar and parishioners elected two each year, their term of office running from Easter to Easter. Their duties were basically to look after the fabric of the church and its possessions. Other duties included overseeing those legally removed to their home parish as a result of a Settlement Order, the allocation of church pews to a family (in return for a payment to the local church), the extermination of vermin, the maintenance of parish arms and payments to the families of parishioners sent to join the militia. They also presented wrongdoers at the local court.

The oldest surviving churchwardens' accounts for Homersfield date from the middle of the eighteenth century. The pages of two vellum-covered books, spanning almost 150 years through to the last years of the nineteenth century, are embellished with the most beautiful handwriting.

The incomings and outgoings are detailed separately in relation to Homersfield Church and its poor. There are huge numbers of entries of all kinds relating to the upkeep of Homersfield Church, to celebratory events and, to a lesser degree, to payments to the poor.

The church rate, collected twice yearly from those

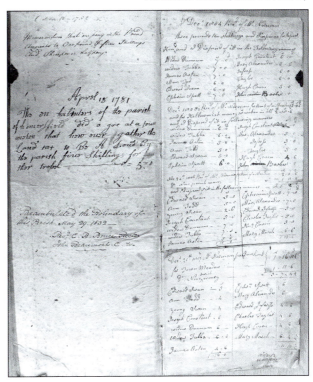

Homersfield churchwardens' accounts showing a parish meeting of 1781, an 1832 perambulation, and many disbursements to the poor from 1804 to 1807.

(REPRODUCED BY KIND PERMISSION OF SUFFOLK RECORD OFFICE, LOWESTOFT BRANCH, REF.: 128/E1/2.)

An Account of Money Recd on the Towns Acc by Bezal[eel] Gooch Churchwarden.

		£	s.	d.
1757				
19 November	*Recd of Mr Morse St Margt Charity Money*	1.	11	-
29 December	*of Mr Brock 1 yrs rent of the Town Meadow*	1.	15	6
		3	6	6

Disbursed to the poor as follows:

		s.	d.
Jno. Lydaman in Cash		2	0
Stephen Stannard d[itto]		1	6
Richd. Goldspink		2	6
George Boswell		2	6
Joseph Bunn		2	6
John Reeve		1	6
Robert Shade		-	6
John Atkinson [a note appears after his name: 'Dead']		2	-
Joseph Hounslea		2	6
Sml. Beddingfield		2	6
Thos. Fuller Senr.		1	6
Margt. Jarvis		1	-
Thos. Fuller Junr.		2	6
Goody Meek		1	6
B. Rust		1	-
Wm. Burges		1	-
Eliz. Todd		1	-
Mary Baker		1	-
Goody Chapman		-	6
Totl. Distributed in Cash	1	11	-
To Goody Breese by the hands of a … Maid		1	-
Totl.	1	12	-
To Mr Aggas for wood distributed to the above	1	11	-
	3	3	-

'Goody' was a word synonymous with 'widow'.

residents who could afford it, was dispensed only in the maintenance of the church and the well-being of its officials. The poor depended on money given to them via the churchwardens from the renting of an area of land known as the 'Town Meadow' and by the Nine Parishes charity. Payments to the poor were generally made on a weekly basis.

In the above table, 3s.6d. was carried over to the following year; often nothing remained.

The entry in the table opposite mentioning the Gunpowder Treason was a regular feature in the accounts over a number of years. The expense was incurred in the purchase of beer for the bellringers.

There are endless entries of the nature 'a (wo)man with a pass', which indicate a goodwill payment to a vagrant in the parish to help him or her on their way, or to someone being legally removed from the parish (via a Removal Order). Other regular entries include trips to courts, bread and wine at Easter, Christmas and Whitsuntide (the seventh Sunday after Easter, originally called 'White Sunday' and occasionally entered in the accounts as such, a traditional time for the baptism of converts who wear white to represent new life), the clerk's wages (paid twice yearly, typically 15s. in the middle of the eighteenth century – a significant sum). Money was regularly paid for removing ivy from the tower, cleaning the church and washing the surplice (the gown worn by the priest). Church repairs feature consistently in the accounts, including 'oyl for the bells' at 6d. per pint, replacement bell ropes (then 4s.6d.), altar rails, fencing and so on.

Towards the end of the nineteenth century, when many jobs had been lost to the ongoing improvements to agricultural machinery, almost every household in Homersfield was 'on the parish' and dependent on the Church for income. The churchwardens' accounts in these times therefore provide a near-complete list of heads of households residing in the village from year to year.

The extracts below relate to a full year in 1748/9.

The Disbursements of George Pearl Churchwarden from Easter 1748 to St Mich[aelmas] 1748 with the Constable.

	£	s.	d.
Disbursements	5	11	7½
Recd. by Rate	5	11	7½

The disbursements of George Pearl Churchwarden from St Mich[aelmas] 1748 to Easter 1749.

	£	s.	d.
For a Journey to Beccles		2	6
paid the Quartridge		2	3
for Bread and Wine		2	0
To A Pass		1	0
To A Journey concerning Atkins for Mr Goddard and Self		4	0
paid Mr Carpenter for 2 Rails		1	6
Brid[get] Rust a Faggot		0	2½
paid Mr Houndslea for mending Bridges		17	6
for Washing the Surplice		2	6
Expences at Gun-Powder Treason		5	0
Bread and Wine at Easter		2	0
The Clerks Half Years Wages		15	0
Excused Jarvis and Atkins Rate		0	6
For Bays for Catchpool		2	3
paid the Quartridge for 25th Mar[ch]		2	3
paid for Stocking the Bells and Oyl		2	6½
for Burying Catchpool		3	0
paid Matt[hew] Swan for a Rail		0	9
Pd. Mr Goddard for a Horse Journey to Beccles		1	6
To Mr Hounslea for a Post and Work		3	0
For making A Rate		1	0
	3	12	3
Recd. By Rate	3	14	1
Disbursements	3	12	3
		1	10
For Signing the Rate		1	0
		0	10
Old Stock		3	2
Town Stock		4	0

A sample of some of the other more interesting entries in the churchwardens' accounts, together with relevant notes are mentioned below.

		£	s.	d.
1749				
6 May	To my being sworn in		3	8
	[the expense probably relates to food and wine]			
	To my journey to Beccles to Take out an Order of Bastardy against George Freston and other affairs.		2	6
	[Bastardy Orders were issued by courts as a means of making the reputed father contribute towards the upbringing of a child born out of wedlock.]			
1754				
11 April	Paid to John Rivett for 9 dozen Sparrows.		2	3
	[Sparrows, hedgehogs and badgers were considered as vermin long before the times from which these accounts date, and the books contain endless entries showing that vast quantities of sparrows were killed by whatever means possible.			

Sparrow Clubs were commonplace in most parishes in the eighteenth and nineteenth centuries and were formed with the sole purpose of killing as many sparrows as possible. Only occasionally (as in the example above) is the payee named. John Rivett took only the heads of the sparrows to the Churchwardens, who then paid him; the entire bodies were decreed unnecessary, and for a great many years, the payments were made on a standard basic unit of a dozen heads, at 3d. a dozen (a farthing each). Payments were made for up to 30 dozen sparrows at a time. Whilst sparrows may cause some damage to crops, the same cannot be said of the entirely innocent hedgehog, but they were widely regarded as suckling cows, and from the mid-sixteenth century were considered worthy of extermination. They appear in the Homersfield accounts, paid at a rate of four pence a head, but badgers do not; probably there were none to be found within the parish. Entries relating to sparrows disappeared from the accounts towards the end of the 1820s.]

6 August	Paid to Jno. Low for Glaseing the Town House window.	3	0

[The 'Town House' was a dwelling in the parish used to house poor families. Almost all rural villages had such a house. It is not known exactly whereabouts in Homersfield this house stood.]

1757

6 October	Paid to Jno. Harvey for Work done at the Town House Nails and Stuff	3	-

1759

20 January	To Mr Morse for Two Coffins for Jno. Gillings and John Atkins.	16	-

[Clearly the families of these two men were unable to pay the costs themselves; later entries show that the cost of burying them was 3s.6d. each.]

1761

[undated]	To the Ringers att Crownation.	5	-

[This entry refers to beer for the bellringers at the coronation of King George III].

1783

30 May	To Expenses of Going the Bounds of the Town.	1	0	0

[A reference to the yearly perambulation.]

25 November	Spent att the Swan when the Bread was Gave Out	1	0

[This is the earliest reference yet found by the author to the Swan public house.]

1784

8 April	For two locks for the town Chest	1	2

[A clear reference to the parish chest, which disappeared from the church during the 1990s.]

	To Carting the Muck from the Steepel	1	0
15 September	To two journeys to Bungay concerning the horse tax	4	0

1788

29 September	Spent at the town meeting	15	0

[A (considerable) Michealmas celebration, commonly featuring in the accounts at these times].

1803

17 November	P[aid] att the Town Meeting concerning the Militia man	5	0

[A rare reference to the compulsory enlistment of men from the village.]

1811

23 May	For taken a List of the poor of Homersfield and where they belong for Mrs Adair	1	0

[The first reference to such a list, which continued for some years.]

1814				
5 June	*Paid for Binding Bible for the Church*	16	0	
1824				
26 September	*Pd T[homas] Smith fetching water for [washing church] and taken away muck*	4	0	
1831				
26 March	*Pd for tolling bell 3 hours King died*	3	0	
1834				
21 May	*Pd Cooper rep[aire]d Bier and Chest*	6	8	
	[A rare mention in the accounts of the parish bier, used for funerals and kept in the church.]			
1836				
22 March	*Guardians Journeys and attendance at Board at House of Industry*	4	10	-
	[The first reference in the accounts of the annual trip to Shipmeadow after the 1834 Poor Law Amendment Act].			
1857				
18 March	*Mr Chappell his Bill for Repairing roof the Church*	30	19	-
1858				
4 December	*Crickmer for catching Moles in the Church*	1	-	
1866				
24 December	*Mr Asten for the New Fence round Churchyard*	10	-	-
1877				
[undated]	*Given away in Coals 8 cwt. to each Cottage*	4	17	6
1879				
27 September	*Collection at Homersfield Church after choral service, for restoration of Bells*	4	10	8
	D[itt]o Saint Cross	5	10	3
1893				
July	*Worn out Harmonium removed from Homersfield Church*	1	-	-
	[It was replaced with a new organ and needed tuning and repairing the following year.]			

Overseers of the Poor

The office of overseer of the poor came into being in 1572, from which date two members of the vestry were elected to look to the finances of the sick, the poor, the unemployed and the elderly, their duties being to decide to whom the Poor Rate should be allocated and how much each should receive. The allocation took the form not only of money, but of clothing, food, wood (winter fuel) and other goods. The overseers' minute-books offer a wealth of detail concerning the ordinary people of the parish, giving their names and what was allocated to them. In some years, the vast majority of a parish were receiving assistance from the overseer.

The oldest Homersfield overseers' accounts exist only from 1838 and continue until 1867. The entries show that many of the expenses relate to trips to the local court in Bungay in connection with the payment of rates, taking individuals to Petty Sessions in connection with their removal to another parish, and presenting a Lunatic List annually.

Terriers

Inventories of the holdings and possessions of a church, known as terriers, give precise details of items held in the church and of land belonging to it (glebe), and were commonly prepared every few years for an impending visit from the governing bishop (known as a visitation). In preparing a terrier, it was standard practice to copy the preceding one, making such alterations as were necessary to reflect any changes that had taken place.

A True Terrier of all the Glebe Lands, Messuages, Tenements, Tythes, Portions of Tythes and other Rights belonging to the Rectory and Parish Church of Homersfield in the County of Suffolk and Diocese of Norwich and now in the use and Possession of the Reverend William Clarke rector there or his Tenants taken made Renewed according to the old Evidences and the knowledge of the Antient Inhabitants at a Vestry holden this seventh day of June in the year of our Lord one thousand eight hundred and one pursuant to due and legal notice given for that purpose and exhibited in the Ordinary Visitation of the Right Reverend Father in God Charles Lord Bishop of Norwich holden at Beccles on the Twentieth day of June One Thousand Eight hundred and One.

As to the Mansion House there neither now is nor by our Antient Evidences do it appear there ever was any.

A	R	P	
3	-	20	*First – One Pightle of Arable Land Enclosed containing by estimation Three Acres and half a rood and it layeth between the Lands of John Brown and the Heirs of Mrs Man towards the North part and the Church Yard towards the South – where of one head abutteth upon the Highway towards the West and the other upon the Church path towards the East.*
1	-	-	*Also one piece of Ground called Gooseland containing by estimation one Acre as it lyeth by the highway leading from Bungay to Mendham on the North upon the ground of William Stanford towards the south one head abutteth upon the Lands of Alexander Adair Esqr. on the East and the other on the Grounds of the said William Stanford towards the West.*
3	-	-	*Also one piece of Land containing by estimation three Acres as it lyeth between the grounds of Alexander Adair Esqr. on the East and West one head abutteth on the Highway leading from Bungay to Homersfield Heath on the North and the Lands of the said Alexander Adair Esqr. on the South.*
4	-	-	*Also one piece of Land called Gandersland containing by estimation four Acres as it lyeth between the Lands of Alexander Adair Esqr. on the East and West, and one head abutteth on the Highway leading from Bungay to Mendham to the North and the other on the Lands of the said Alexander Adair Esqr. towards the South.*
5	-	-	*Also one piece of Ground now in several partitions containing by estimation five Acres as it lyeth between the Lands of Alexander Adair Esqr. as well East as West the one head abutteth from the old river towards the North and the other upon part of Homersfield Heath towards the South, all the above pieces of Glebe are now in the Occupation of Jeremiah Cock.*
16	-	20	

Item. All those Tythes in the said parish of Homersfield are paid to the said rector or his tenants in their proper kinds, and there are no customs in the said Parish but only eight pence for every Cow and calf two pence per Acre for Meadow ground when tis Mowed, Garden one penny, Hearth Silver two pence Orchard two pence – The Glebes Tythes and Profits of the said Rectory may be Computed worth Corbus Annis p[er] Ann[um] or something better.

There is also belonging to the said parish of Homersfield one piece of Land lying in saint cross alias saint George alias sand Croft containing about Two Acres now lett to Robert Shearing at two pounds and ten shillings p[er] Ann[um] which is distributed amongst the Poor Yearly by the Churchwardens as by the Enfeoffment more fully appear.

Also a piece of Land left in the use of [blank] at the Yearly Rent of two Shillings and Sixpence.

Also a Cottage long since wasted.
Wm. Clarke Rector

Wm. Squire   Chief Inhabitants   Jereh. Cock

A True and perfect Note of all the Goods, Books, Ornaments & Utensils belonging to the parish and parish church of Homersfield Aforesaid.

First one Silver cup thereunto weighing about twelve ounces and large pewter flagon,
One pulpit Cloth and Cushion of the same, one large Surplice of Holland cloth, one fine
linen Cloth & Napkin for the Communion Table – also one more ditto a Barrying Cloth
– one Common Prayer book, one large Bible of the old translation, one Book of
Homilies, Three Bells with their Frames, the least thought to Weigh about four hundred
– and the second about five hundred and the third about six hundred pounds.

In testimony of the truth of the above mentioned particulars We the Minister,
Churchwardens and Chief Inhabitants have hereunto set our hands the Day and Year
above written.

Jereh. Cock Churchwarden

[The Mansion House mentioned refers to a rectory; in fact, there had been one in Homersfield, long since
disappeared by the time this terrier was produced].

There exist ten Homersfield terriers prepared during the nineteenth and in the first decade of the twentieth century. In the table (opposite and above), the oldest is detailed in full. Areas of land are given in acres, roods and perches, denoted by the letters 'A', 'R' and 'P' respectively.

Tithes

In medieval times, under the manorial system, people paid taxes both to local government (the lord of the manor) and to ecclesiastical government (the Church). As the manorial system declined during the sixteenth century, the Church gradually took control and consequently received all tax payments. Known as tithes, these were largely superseded at the end of the nineteenth century by the local and national taxes still paid today, although some tithes were finally repealed only in 1936.

The tithe was a ten per cent tax levied to support the clergy and the Church. It was calculated on a person's yearly income from produce, labour, or both, whichever was applicable, and in Homersfield was payable directly to the incumbent. The produce levied from the tithes was stored in a tithe barn which could often be as much as 50 yards long and 10 wide. Ancient documents refer to such a tithe barn in the thirteenth century in Homersfield and, although its exact location may never be known, it would have been built close to the rectory, which in turn would have been close to the church. Both the rectory and the tithe barn have since long disappeared from the village.

In 1836 the Tithe Commutation Act meant that payments could be commuted to money settlements instead of goods and commissioners were empowered to negotiate land values for this purpose. Consequently, between 1838 and 1854, a Tithe Map was drawn up for every parish, showing every dwelling, outbuilding and field. Each was allocated a number which could then be cross-referenced to the accompanying Tithe Apportionment, a hand-written

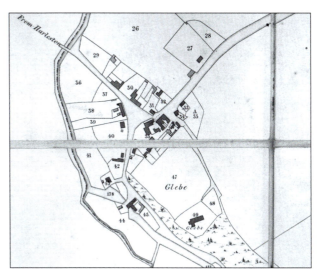

Part of the Homersfield Tithe Map of 1839, showing the village centre.

(Reproduced by kind permission of
Suffolk Record Office, Lowestoft branch, ref. 947/A/10/2.)

A page from the Homersfield Tithe Map Apportionment of 1839, detailing some of the dwellings shown in the photo of the map. (Reproduced by kind permission of
Suffolk Record Office, Lowestoft branch, ref. 947/A/10/1.)

book which, for each dwelling and field, gave the name of the owner, name of the occupier, a description of the land and premises, the area of land involved in acres, roods and perches, its value and the amount subsequently payable to the vicar. Though the purpose of the Tithe Map, on which every dwelling and field in the parish were represented, together with its apportionment, was purely to calculate the revenue due to the vicar, it is an extremely valuable document for any local historian.

The Homersfield Tithe Map is drawn on individual panels which have then been pasted onto a large canvas with a small gap between each panel to enable easy folding. It measures approximately 6ft x 5ft 6ins and comprises eight rows of five panels, each panel measuring 8 x 12ins or thereabouts. Houses and cottages are coloured in red, outbuildings in black. The Apportionment Book, dated 7 March 1839, together with the map provides an invaluable snapshot of Homersfield as it then was, with every landowner, occupier and field named, and depicts some houses which are no longer standing. It is difficult to imagine now, but some of the smallest houses in Homersfield housed more than one family when the Tithe Map and Apportionment were produced.

The Court

The Church had uses other than for worship, baptisms, marriages and burials. In medieval Homersfield, one use was as the ecclesiastical courtroom for the Deanery of South Elmham (until 1540) and dealt with matters concerning marriages, breaches of public ethics and church discipline. Incontinency was a common reason for appearing in court, as can be seen from the following examples from 1525, at which time incontinency referred to a lack of restraint in the indulgence of sex.

Margaret Wenyor of Flixton was presented as a gossiper in church during the time of Divine service. She was ordered to purge herself by four women as compurgators, in St James parish church on 27 July 1525. She brought as compurgators Margaret More, Joan Blanchard, Margaret Hill and others, and so lawfully purged herself.

William Venor of St Peter was presented at the court for incontinency. He was ordered the following Sunday to head the procession into the church with his head, legs and feet bare, holding a candle in his hands to the value of one penny. He was then to kneel before the principal image in the church until after the offertory, and to subsequently offer the candle into the hands of a priest. At the conclusion of all this, a certificate of the performance to prove he had carried out the order as directed by the court was to be given to him.

John Awers of St Margaret was presented for practising diabolical acts, but as he had been able to find three compurgators, was let off with a caution in the hope that he would amend his bad ways. One is but left to wonder just what these diabolical acts may have been!

Margaret Hoode of Sancroft (South Elmham St Cross) was presented for incontinency and was ordered during penance to walk with bare feet, kneeling before the image in the chancel, saying the salutation of the Angels 'cum cimbale' five times, and afterwards to retire to her customary place.

John Woodward of Homersfield, presented to the court on 28 September 1525 for incontinency, was ordered to carry out his penance on two consecutive Sundays, heading the procession in church with bare feet and legs, his body covered with a sheet instead of a tunic.

John Toftys, also of Homersfield, was presented for refusing to pay his portion towards the wages of the parish clerk.

Stephen Legate, again of Homersfield, was charged with adultery but received absolution from the rector as he had received correction for the offence in the presence of the Lord Bishop of Norwich.

Punishment

In medieval times, the Church was also responsible for maintaining the objects used for administering punishments, and reference is sometimes made in the churchwardens' accounts to them being in need of repair. In rural parishes, these normally comprised the stocks, the whipping post and occasionally the gallows, although these were much more common in towns. They had all been abolished by 1840, by which time the justice system had become more centralised rather than administered at parish level.

The Stocks

An Act passed in 1405 directed that for the punishment of wrongdoers every community should have stocks, which were to be maintained by the parish. The Homersfield stocks have long since disappeared (although they are still to be seen at nearby St Margaret) and would almost certainly have been

The stocks from South Elmham St Margaret, photographed in 1995.

sited on the green in order to cause the maximum humiliation to the person or persons detained in them. To add to the embarrassment, a nearby notice-board would sometimes hold details of the crime committed. The majority of village stocks consisted of a pair of boards which clamped together like jaws, hinged at one end with a padlock at the other. The boards were supported at each end by upright posts made from tree trunks, the Old English word for which was 'stocc', hence the name. Wrongdoers were secured with their ankles through apertures cut as semi-circles on the inner edge of each board. Stocks were commonly used to detain troublemakers

A medieval whipping-post similar to that which would have been used in Homersfield centuries ago; this example, photographed in 2005, is in New Buckenham, Norfolk.

A possible site for the Homersfield gallows on the road to St Cross, photographed in 2007.

prior to their appearance in court. A period of four hours was a standard term of confinement for the more petty offences such as blaspheming, being drunk or indulging in sports on the Sabbath. This well-known method of punishment was commonplace during the whole of the medieval period and continued into the first half of the nineteenth century.

The Whipping Post

In addition to the stocks, every parish had its whipping post. This was a single iron plate attached to a post with semi-circular loops at right angles along its length. Like the stocks, the Homersfield whipping post was probably on the green, designed to attract the most attention to those manacled to it – almost always women – whose punishment was to be whipped bare-back. The women punished in this way were often beggars and vagrants and, having undergone this deterrent, were afterwards returned to their place of origin.

The Gallows

This wooden scaffold, made from two upright posts set several feet apart and joined by a cross-piece, was for hanging those who committed very serious crimes. The condemned man or woman, along with their coffin, would be driven between the posts in a wheeled cart and then strung up. As death occurred as a result of slow strangulation over a period of days, the degree of suffering was undoubtedly extreme. In the eighteenth century, gallows were altered so that a drop resulted in a broken neck and instant death.

Gallows were usually built at crossroads and, although they were not common in the countryside, there was one on the road between Homersfield and St Cross, on the hill, where it could be seen for some considerable distance in all directions – a clear warning to potential law-breakers.

Like the Homersfield whipping post, the gallows have not survived.

Church Ales

In medieval England, the Church not only prohibited work on festive days but obliged parishioners to attend church services rather than have a day to themselves. The Church, via the churchwardens, therefore needed to provide entertainment for the people of the parish on these holy days, which are the origin of what eventually became the holiday. By the end of the fifteenth century the church ale was the most popular activity at these religious gatherings and remained so for a further century or more before it gradually died out as a result of Puritanical influence. The ale was normally held in the church-house, a building close to the church equipped with the necessary utensils for making various kinds of food, and of course, for the brewing of ale – all paid for by the parishioners through taxes. The churchwardens bought malt and brewed the ale, which was then sold, the resulting feasts being known as 'church ales'. These were held at least three or four times a year, and were extremely popular events. The ale was weak and barely intoxicating, but nevertheless much revelry and socialising took place. Bride ales were held to celebrate the weddings of those too poor to provide their guests with food and drink. Lamb ales, to celebrate the lambing season, were also held, as were harvest ales, to celebrate a bountiful harvest. There were clerk ales, to help fund the parish clerk's wages, and bid ales, to help a poor man desperately in need of money. These ales, for many different causes, all helped swell the church funds.

The Homersfield churchwardens' accounts from these times have unfortunately not survived, so it is not possible to see the different kinds and the frequency of church ales in the village, but that they did take place is beyond doubt.

Rogation

Rogation days, introduced into England in the eighth century, comprise the three days preceding Ascension Day (the fortieth day after Easter, marking the last earthly appearance of Christ). This festival was a time of fasting and prayers for a good harvest. The pagan festival of 'Robigalia', from which the Christian 'Major Rogation' was derived, involved a procession through the cornfields praying for protection of the crops. The two minor Rogation days were associated with protection of the land from earthquakes and other natural disasters. The festival also included a perambulation whereby boughs and crosses were carried, the land and crops were blessed and the parish boundaries confirmed by tracing crosses in the ground. The parish priest would read from the Bible at traditional local stopping-points, often at a prominent tree on the parish boundary, or at a corner. The terms 'gospel oak' and 'amen corner' survive as relics of this ancient festival. The festivities during the three days of Rogation, having their roots buried in paganism, were excessive and, after the Reformation became merely days of fasting and abstinence, while the procession was limited to the 'beating of the bounds', a tradition which later became the formal perambulation.

The Homersfield churchwardens' accounts for years when Rogation was practised have not survived but, as with church ales, Rogation undoubtedly did take place in Homersfield.

Perambulation

Rogation Sunday, the fifth Sunday after Easter, was the day when the vestry arranged for the annual perambulation to take place. It was the vestry's responsibility to ensure that no boundary marker stones had been moved during the last year, that there was nothing obstructing the boundaries and that no new buildings had been put up without their knowledge. In times when detailed maps were not available, this was a very important and popular event in the parish calendar and continued until well into the latter half of the nineteenth century. For the purposes of deriving income from its parishioners, it was important to know the exact boundaries and therefore the houses contained within it. A procession, headed by the priest and members of the vestry, with prominent people and all the children of the village dressed for the occasion following behind, walked around the entire parish boundary. Along the way, the congregation would stop occasionally while the priest held prayers for a plentiful harvest. Any obstacle in the way, such as an overgrown bush, was broken down and removed. Where the boundary was a river the priest would commonly get into a boat and row along it. The children carried wands of willow branches with which to beat the boundaries as they walked, hence 'beating the bounds'. These wands were a remnant of the earlier Rogation festival, and sometimes involved the 'beating' of boys along the parish boundary (sometimes held upside-down over a pond or bumped against boundary stones) as a way of instilling these boundaries into the children's minds. The intention of these beatings was that the boys' outcries would drive away evil spirits and so help ensure a good harvest at the end of the summer.

With the introduction of maps, commencing with the Tithe Map from the end of the 1830s and followed by Ordnance Survey maps in the 1870s, together with estate maps, all of which showed parish boundaries in clear detail, the practice of perambulation started to decline. Nevertheless, in some parishes it continued for some considerable time, even though it was unnecessary.

That it took place in Homersfield is confirmed by a parish magazine from towards the end of the nineteenth century, as well as the surviving churchwardens' accounts, where an entry reads: 'Perambulated the Boundary of this Parish May 29 1832.' It is signed by the incumbent, Revd C.B. (Courtenay Boyle) Bruce, and by John Beaumont, one of the Homersfield churchwardens.

Non-conformism

Dissenters, those dissatisfied with the Church of England, are known to have existed from medieval times. The Acts of Supremacy and Uniformity in 1558 and 1559 defined conformity as regards the Church of England, and those who refused to conform were labelled 'recusants', a term applied to Protestants and Catholics alike. Recusants had their own chapels, where priests and followers could worship, and built hiding-places in houses (priests' holes) to avoid being arrested and prosecuted for their faith. Prayers were said in secret and behind locked doors for fear of discovery.

Following Oliver Cromwell's removal from power in 1660, the monarchy and the Church of England were restored to their former glory. The Act of Uniformity in 1662 formally expelled groups of recusants from the Church of England and the term 'Non-conformist' came into being. Non-conformists were forbidden from worshipping in groups of five or more unless they were conforming to Anglican rules, and Non-conformist ministers were banned from returning to within five miles of where they had previously preached. Persecution was the order of the day, and while those caught were fined or imprisoned, those who escaped such treatment not uncommonly went on to found independent chapels with ready-made congregations waiting to fill them.

Acceptance of the growing Non-conformity in England was eventually marked by an Act passed in 1689. The Act of Toleration enabled people to worship and to build chapels legally for the first time. Punishment of recusancy declined and was eventually abolished altogether as a result of three Acts: the Roman Catholic Relief Act (passed in 1781), the Places of Worship Act (1789) and the Catholic Emancipation Act (1829).

Non-conformity in Homersfield

James Whiting, a Homersfield farmer, paid for the United Reform Chapel to be built in Wortwell. In 1773, when he was in his early seventies, it was opened in the presence of local Non-conformist ministers. Whiting passed away some 14 years later in 1787, aged 85 years. In the 1930s, a Homersfield railway stationmaster was the chapel's minister.

From the end of the 1700s Homersfield residents who were not willing followers of the Church of England were able to meet and worship at a Non-conformist meeting-house within their own village, such a dwelling being authorised by the Bishop of Norwich.

John Larke, christened on St George's Day, 1758, in Ringsfield, near Beccles, was living 20 years later in Woodton, having married Susanna Spratt of Homersfield on 13 October 1778. Seven of their children, twin daughters and five sons, were baptised in Homersfield Church in the 15 years from 1783 to 1798. All but the first were baptised at home, a common practice at a time when children died young and were baptised as soon as possible rather than waiting for a church baptism. Two of their sons did die very young, aged three and 14 months respectively. Six months or so after their last child was baptised, John and Susanna opened their home (with their landlord's permission) as a Non-conformist meeting-house.

A document referring to a certificate granting permission from the Bishop of Norwich for John Larke to open his house (with the owner's consent) as a Non-conformist place of worship for Protestant dissenters, 1798.

Wortwell United Reform Chapel, 2007.

John passed away in 1837 and was buried in Homersfield churchyard on 27 January, aged 83 years. His wife, Susanna, was living in Wortwell when she died on 14 December 1842, aged 88 years.

The Parish Magazine

It seems that the first Homersfield parish magazine was published quarterly from 11 November 1890. *Our Quarterly Messenger*, for the parishes of Homersfield and St Cross, was available from St

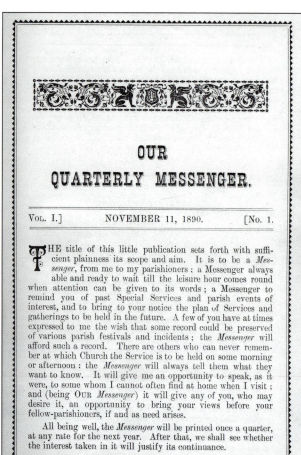

OUR
QUARTERLY MESSENGER.

VOL. I.]   NOVEMBER 11, 1890.   [No. 1.

THE title of this little publication sets forth with sufficient plainness its scope and aim. It is to be a *Messenger*, from me to my parishioners; a Messenger always
able and ready to wait till the leisure hour comes round
when attention can be given to its words; a Messenger to
remind you of past Special Services and parish events of
interest, and to bring to your notice the plan of Services and
gatherings to be held in the future. A few of you have at times
expressed to me the wish that some record could be preserved
of various parish festivals and incidents; the *Messenger* will
afford such a record. There are others who can never remember at which Church the Service is to be held on some morning
or afternoon: the *Messenger* will always tell them what they
want to know. It will give me an opportunity to speak, as it
were, to some whom I cannot often find at home when I visit;
and (being OUR *Messenger*) it will give any of you, who may
desire it, an opportunity to bring your views before your
fellow-parishioners, if and as need arises.

All being well, the *Messenger* will be printed once a quarter,
at any rate for the next year. After that, we shall see whether
the interest taken in it will justify its continuance.

OUR
QUARTERLY
MESSENGER;

THE CHURCH OF ENGLAND

MAGAZINE AND RECORD

FOR THE UNITED PARISH OF

HOMERSFIELD

WITH

ST. CROSS.

Beccles:

A. W. JORDAN, PRINTER, HUNGATE WORKS.

OUR
QUARTERLY MESSENGER;

THE CHURCH OF ENGLAND

Magazine and Record

FOR THE UNITED PARISH OF

HOMERSFIELD

WITH

ST. CROSS.

No. 75.   March 1st, 1911.   Price, 3d.

SOLD AT ST. CROSS RECTORY,

AND BY

MR. DEBENHAM, HOMERSFIELD.

H. W. SHORT, PRINTER, BUNGAY.

Cross rectory and from Henry Debenham's shop in
Homersfield (now Waveney House) priced at 3d.
Instituted by the Revd William Morley Smith, it
constitutes a priceless mine of information regarding
the social life in the two villages towards the end of
the Victorian period and beyond. The magazine ran
until at least 1911, by which time 75 issues had been
produced and the good work of Revd Morley Smith
was being carried on by his successor, Revd Wilby.

The magazines naturally exhibit a strong religious
leaning and abound with the names of local residents. Many small clubs and societies of Victorian
Homersfield – local branches of the Church of
England Temperance Society, the Band of Hope, the
Girls' Friendly Society, the Boys' Friendly Society, the
Clothing Club, the Cricket Club and many more – are
all to be found in the pages of the magazine. As well
as detailing the minutiae of everyday life, these
magazines carry articles on local history, on events
throughout the Empire and on missionary work
undertaken abroad.

Top left: *The opening page of the very first parish magazine, 1890.*

Top right: *An early cover of the parish magazine from
1895.*

Left: *A much later parish magazine cover, showing it little
changed in design.*

CHAPTER 5

From Pillar to Post

Vestries

During medieval times the lord of the manor and his court took care of administering local goings-on and the law, including dealing with those who broke it, via the manorial court. From the sixteenth century, manorial courts receded in importance and the Church gradually took control, administration then becoming the responsibility of individual parishes. Amongst its many responsibilities, the parish became accountable for the care of the sick and the poor, and levied a rate to cover the cost of doing so. This administration was carried out by the vestry (a parish council) and the Justices of the Peace.

Vestries came into being from the fourteenth century onwards. Minutes of their meetings were recorded in vestry books, which detail matters such as the care of the poor, church repairs, charities, schools and so on. Vestries continued these functions until 1834, at which time responsibility for the poor was transferred to Poor Law guardians and many other duties were transferred to new civil local authorities. Parish Councils ultimately replaced vestries from 1894.

In 1597/98 an Act of Parliament empowered vestries to collect a poor rate from householders in their parishes, the duty of collection falling on the overseers of the poor.

SETTLEMENT AND REMOVAL

An Overview

In 1601 the Poor Law Act, which remained in force with various amendments until 1834, provided for relief to be approved for those incapable of looking after themselves in their parish of legal settlement – and in no other. This constraint was intended to prohibit a mass arrival of paupers into parishes where there may be work of a temporary nature, but whose finances were already stretched by the considerable number of impoverished people they were already looking after. Under the Act, parishes could provide housing for the poor. Overseers would commonly pay such poor peoples' rent, but in some parishes houses for individual poor families were built or an existing dwelling, used as a parish poor house, was commonly referred to as 'the town house'. Parishes often had an old, uninhabited cottage or two that could be used for this purpose, a single-roomed dwelling, often no more than a damp

hovel. The churchwardens' accounts show that Homersfield had such a town house, which provided accommodation for the old and sick and for widows and children.

At any time, the head of a household could fall ill, die or become unemployed and the family could find themselves having to go to the parish to be looked after. Poverty could always be just around the corner. Under the terms of the Poor Law Act it was essential that people ensured they were legally settled in the parish where they lived in order to claim relief from the overseers.

The Act stated that a person was considered to be legally settled in a parish after he or she had lived there for one month. However, this stipulation presented an opportunity for outside workers or homeless people to move to a new parish and acquire the right to receive money, clothing, food and other commodities from their new parish quickly. This became a huge burden on some parishes and the 1662 Settlement Act (correctly known as the Poor Relief

A 1764 Settlement Examination for Mary Jessup of Bungay, who at one time lived at a farm in Homersfield with her husband, John. Frustratingly, the farm is not named! (REPRODUCED BY KIND PERMISSION OF SUFFOLK RECORD OFFICE, LOWESTOFT BRANCH, REF.: 128/G4/5.)

A charming view of agricultural labourers with their horse and cart outside Barnfield Cottages, c.1925.
(REPRODUCED BY KIND PERMISSION OF FRANK HONEYWOOD.)

Act), together with later Acts, changed the rules considerably in order to alleviate such problems, granting a legal right to settlement and to relief from that parish to individuals provided that one of the following conditions was met:

i) the individual holds a public office in the parish, or pays the parish rate
ii) the individual rents property in the parish worth more than £10 a year
iii) the individual has been apprenticed to a master in the parish
iv) the individual is a woman who has married a man of the parish
v) the individual is unmarried and has worked in the parish for at least one year
vi) the individual is a legitimate child, aged under seven, whose father lived in the parish
vii) the individual is an illegitimate child and was born in the parish, or
viii) the individual has resided in the parish for 40 days after having given the parish authorities prior written notice of his or her intention to do so

The rules were often strictly applied. Parish officials (or Justices of the Peace) were entitled to question new arrivals on oath as to their place of settlement. As a result, removal from a parish might be enforced if an individual (together with his or her family) was not legally settled there and thus regarded as a potential burden on the parish. Several Homersfield settlement examinations still exist, and record much information, such as people's place of birth, their places of employment or apprenticeship and the places where they lived for a significant period of time.

A much-changed view of Homersfield railway station, c.1930. The car and dog probably belong to the photographer. (REPRODUCED BY KIND PERMISSION OF FRANK HONEYWOOD.)

At the Quarter Sessions, Justices issued a removal order if it could be satisfactorily shown that a person or family needed (or were likely to need) poor relief and had no settlement rights in the parish. Such a removal order stipulated the return of a person or family to their parish of legal settlement. Justices issued a pass, which recorded a pauper's place of legal settlement and meant that the person, together with any family, would be escorted from the start of the journey to the end to ensure that the removal was successfully executed. Homersfield churchwardens' accounts from the eighteenth century contain hundreds of examples where money was given to help those with a pass out of the parish. Clearly, pauperism was a huge problem. The procedure was that a parish constable would escort a person or family as far as his parish boundary, where the constable in the neighbouring parish would take

The back of Homersfield Mill and two haystacks can be seen in the background of this view of the river from near Mendham Lane, c.1940. The motorcycle appears in several similar views and belonged to the photographer.

A postcard from about 1907 showing the topiary at No. 83 and the entrance to the pub bowling green, with the railway line and Dove Hill in the distance.

Mrs Mary Ann Gower and her daughter Alice seated outside the Post Office, c.1908. Note the maid posing for the camera at the back.

charge and convey them to the next parish boundary, the process being repeated until the destination was reached. On reaching their parish of legal settlement, the paupers might receive relief, but it was also possible that the receiving parish would deny liability and apply to the court for another removal order. Disputes among parishes over the liability of paupers were commonplace, and in such instances the courts had to make the decision as to which parish was liable.

Apprentices were usually orphaned children, or the children of unmarried mothers or widows. The purpose of the system was to teach these children a trade so that they could later go out and earn a living, but in reality, by the eighteenth century, apprenticeships were generally thought of by parish officials as a way of relieving themselves of responsibility and saving ratepayers' money. Children were commonly apprenticed to farmers or innkeepers, and were a convenient source of cheap labour.

Although the Settlement Act, by and large, improved matters considerably for overburdened parish finances, one unintentional side effect was that it effectively prevented many folk from moving to another parish to find employment, especially in cases where they had been treated well. The potential difficulty of obtaining a legal settlement, the uncertainty and fear of the old parish denying liability after a person or family had moved away, the distrust of parishioners and parish officials towards any new people who may need relief at some point in the future, all combined to restrict the movement of

A delivery boy, a maid and a young man pose for the camera outside the Dove, c.1912.

Farmhands inspect their stock, c.1910, while leaning on movable sheep pens which are still used today.

Henry Debenham's general stores (on the left) *with Homersfield Mill* (centre background), *c.1912.*

those genuinely in search of work in neighbouring parishes. New arrivals were positively discouraged in some parishes and, where one family ruled over them from a large house (such as in Homersfield), there was a tendency to pull cottages down to prevent their occupation by potential paupers and thus potential future claims for relief. Another common method of denying relief to unmarried persons new to a village was to hire them for 364 days rather than the all-important full year.

This problem was addressed by the Settlement Act of 1697, which empowered overseers to issue settlement certificates to parishioners relocating to another parish. These guaranteed that the person or family would be taken back if things didn't work out and they subsequently needed to claim relief. This system made things easier for parishes receiving outsiders, as they could now permit people with a

An early motor car travels towards Homersfield Mill, having just passed St Mary's Cottage and Waveney Cottage, c.1920.

John Borrett's name is on the board above the door in this view of the Black Swan, c.1908.

settlement certificate to move in, knowing that they could be returned to their old parish if they fell on hard times, which they not uncommonly did. Incomers normally passed over their settlement certificates to the new parish officials so that they (the officials) could prove their case against the old parish if the new people should become a liability.

One unpleasant aspect of the 1697 Settlement Act was that paupers were required to wear a large badge on the right shoulder of their outermost garment bearing the letter 'P' and the first letter of the name of their parish. In theory, until 1810, failure to comply with this (although those of good behaviour were exempted in an Act of 1781/82) resulted in the offender losing their poor relief or being whipped and committed to a 'house of correction' (prison) for a period of hard labour. In practice, however, it was often not enforced, no doubt because paupers already had more than enough to contend with in the form of feeding and clothing themselves, let alone anything else.

Another unpleasant aspect concerned illegitimate children, who were entitled to legal settlement in the parish of their birth. Such children were thought of by parish officials as potential future claimants of poor relief. Overseers often got around this problem by having pregnant migrant unmarried women removed to a neighbouring parish before the birth. An Act of 1732/33 prevented such removals of women during pregnancy and in the month following childbirth. Women were also required to name the child's father with a view to him providing

financial support. Another Act 11 years later stipulated that an illegitimate child's parish of settlement should be designated the mother's parish of settlement (and not the parish where the mother gave birth). From the point of view of a child's settlement rights, it therefore did not matter if a woman was allowed to stay in a parish for her confinement. Yet another Act in 1794/95 reduced many of the undesirable aspects of the Settlement Acts by prohibiting the removal of paupers unless they required relief. Removal was no longer possible simply because parish officials were apprehensive of someone requiring relief in the future. This same Act also authorised Justices to suspend removal orders issued against those who were sick, which had hitherto provided another means by which overseers reduced the amount of poor relief given to needy people.

A small group of associated families who lived in Homersfield in the middle of the eighteenth century and who were subject to settlement and removal is now considered.

The Leman Family

Robert Leman was a carpenter in the village of Upwell in Norfolk and in about 1705, his son, Thomas, was born there. Thomas was later hired on a yearly basis to work for John Chamberlain, an overseer of the poor in Upwell, for whom Robert also worked as a servant for a couple of years. Thomas learnt his father's trade and, when he was about 24 years old, moved away and came to live in

A lady stands in her garden at No. 67 in this view of the village, c.1925. A board is at the front of the garden in the police house (No. 68) and a well-trodden path can just be seen going across the green to Nos 79 and 80.

Homersfield. When his first wife died young, he met and fell in love with a girl in his new parish. Ann Chapman was the last of at least six children of Richard and Elizabeth Chapman to be baptised in Homersfield. Their banns were read out in church on three consecutive Sundays from the middle of July, and Thomas and Ann's wedding took place in Homersfield Church a couple of months afterwards, on 5 October 1756. A gap in the parish registers between 1742 and 1760 no doubt explains why the baptism of their son, Thomas, is not recorded; neither are the baptisms of any other children they may have had until their daughter Ann appears, baptised on 12 May 1760. Possibly there were no others, but as there is a similar gap in the dates of burials, it cannot be seen whether any other children they might have had subsequently succumbed in early infancy.

It seems that the family fell on hard times, as Thomas tried to obtain a settlement certificate so that they could remain in Homersfield and subsequently claim relief from the overseers if they needed to. His settlement examination, dated 12 December 1761, shows that he based his evidence of having met the legal requirements for obtaining such a certificate on the fact that, in 1743 or thereabouts, he lent £10 to one Thomas Todd as a mortgage on the security of a cottage with some land in Homersfield. He later paid a further £8 to Thomas Todd's son and heir, John, for the cottage and land. He then lived in the cottage, although possibly he had lived in it from the time of the mortgage.

For whatever reason, it is apparent that his much-needed settlement certificate was not forthcoming, as a removal order was issued against him by the Homersfield overseers five weeks later, on 19 January 1762. He, his wife Ann and two children were ordered to return to Upwell, Thomas' birth-place. They are not heard of again in the Homersfield parish registers.

Mary Mayes

Mary Mayes' settlement examination, on 8 February 1755, states that she was about 17 years old and was born in Homersfield. She wasn't baptised there, but that is not uncommon, as not every child was baptised. She claimed her place of settlement to be at Carlton in Norfolk, where her father lived, and had had a settlement certificate issued there, as she felt she had done nothing specified within the rules to gain a similar certificate in Homersfield; she hadn't lived in any parish nor been hired for work for a whole year.

Somewhat frustratingly, whether the outcome of this examination was successful or not isn't known, but if she did leave Homersfield at some point, it appears she returned to the village. She is very probably the Mary Mayes who married shoemaker Samuel Bunn on 10 October 1773. She would then have been about 35 years old and on her wedding day had been with child for six months. Ann was baptised in Homersfield Church on New Year's Day 1774 and another daughter, Mary, was baptised there

The photographer stood in the garden of No. 70 to take this photograph of the Post Office, c.1920.

Some outbuildings can be seen on what is now the playing-field in this view of Waveney House, c.1932.

A grand-looking Mill House, c.1930.

on 19 December 1776. Their joy at the birth of another daughter was abruptly curtailed, as she was buried later the same day. Probably she had been born poorly and died within a few hours. Samuel passed away only six years later and was buried in the churchyard on 17 March 1782.

Mary Bullock and the Rust Family

The settlement examination for Mary Bullock is probably the most interesting of all those that still exist, if only for the potential scandal it would have incited when a certain event became common knowledge in Homersfield. A clue to the underlying revelation in this examination is contained in the way in which she is repeatedly referenced in the document, as 'Mary

Bullock, alias Rust'. The use of an alias in settlement and removal documents is unusual.

The examination is dated 1 October 1760, when Mary Bullock was about 65 years old, so she was born c.1695. In her late twenties, she married a journeyman shoemaker (one who was paid by the day) by the name of John Rust, at Biggleswade in Bedfordshire on 18 January 1722. Prior to marrying her, he had told Mary he was a widower and that his wife and children had died of smallpox in Homersfield. He also told her that he had been granted a settlement certificate whilst living there. John and Mary were married for about 24 years; he passed away c.1746, probably aged about 65 years. The revelation comes from a daughter of John's first marriage, Bridget Rust, who was baptised in

An early view of the entire Barnfield Cottages, c.1930.

Homersfield on 20 January 1711. She states that her mother, Margaret, died in 1734, some 12 years after her father married Mary Bullock!

The settlement examination is supported by three additional statements. Bridget Rust reiterates that her mother died in 1734 and also that her father left her mother in Homersfield when Mary Bullock was very young. Whether John Rust actually knew Mary Bullock at this time is not made clear, but the inference is that he did. Mary May[e]s and Elizabeth Chapman (younger sister of Ann Chapman, who married Thomas Leman) also both confirm that Margaret Rust died in 1734, Elizabeth adding that it was John Rust who buried her!

John claimed that his wife and children had died in Homersfield. The implication from this is that all his children had died. There is some evidence to support the claim that one, possibly two, of his children died in Homersfield, but certainly not all. Between 1705 and 1711 the parish registers show baptisms for three children whose father was named as John Rust. One was buried less than a year after being baptised, and another possible child, who is not shown as having been baptised in Homersfield, was buried in 1714. One of the remaining two baptised in the village is not mentioned in the registers after his baptism, implying that he survived. Bridget Rust clearly did survive childhood, smallpox or not, and died unmarried; she lived past her sixtieth birthday and was buried in Homersfield on 12 October 1773.

John's wife, Margaret, may have died in Homersfield but the burial registers do not include

If only all main roads were like this one; from a postcard photograph taken around 1937!

her name, nor, for that matter, do they include her husband's.

The evidence from the settlement examination and the use of an alias when referring to Mary Bullock very strongly suggest that when John Rust married her in Biggleswade, he became a bigamist; the marriage being illegal, it was therefore not recognised by the Judge, William Adair of Flixton Hall. In these times, bigamy was not as uncommon as one might think.

It would seem that Mary Bullock's application for a settlement certificate to be issued to her in Homersfield was unsuccessful, as a removal order was issued against her on 7 October 1760, sending her via the parish constables all the way to Mundford, in Norfolk.

✦ CHAPTER 6 ✦

Christmas Day in the Workhouse

The state pension came into existence on New Year's Day, 1909; before then, those who could not afford to stop work at any point in their lives had a choice to make: either they carried on working, often until they dropped, or they went into the local workhouse. It was as simple as that. Even to this day, many families shy away from revealing that their ancestors may once have been in the workhouse, but the plain truth is that for the vast majority of those who need to work for a living today, almost invariably some of their direct ancestors spent time in such an institution.

Before 1834

In 1723 an Act of Parliament gave a parish or group of parishes the power to build workhouses, where those who were admitted would be put to work. This legislation, widely known as the 'Workhouse Act', permitted parishes to deny relief to those who refused to go into the workhouse. To minimise costs in funding the poor, paupers could also be put under the control of a contractor (in return for a fixed sum), whose responsibility it was to maintain these impoverished souls and find employment for them. In general, the building of workhouses resulted in significant financial savings for parishes.

As a more efficient and less financially draining means of administering the needs of the poor, local magistrates and the more affluent residents made a decision to create 'Incorporated Hundreds', which encompassed several parishes and were controlled by a Board of Guardians. These guardians, elected by those parishioners who paid the poor rate in the relevant parishes, typically consisted of clergy, gentry, principal landowners and businessmen. These organisations could borrow money (within limits) in order to build 'houses of industry', large, imposing buildings capable of housing considerable numbers of paupers from parishes within their own Hundred. The board appointed a workhouse master and a relieving officer to oversee the poor. The Wangford Hundred, of which Homersfield is one of 27 parishes contained within it, did build such a house.

Another Act, passed in 1782 and known as Gilbert's Act, made provision for outdoor relief, given to those who were not resident in a workhouse but needed to go on the parish in order to survive. This relief took the form of fuel, clothing and medical help, in addition to cash.

There were thus two separate systems of providing for the poor, one parish based, the other hundred based. Out of principle, many people understandably did not wish to leave their own homes and be admitted into a workhouse. More often than not, the local house of industry was, in fact, a very comfortable place in which to live. In particular, those in East Anglia generally gained a reputation for offering a quality of life far better than that available outside.

In a period of about 50 years, between 1760 and 1810, around five million acres of common land in England were acquired legally and enclosed by landowners, depriving the ordinary labouring family of precious land on which to grow food, keep cattle and collect winter fuel. In another period of about 50 years, roughly between 1780 and 1830, the amount of outdoor relief given to the poor rose greatly, due to population increase, the agricultural and industrial revolutions and rising prices as a result of the Napoleonic Wars, which led to an increase in the numbers of unemployed and a recession.

In 1795 another system introduced was taken up by a great many parishes, to the point of being almost universal. Named after the first village in which it was introduced, the Speenhamland (in Berkshire) system (also known as the Berkshire Bread Act) worked on the principle that those labourers not earning enough to support themselves and their families would have the difference made up by the overseers out of money collected by way of the parish poor rate. The minimum level of income for a person depended on two things: the size of his family and the cost of flour or bread. The rate money was paid to those in work as well as to the unemployed, the latter receiving all their income from the parish. The system, well intentioned in theory, in practice was a disaster. Employers were not slow in seeing a major loophole in the system, nor were they slow in taking advantage of it.

Wages were deliberately kept low and employers did little or nothing when the cost of a loaf of bread rose (as it did in the last decade of the eighteenth century), knowing that their employees would be subsidised by their parish overseers. The 'bread money' as it became known, soon came to be thought of as the poor man's entitlement; compensation for the Settlement Act, which prevented him from seeking work elsewhere, even when his own parish was unable to employ him. As things went from bad to worse it became clear that the existing system of maintaining the poor wasn't working; something had to be done, and in 1834 came a change which was to affect life in the workhouse forever.

1834 and After

In 1834 the Royal Commission produced a report of the current state of the poor laws in England and Wales. Their proposed changes resulted in the Poor Law Amendment Act later the same year. This revolutionised the administration of workhouses and the people in them. The Act permitted the formation of new Poor Law Unions, consisting of a group of parishes, and did away with outdoor relief almost altogether. The responsibility of the poor was transferred by the Act from the parish to the union. Anyone unable to support themselves had to go into the workhouse whether they wanted to or not, those who refused being denied any relief at all. This resulted in the poor living in dread of the workhouse, an emotion that lingered well into the twentieth century. Only through sheer desperation did people enter the workhouse when the Act became law.

There was much cruelty in the new regime. On entry, the new arrival was searched and his or her clothes removed and stored away. The inmate was then thoroughly washed and workhouse dress issued. Though not compulsory for a union to have a uniform for its 'guests', it invariably did.

Families were split up, with husbands separated from wives and children from their parents. They were often allowed to see each other only for a very short time once a week; being caught together or even speaking to each other would result in a harsh punishment. Comforts were reduced to a minimum. The basic item in any room was a cheap wooden bed with a sacking mattress and a couple of blankets. Pillows were deemed unnecessary and, if there were sheets, they were of the most coarse and uncomfortable kind. Many had to share a bed, some of which were in two tiers, one above the other. Any chairs would be both armless and backless, and there would be none in the working areas, while for meal times there were rough tables with benches to sit on. The otherwise bare walls would display workhouse regulations and weekly diet tables, and reading matter was confined to the odd religious tract, lecturing the pauper on ways to improve himself. Children did not have the luxury of toys or games; there were none provided.

Residents, expected to work and earn money for their institution, were ruled with a rod of iron, and discipline was severe. The women and young girls commonly sat spinning hemp, or spinning and carding wool. Spinning wheels, supplied by overseers of the poor, were in almost constant use and in need of frequent repair. The women also did much of the domestic work, while the men and boys worked in the fields for local farmers or helped maintain the public roads (at least until the responsibility for their upkeep was transferred from the parish to the local authority). From the fields they would collect stones used to fill holes in the roads, breaking the larger ones into more manageable pieces. Men, women and children were commonly seen picking oakum – a loose fibre from old rope, most commonly from ships' rigging. Used to seal the hulls of ships, this was soaked in water and picked apart with bare fingers, which quickly became very sore.

The Poor Law Board recommended half a dozen different diets for the residents, which were almost universally adopted by individual unions. Their diet, poor to say the least, consisted typically of daily gruel, bread and cheese, with soup, bacon and potatoes, and meat and potatoes once a week. The women often had less to eat than the men. The only permitted drink was water, beer being prohibited, although in some workhouses a small concession was made to those aged over 60 in the form of tea, sugar and butter. Often no cutlery was provided and residents had no choice but to eat with their fingers.

One of the saddest sights to be seen was that of a pauper being carried to a grave, having died in the workhouse. Before the 1834 Act, paupers were given a decent funeral as standard practice, but the Act changed all that. Such a funeral was now a very visible reminder of the depths the poor soul had plumbed in not providing for his or her later years.

These huge changes in workhouse life were brought about to discourage paupers from entering the workhouse and to encourage those already there to seek work outside. In effect, these institutions were prisons; once behind the walls, it was very difficult to get out again. Though free to leave of their own accord at a day's notice, inmates would get no relief from their parish if they had no work and were therefore likely to be arrested and imprisoned for vagrancy, an even worse fate. The Act created miserable existences for a great many people, the system dealing with the problem of the poor by a continuing policy of cruelty and rejection.

The Demise

Residency in workhouses, which decreased very significantly during the First World War, rose again just as significantly when the war ended and massive unemployment swelled the numbers of those claiming relief, both in and out of the workhouse. The unions had a serious problem on their hands and eventually something was done about it. The government of the day believed that the solution was to do away with the boards of guardians and the unions and pass the problem on to county councils, which in turn would pass all claimants – the sick, the elderly, the demented, the destitute, the incapable and children, to more specialised authorities. After a little over two centuries, workhouses officially ceased to exist from 31 March 1930. Although this should have been an occasion of great celebration for ordinary people, they were too busy facing their next major obstacle; the Great Depression of the 1930s.

SHIPMEADOW HOUSE OF INDUSTRY

Beginnings

The guardians having been elected by the 'poor rate' payers in each of the 27 parishes in the Wangford hundred, their first meeting took place at the Three Tuns public house, Bungay, in June 1764. The principal officers were elected, the chairman being Sir Thomas Gooch of Benacre Hall. The original directors had quite a few members of the clergy and two local gentry among them, one of whom was William Adair of Flixton Hall. The House of Industry was to be built 'for the better Relief and Employment of the Poor in the Hundred of Wangford, Suffolk'.

The next step was to find the necessary land and raise the money to buy it. Suitable land, located in Shipmeadow, was purchased and tenders invited for the construction of the house, to hold up to 350

The opening page of the first minute-book of the Shipmeadow House of Industry, 13 June 1764.
(Reproduced by kind permission of Suffolk Record Office, Lowestoft branch, ref.: 36/AB1/1.)

people. The governor and his family were also to live on the premises, and other buildings were needed for the people to work, conveniences, cooking, washing, drying and so on. There would also be a granary, a linen-house and a place to house and treat the sick.

Built in the shape of the letter 'H', the house was of two storeys with attics. Outhouses stored animal food and farm vehicles, and there were stables, a cow-house and various other small buildings.

Matthew Spilling was appointed the first governor, and Martha his wife, was appointed matron. They were to be responsible for the efficient day-to-day running of the house, which would require much work and careful management. They were responsible for just about everything with the exception of maintenance, any needs for which were to be conveyed to the guardians and directors at their weekly meetings. The house opened for business in the autumn of 1767.

The incorporated hundreds that initially established houses of industry were gradually replaced by unions, the Shipmeadow House of Industry being taken over by the new Wangford Union, which came into being in 1835. Until its closure, the house was subsequently known as Shipmeadow Workhouse.

Administration

The Shipmeadow minute-books describe the goings-on at yearly, quarterly and weekly meetings in meticulous detail; 101 of these books survive, dating from 1764, when the first meeting took place.

The AGM

Such an establishment required much looking after and in turn, required many meetings. The annual general meeting was normally held at the end of June in the Bungay King's Head and comprised one of the four quarterly meetings every year. Included in the regular agenda items at the yearly meeting was the directors' and guardians schedule of tasks for the coming year.

Shipmeadow House of Industry, 2007. Although completely redesigned internally and converted into modern dwellings, it largely retains its original external appearance.

Quarterly Meetings

Financial costs were discussed at quarterly meetings, which, unlike the weekly meetings, were not held in the Shipmeadow Committee Room, but in comparative luxury at public houses in Bungay or Beccles. They regularly took place in the morning, and one might not unnaturally suspect that, after the meetings had concluded, there was a significant delay before the attendees left the local watering-hole! The overseers' bills for outdoor relief and tradesmen's bills for essential supplies to the house were inspected, after which the current balance in hand determined whether the house could afford to make any repayments on the money borrowed to fund its building, furnishing and equipping.

The quarterly meetings also dealt with other matters, matters of a more personal nature. Removal certificates were granted by the directors to relocate paupers from their current parish to their legal parish of settlement. Warrants concerning bastardy orders (whereby the acknowledged father of a base-born (illegitimate) child paid regular weekly sums to the child's mother) were also reviewed. Individual payments were sometimes made for work done by those resident in the house, which saved the corporation expenditure on local tradesmen.

Weekly Meetings

Committee meetings held at the house dealt with the day-to-day minutiae. Commonly noted were details of the governor's weekly report of commodities delivered and payments received as a result of farmers and other local businessmen employing resident paupers. This report also specified any maintenance that needed to be carried out, such as broken windows and missing roof tiles. New entrants and those who had left were mentioned, together with their parish of residence, and the passing away of others was also discussed. Fathers who failed to pay maintenance for illegitimate children in the house were ordered to be sought and payments by over-

Next to the house stands St James' Chapel, now a private house. Photo taken February 2007.

seers to those claiming relief in their parishes were also sanctioned.

Apprentices

The house saved money by apprenticing children to local tradesmen, and they returned once a year for a special dinner. The minute-books occasionally note that the dinner had to be cancelled. For some, it was a chance to be in the outside world, as children were rarely allowed outside the forbidding walls. Some, of course, must have detested being away from their parents for such extensive periods of time.

Naughty Boys and Girls

Punishments meted out to those who disobeyed were detailed in weekly meetings. The most common wrongdoing by far was leaving the house without permission from the governor. For this, the individual went without meat during the following week, and repeating the offence continually would result in having to wear a distinctive yellow jacket at dinnertimes. Another common offence was refusing to work. These wrongdoings were commonplace throughout houses in England.

Later Uses

Shipmeadow Workhouse, along with all others, closed its doors for the last time on the last day of March, 1930. When war broke out in 1939, the buildings were used for storage, but a more pressing need came in the form of around 400 evacuees. Boys and staff from a school in Gravesend, Kent needed somewhere to stay and to further their education. The old workhouse was used and the boys were taught for a couple of years before returning to Kent halfway through the war.

Some time after the war, Shipmeadow Workhouse became a farm for some years, housing chickens and pigs. Towards the end of the 1980s it was renovated and converted into more than 20 dwellings. The inside of the principal building was completely rebuilt, although it largely retains its original external appearance. The workhouse chapel, dedicated to St James, is now a private house.

The lives of an individual and a family, selected at random from a good many that lived in Homersfield over the years and who, for different reasons, were admitted to a workhouse, are now presented.

Samuel Calver

Shadrach Calver, a labourer, married Jane, her last name also Calver, at Flixton in 1794. Not long after their happy day, they moved to Homersfield, where they had at least six children, all boys. Daniel, their first child, was born in 1796, followed three years later by William, who lived for only three months. Their third son was named after the second, and had better luck than his brother. Two more sons, Robert and James, were born in 1807 and 1808 respectively. Robert followed his little brother William to a very early grave, surviving for just nine days.

The last of their six sons, Samuel, was born on 25 May 1811 and baptised two and a half weeks later in Homersfield Church. Like many young Homersfield men, he became a farm worker. In his early twenties he married Hannah Borrit, and together they had at least seven children in Homersfield. Their first, born in 1833, was named after Samuel's father. Their second, Thomas, sadly died before his second birthday. Charlotte, their first daughter, was baptised in 1839. Another probable son, Charles, was buried unbaptised in 1840, having lived just seven weeks. George was born a couple of years later, followed in 1845 by Samuel. They were both baptised on the same day in 1847. Later the same year, Samuel's grandfather, Shadrach, who was then living in Flixton, passed away aged 85 years and was buried in Homersfield churchyard. Their next child was named after the child they had lost earlier, but fate took a hand once again and Thomas lived for fewer than two weeks. Their last child, Jane, born in 1851, suffered an equally tragic fate, living just a few days.

During the 1850s the family moved from Homersfield to St Cross. Hannah, Samuel's beloved wife, died during that same decade and within a few years Samuel had moved and was a lodger in a little house near the Dove in Wortwell. By 1881, having reached his seventieth year and seemingly unable to support himself any longer, he had been admitted to the Depwade Union Workhouse in Pulham Market, Norfolk. He spent his final days there and passed away early in 1895, aged 83.

Of all the Calver family who were born or lived in Homersfield and who are buried in the churchyard, no headstones are to be seen for any of the 14 who were laid to rest. For the majority of ordinary working people such costly items were simply beyond their means and those sleeping quietly in their graves go unmarked for time eternal.

The Todd Family

Anne Todd never walked down the aisle, but a detail such as that didn't stop her from having children. She had three. Her first, a girl, was born on 18 February 1792, when Anne was 24 years old. Also named Anne, the child was baptised when almost two years old. By the time she was three, her mother had become incapable of supporting herself and, on 13 May 1795, she and her child were ordered to be received into the Shipmeadow House of Industry for the first time. It wasn't to be Anne's only visit; far from it. They were discharged and readmitted twice more later that same year. In February 1796, they

were discharged once again.

Anne's son, Robert, was born on 14 September 1798 and baptised a month later. By October of the following year, Anne Todd and her two children were back in the house. A little more than four months later, they spent a further two months in Shipmeadow before being discharged. True sadness entered Anne Todd's life when Robert was buried in 1801, aged two and a half years. Two years later, on 21 July 1803, her third child, Harriet, was born.

Anne Todd senr managed to keep out of the house, although she was dependent on it for payments made to her, some of them from the fathers of her children. Anne Todd junr returned to Shipmeadow on 1 November 1815. Three months later her sister, Harriett, was also admitted. Harriett went back towards the end of 1816 for a different reason. At the Shipmeadow Christmas quarterly meeting, held at the Three Tuns in Bungay on New Year's Day, 1817, she was bound as an apprentice to John Doggett. No details of his trade or address were given, but undoubtedly it is the same John Doggett who owned Holehouse Farm.

Anne senr and Anne junr were ordered to be admitted one more time, on 12 March 1817. The authorities had by then seized their possessions towards the cost of their board and lodgings; they cannot have been valued at much. The two women were discharged four weeks later.

Although the baptisms in Homersfield parish registers give no indications of the names of their fathers, Anne's three children were the offspring of three different men. Their names are revealed in a Shipmeadow Workhouse Bastardy Book, which gives details taken from bastardy orders against the fathers. Such an order was the forerunner of modern-day child support. Where fathers refused to marry the mother of their child or pay money towards their upbringing, an application could be made to the courts and a bastardy order would then be issued. The money was paid not to the mother, but to either the overseers (if the mother was living in

One of several entries admitting Ann Todd into Shipmeadow. This dates from 18 November 1795.

(REPRODUCED BY KIND PERMISSION OF SUFFOLK RECORD OFFICE, LOWESTOFT BRANCH, REF.: 36/AB1/21.)

A view from around 1905 of Anne Todd's one-time home, one half of St Mary's Cottage, on the left in this picture. In the foreground on the right a gate in the picket fence leads into the garden of Nos 75 and 76.

a parish) or to the workhouse. Anne Todd is the subject of three different maintenance orders. The father of her first child, Anne, was Christopher Slapp, who lived just the other side of the river in Wortwell. The aforementioned book shows that the 'going rate' for weekly payments was 1s.6d., but Christopher was so poor that he was ordered to pay 1d. a week. Even so, he absconded from Wortwell and his fatherly duties and the Shipmeadow minute-books show that he was being looked for. The father of Anne's second child, Robert, was named as Robert Burgess of Flixton, and of her last child, Harriet, the father was George Todd, probably a distant relation of Anne's. Baptised in Alburgh, Norfolk, in 1782 he had come to Homersfield with his parents prior to meeting Anne and becoming a father. The fathers of Anne's second and third children were ordered to pay 1s.6d. a week.

Anne Todd the younger followed in her mother's footsteps in certain respects. She too had three children, all born out of wedlock. Robert, her first child, was born in 1824, followed by Harriet in 1831 and William in 1834. In 1841 Anne junr was living in Homersfield with her mother and two of her children. Robert was then learning to become a brick-layer. Harriet had possibly already died. It was not until 1845 that someone made a decent woman of

Anne Todd the younger, and it is from her marriage that we have confirmation of her father's name. The parish registers name him as Christopher, a labourer, with no surname divulged. She married James Plumb, a butcher in Homersfield, who was possibly the father of Anne's last child, William. He was 60, and Anne was 53. Her first child, Robert, had by then married Maria Calver and given his mother two grandsons and a granddaughter. He and his wife were witnesses at Anne and James' wedding. For Anne's new husband, it was his second marriage, his first wife, Mary Keely, having passed away in 1840, aged 51. Anne Todd senr died in 1847, aged 80 years, and was interred in Homersfield churchyard. Other than a few spells in the workhouse, it seems she lived her whole life in Homersfield.

In the early 1850s, James Plumb, his wife Anne and her son William were living in one half of the house now known as St Mary's Cottage. William followed his grandmother into Homersfield churchyard in the July of 1852, aged only 18. Anne was left a widow in the middle of the same decade, when James was laid to rest, and lived on alone in the same little cottage.

CHAPTER 7

The Big House

In times gone by, Homersfield was known as a 'closed' village, one which was part of an estate (as opposed to one which wasn't) and was administered by the family living at the nearby hall. The Tasburgh and Adair families acquired property and land over several centuries, their estate eventually comprising most of several local villages and other areas besides. Many Homersfield people lived in houses owned by the governing family and paid them rent; many were also employed directly by the family in various capacities. Flixton Hall was therefore a very important part of their lives indeed.

HUMBLE BEGINNINGS

In 1258, a priory of the Augustinian order was founded by Margery of Creke in Flixton and dedicated to St Katherine. This priory directly controlled the manor of Flixton, but its income was never enough to make it self-supporting and Henry VIII closed it in 1538, one of many such buildings to undergo a similar fate during the Dissolution of the Monasteries. At the time of its closure it housed only a handful of nuns, and its remains can be seen to this day in a field close to Abbey Farm, one upright wall standing proudly on a raised rectangular mound

forming the outline of a once impressive ecclesiastical building. It is said that part of another wall is inside the Abbey Farm itself.

TASBURGH

The manor of Flixton was offered to Cardinal Wolsey, but he turned it down. It was subsequently leased to Richard Wharton and, around the middle of the sixteenth century, was bestowed on John Tasburgh, whose ancestors had originated in the Norfolk village of the same name a few hundred years earlier, and who had lived in St Peter's Hall since 1220. When Tasburgh was granted Flixton, living in the manor house were the Batemans, themselves an old and well-known local family of some standing, one of whom, one William Bateman, was consecrated Bishop of Norwich in 1343.

Flixton Hall was built on the site of this manor house in around 1615. Approximately 40 years or so after it was built, the hall was admired by Charles I, who was journeying from Yarmouth – probably on the road from Homersfield to Flixton, which then ran in front of the hall. He enquired of one of his entourage as to who owned the house, and was told, 'It belongs to a Popish dog, your Majesty', a reference

An excellent view of the front of the hall, c.1906.

An uncommon view of the hall, c.1908.

to the Tasburgh family's Catholic faith. The king was said to have replied, 'Well, the dog has a very beautiful kennel'.

The Tasburgh family were in residence at the hall almost until the mid-eighteenth century, at which time there was no male heir to continue the line.

WYBARNE

The estate passed by a daughter's marriage to the Wybarne (also spelt Wybarn, Wyburn or Wyborne) family, who were there for less than two decades. The year before they left, Thomas Sandby, a well-known artist, was commissioned to paint a picture of the house, the earliest known image. It showed that the hall had two wings with a central entrance and was shaped like the letter 'E' – common in large sixteenth-century houses. Entrance to the hall was via an arched brick-built bridge over a moat, which enclosed the house.

ADAIR

Early in the seventeenth century, the Adairs, who were descended from a branch of the Fitzgerald family, were seated in Scotland, at Dunskey Castle, Portpatrick, in Wigtonshire. As a result of civil unrest in Ulster, Ireland, James I decided to offer gentle incentives to English and Scottish people settling there. In 1610 he gave the Adairs some land in Ballymena, County Antrim, to where a branch of the Adair family subsequently moved from Scotland. About 100 years later, the family had instituted a seat at Ballymena Castle.

Dates shown next to the following Adair family members relate to the periods when they governed the Flixton estate.

William Adair (1753–83)

In 1700, William Adair was born in Kirkmaiden, Galloway, in Scotland, the first child of a large family. He was schooled at Carrickfergus in Ireland. By the early 1740s, William had become an Army agent in London, providing an administrative function for colonels, often local gentry, wealthy individuals who had civilian responsibilities and who had raised a regiment with money subsequently allocated to them through a parliamentary voting process.

Like many other agents, William set up offices in a London residence. Adair House, on the corner of Pall Mall and George Street, was a typical Georgian town house, with four storeys and a basement, built around the middle of the eighteenth century (it was demolished in 1886). Around the same time, Alexander Adair, William's nephew, came into the business and carried it on long after his uncle had taken retirement and passed on to the next world.

In 1753 William bought Flixton Hall from the Wybarne family. His purchase gave him the status of landed gentry, and he spent a lot of money furnishing it and made significant alterations. Within 35 years of having bought Flixton Hall, the moat had been filled in and the bridge had disappeared. An open portico and colonnade at the south of the building had been closed up and made into separate rooms.

William died in May 1783 and left two wills, one relating to his personal possessions and the other to his property. Though he never married, it appears he may have fathered an illegitimate daughter, the mother of whom was well provided for. The majority of his fortune, however, was left to his nephew. He also left a charity to provide red cloaks for the girls and blue jerseys and boots for the boys of the village.

Alexander Adair (1783–1834)

Alexander, born in the early 1740s, inherited the Flixton estate from his uncle, complete with its furnishings and family heirlooms, for his lifetime, in addition to which he was left his uncle's business and office premises, Adair House. At one time he served as a Captain with the 9th (or South Elmham Troop) Suffolk Yeomanry.

Alexander married Lydia Thomas, in memory of whose death in 1814 a monument was placed in Flixton Church. He died childless, nine years short of his century, in 1834, at which time the estate went to his cousin.

William 'Hugh' Adair (1834–44)

The benefactor was William Adair, then 80 years old and living in Ballymena, County Antrim. He was known in the family as 'Hugh', to distinguish him from others in the family who were also called William! Hugh was a captain in the 25th Regiment of Foot, later renamed the King's Own Scottish Borderers, which took part in the Siege of Gibraltar in 1781. Hugh's uncle, William Adair, was the Army agent to this regiment during Hugh's service. The name that has been subject to stories and speculation

Lady Adair, possibly the wife of Sir Hugh Edward Adair.
(Reproduced by kind permission of Charmian Smy.)

A bookplate measuring 3.5 by 2.5 ins, dating from 1866.

in later members of the family was due to Hugh's marriage. In 1784 he married Camilla, heiress and daughter of Robert Shafto, of Benwell in Northumberland, and her family arms were added to the three red hands of the Adair family. They had two sons, the younger of whom decided to enter the clergy and became Revd William Adair of Portsmouth, in Hampshire. In 1844, aged 90, Hugh died, 60 years after he had married.

Sir Robert Shafto Adair, 1st Baronet (1844–69)

The Flixton estate then passed to Hugh's elder son, Robert Shafto Adair, born on 26 June 1786 in Ballymena. On 17 September 1810 he married Elizabeth Maria Strode, daughter of the Revd James Strode of Berkhampstead in Hertfordshire .

At one time a captain in the Royal Life Guards, he undertook a dangerous mission escorting Sir Francis Burdett (a political reformer arrested for publishing a libellous book on the House of Commons) to the

Tower of London. For dealing with rioters along the way, Robert was made a baronet in 1838.

Shortly after moving into the hall, Robert began to carry out repairs and improvements, employing architect Anthony Salvin on the project. He was responsible for kitchen offices in a new wing on the east side of the house, and for renewing the windows and their frames, together with some internal modifications. The new wing was probably complete by the end of 1846, at which time the key part of the work was being carried out in the main part of the house. Window frames were replaced with others of heavy stone, a square cupola was added to the roof in the centre and the main entrance was altered slightly. The family had gone to their home in London while this part of the work was being done, leaving the staff in residence, and it was during this time that a most horrendous event took place.

At about a quarter before one on the Sunday morning of 13 December 1846, a man walking along the road past the hall saw sparks coming out of the chimneys in the centre of the building. He ran towards it in order to raise the alarm, and found only a few of the staff in residence, at the back of the house. Messengers were sent to call out the fire engines at Harleston and Bungay; the residents of the latter town were awakened by the sound of church bells and cries of 'Fire'. While the fire spread rapidly to many other parts of the building, the engines were hampered by snow, which lay several feet deep in places. The first to arrive was from Bungay, another came from the silk mill at Ditchingham and a third from Harleston. By the time they were ready to deal with the fire, the whole of the inside of the hall was a mass of flames. The firemen put their best efforts into saving the east wing and the newly constructed buildings nearby. A man from the Bungay engine managed to reach the top of the house, and stayed there for seven hours, pouring water onto the flames. Between three and four on Sunday morning, flames could be seen emanating from every window. By five o'clock the building was a mere shell, all the ceilings having been consumed, and what remained was open to the heavens. The roof had completely gone, some 25 or more tons of lead having melted, and the supporting joists had been heard to collapse with a thundering crash. The fire crews' valiant efforts went largely unrewarded; some kitchen offices were saved but very little else. The rest of Sunday and most of Monday were spent damping down the smouldering remains. At the height of the fire the flames could be seen for many miles around, and those in Homersfield would have seen it, heard it and smelled it. During the course of the night and throughout Sunday, thousands of people came to see the spectacle; undoubtedly many walked from Homersfield to see the inferno.

The fire had started high in a chimney in the entrance hall, and flames were first seen in the attics. The floors subsequently gave in, falling through the ceiling of the entrance hall onto workmen's benches. Repairs had been going on in the house for several months and many workmen lost their tools in the blaze. The west wing and the centre of the house, including the fine staircase, were all destroyed. Many of the treasures were in the salon on the second floor, where everything was lost. Some of the remaining walls were so badly cracked they had to be demolished before any clearing up could be done.

Many precious works of art were lost, including examples by Gainsborough, Sir Joshua Reynolds, Canaletto and Raphael. The fire also consumed bronzes, marble busts, items of furniture and rare books. The losses incurred were estimated at £40,000–£60,000, a vast sum in those days. However, not everything was destroyed; one item to survive was a 'black jack', a leathern jug which held eight gallons of ale and which, to this day, is still in the possession of the family.

Sir Robert Shafto Adair, in London at the time of the fire, was informed of the calamity when a messenger was sent to Norwich and the news conveyed by telegraph. The following morning, Alexander Shafto, Sir Robert's elder son, arrived. When his father arriving that afternoon he immediately decided to rebuild his desecrated home.

It was rebuilt in the same style, with 60 rooms, and was said to have 52 chimneys and 365 windows. Sir Robert made alterations every now and then, including the addition of his initials and the date (1863) at one end of the great hall. Within a decade,

a brick wall was erected around the house and its gardens, with an iron gate at the main entrance.

Sir Robert is also remembered in connection with Flixton Church. During his time at the hall, the chancel collapsed and in 1861 the Saxon tower also fell down. Most of the church was rebuilt at Sir Robert's expense.

When he died at his home in Suffolk at the end of February, 1869, aged 82 years, the estate passed to his eldest son.

Sir Robert Alexander Shafto Adair, 2nd Baronet (1869–86)

Robert, born on 25 August 1811, married Miss Theodosia Meade, eldest daughter of General the Hon. Robert Meade in 1836. He became Sir Robert upon inheriting the Flixton estate from his father. His wife died in 1871 and in the same year he took a peerage and became Baron (Lord) Waveney of South Elmham. He was a lieutenant-colonel in the East Suffolk Militia Artillery from 1853 to 1881, and an honorary colonel of the same for the following five years, until 1886. As Liberal MP for Cambridge from 1847 to 1852, and again from 1854 to 1857, he unsuccessfully contested East Suffolk more than once. He was also a magistrate, the Lord Lieutenant of County Antrim, the military aide-de-camp to Queen Victoria from 1857 onwards, and as well as all this, managed his estates in Ireland and Flixton.

Sir Robert decided to re-route the Homersfield to Flixton road, which ran in front of the hall, further away from his home in order to acquire some privacy. The 'New Road' as it was called (the current B1062) was constructed in 1870.

When Sir Robert died on 15 February 1886 at his residence in Audley Square, he had no heir or heiress to inherit his estate, as a result of which the title of Lord Waveney became extinct.

Sir Hugh Edward Adair, 3rd Baronet (1886–1902)

The baronetcy and Flixton estate passed to Sir Robert's younger brother, Sir Hugh Edward Adair. Born on Boxing Day 1815, on 10 July 1856 he married his cousin, Harriet Camilla, eldest daughter of the late Mr Alexander Adair of Heatherton Park, Somerset, a barrister and MP for Ipswich for several years. His reputation was that of an aristocratic, kind, generous and courteous man.

Like his predecessors, Sir Hugh made changes in his new home. Carried out between 1888 and 1892, these were overseen by the architect Mr F. Wade. The kitchen offices adjacent to the east wing were replaced with others which, as well as being bigger, were much more in keeping with the appearance of the hall. Several alterations were made externally, in particular a new entrance to the main hall. The colonnade, closed up many years earlier, was made into a conservatory, where oranges and passion flowers were grown. The cupola that Salvin had installed was replaced with a stone tower housing a clock and resembling a wedding cake with tiers. The west wing received an ornate entrance portico, with staircases to the front of the house and gardens.

Sir Hugh purchased paintings to replace some of those lost in the fire of 1846. The central area between the wings was changed so that it was one open area, while the new great hall was constructed from what had been the dining-room and the previous great hall. A wall separating the dining-room from the east wing was replaced with three arches. A new, intricately carved wide staircase was also installed, with Sir Hugh's initials entwined. At night, the menservants would go up to their quarters on one side of the stairs, and the women would go up to theirs on the other side. At the bottom, counting them, would be the housekeeper, whose duty it was to ensure there were no absentees!

Sir Hugh funded alterations to Flixton Church, including some restoration of the chancel in 1893. A marble floor was installed, together with a carved and panelled reredos. Two years later a chapel was built at the north-west corner of the church. In it is a marble statue of Lady Theodosia Waveney kneeling on an alabaster pedestal, sculpted by John Bell.

For a ten-year period beginning in 1887, the agent for the Flixton estate was Captain Charles Cunningham Boycott, an Irish land agent. In 1879 he had opposed demands for land reform by the Irish Land League in 1879, and the fact that local people would not work for him resulted in his surname becoming a word in the English language. He lived at the Priest's House in Bungay.

Sir Hugh passed away early in 1902.

Sir Frederick Edward Shafto Adair, 4th Baronet (1902–15)

Sir Hugh's son inherited the Flixton estate. Frederick was born on his father's birthday in 1860 and was educated at Harrow, Christ Church and Sandhurst.

In his time, he was a captain in the Rifle Brigade, a JP in Norfolk and Suffolk, and served as High Sheriff of Suffolk. Well known for being a man of leisure, he enjoyed sport and spent a lot of time in foreign lands, writing books about his travels and experiences. He also enjoyed painting and acting. Sir Frederick was very competent in the then still relatively new hobby of photography, and took many excellent pictures of his home.

When war was declared on 4 August 1914, the Shropshire yeomanry were temporarily stationed at the hall.

Alterations made by Frederick to the hall involved the exterior, where he added a rockery, the design of which was based on one of his paintings.

The Flixton sign, shown in its original position on the green, erected by Sir Shafto Adair in 1921.

He also created new gardens based on the four seasons, completed just before his death.

Sir Frederick was another Adair who had no children to whom he could pass the baronetcy. He died at Flixton Hall on 8 April 1915 at the young age of 54, unmarried and childless.

Sir Robert Shafto Adair, 5th Baronet (1915–49)

Sir Hugh's brother, Robert Shafto Adair, became the fifth baronet. Born in 1862, in 1890 he married Mary, daughter of Henry Anstey Bosanquet.

Commonly known as 'Sir Shafto', he was basically a shy man with a reputation for being very generous. Unlike many others in his family, he never joined the military but was educated at Oxford University and became a barrister and a director of the Royal Academy of Music.

One of the earlier Suffolk village signs is attributable to Sir Robert. The Flixton sign, which stands outside the main entrance to the hall, by Flixton Lodge, was erected in 1921, and depicts a model of the church being held by St Felix, after whom the village is thought to be named.

Sir Shafto often related this favourite story to

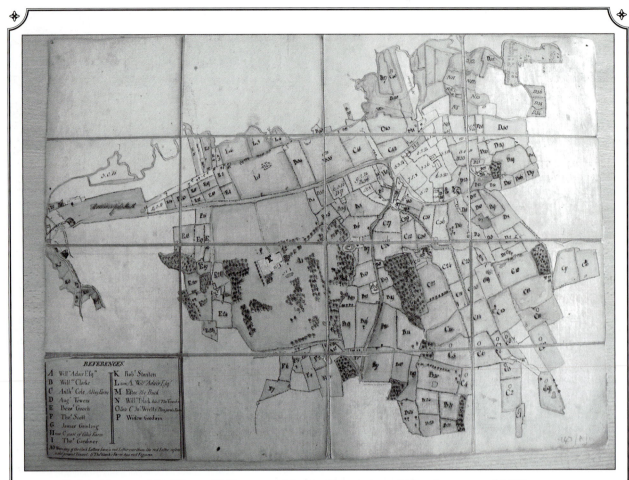

A wonderful old map of the Flixton Hall estate, with named occupiers, dating from around 1800.
(REPRODUCED BY KIND PERMISSION OF SUFFOLK RECORD OFFICE, LOWESTOFT BRANCH, REF.: 947/A/1.)

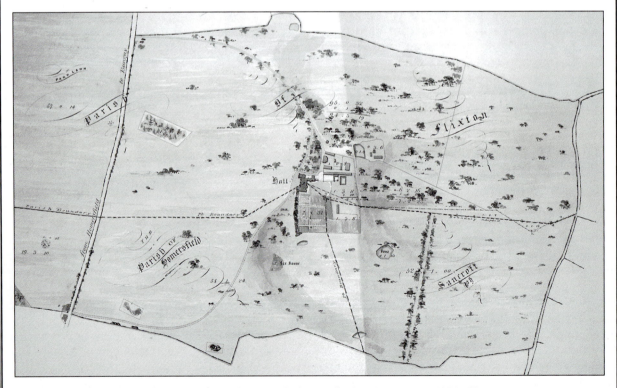

Flixton Hall from a Deanery and Manor of South Elmham roll of various maps, 1838–40.
(REPRODUCED BY KIND PERMISSION OF SUFFOLK RECORD OFFICE, LOWESTOFT BRANCH, REF.: 613/1.)

The saloon (or salon), rebuilt after the fire of 1846, c.1906.

A splendid view of the typically Edwardian library.

The popular Victorian art of taxidermy is well in evidence here in this view from around 1905. The bear must have presented a not inconsiderable challenge!

dinner guests at the hall: when he was riding on horseback around his estate one day, he arrived at a closed gate. On it was sitting a young boy, whom Sir Shafto knew to be the son of a shepherd new to his employ. When he asked the boy to open the gate for him, his request was turned down flat.

Sir Shafto asked: 'Young man, do you know who I am?'

'No,' replied the shepherd's son.

'I'm Sir Shafto Adair, Baronet, Knight of the Garter.'

The boy's reply was certainly to the point, if nothing else. 'I dun't care if yer t'noight, t'morrer noight or the night arter, you kin oopen the bugger y'self.'

The Adair family coat of arms included the three bloody hands of Ulster, a reference to the family's origins. Several stories have circulated over the years as to how these blood-red hands came to be. One involves the death of a young black man, but the most common concerns a young boy who was thrashed so badly by his Adair master that he died of his injuries, first leaving a bloody handprint on the wall. This was incorporated in the family crest as a constant reminder of the appalling deed.

One alternative, and much less commonly heard story, was told by a gardener who worked at the hall

during Sir Shafto's time there. Known affectionately as 'Major' Clarke, he lived in the house now called Plumtree Cottage in Homersfield. He related that a servant boy found beaten almost to death in a small, empty bedroom at the hall had tried, without success, to get up from the floor. The imprints of his bloody hands were left on the wall, four of them in all. The identity of the murderer was never discovered, but from that day on the family was cursed by having the bloody hands incorporated into their crest. No doubt this story is the result of a colourful imagination and a mischievous sense of humour!

Very popular point-to-point meetings held at the hall from at least the 1920s were abruptly brought to an end on the outbreak of the Second World War in 1939. When the United States joined the war a few years later the American Air Force was stationed at Bungay airfield, constructed during 1942 and sited in the grounds of Flixton Hall. Known as Station 125, it had three runways and was still in the process of being built when its first occupants arrived. They did not stay long, nor, for that matter, did a second group of occupants, before the 446th Bomb Group came in November 1943. They stayed until the end of the war, returning home in the middle of 1945.

Sir Shafto and Lady Adair knew the vicars of Homersfield and St Cross well. The Revd Robert Skene's daughter, Rosalys, who became known to the Adairs, would occasionally tell a story from her early life involving this titled family. One such story, in Rosalys' own words, recalls Lady Adair:

Lady Adair gave quaint tea parties for anyone connected with the war effort. At one of these the American airmen's wives and American Red Cross were there, and my friend who ran the Land Girls at [South Elmham] St Margaret's. We'd have tea, and the older ones tottered around the rose garden, the younger ones played tennis and that sort of thing. Lady Adair would receive them and then go upstairs and retire to her bed. Once, the bedroom window was flung open, and she was wearing a very voluminous old-fashioned nightdress, she always called me 'Rose' and she shouted, 'Rose, Rose, have you met Mrs Rogers?' Well, she was the one who ran the Land Girls, so I said, 'Well,

One of the ponds at the hall, c.1915.

The deer herd in the early years of the twentieth century.

I did see her earlier,' and she said, 'I want you to be friends, she is lonely.' She knew everything that was going on. She operated a real feudal system, and sent out her spies (the maids) to find out, and if there was any illness she would send out soup, and once when my father was very ill, she sent a £5 note as well as soup. He was thrilled. She was eccentric, quaint, a lovely lady.

Not long after the end of the war, a children's film was made, some of it shot on location at the hall and in surrounding villages. Sir Robert took a great interest in the film, his house and gardens providing some beautiful views. The story for the film was based on a book by Mary Cathcart Borer, called *The House with the Blue Door*, in which two young boys discover that their father's housekeeper is not trustworthy at all. A gang of thieves, with whom she is associated, have stolen a work of art by Rembrandt and plan to steal more items from the boys' father via

a secret tunnel in the house. Their eventual downfall is due, of course, to the efforts of the young boys. Homersfield Bridge appears in one scene, in which a horse and trap cross it on the way to the police house. However, it was not the Homersfield police house that was shown, but one in Ditchingham, a few miles away. The film, a little over three-quarters of an hour long, was released in 1947.

Sir Robert died on 9 October 1949, aged 87 years, and his wife followed him a mere three months later on 3 January 1950, also aged 87.

Major-General Sir Allan Henry Shafto Adair, 6th Baronet (1949–50)

Allan Henry Shafto, Sir Robert's only surviving son, born on 3 November 1897, became the sixth and final baronet. He had a very distinguished military career. His first school was at Broadstairs, Kent and, like several Adairs before him, he was then educated at

The Henham Harriers at the hall, c.1908.

A marble statue in Flixton Church of Lady Theodosia Waveney , c.1905.

Sir Robert Shafto Adair in the grounds of his home, c.1925.

(PROVENANCE UNKNOWN, BY KIND PERMISSION OF GLEN EARL.)

A large gathering at the Hall, thought to be in 1932.

(REPRODUCED BY KIND PERMISSION OF LADY DARELL.)

69

A rare view of the rock garden.
(Reproduced by kind permission of Lady Darell.)

An excellent view of some of the ornate chimneys at the hall. (Reproduced by kind permission of Lady Darell.)

A pretty young lady poses with a book in the pergola, c.1930. (Reproduced by kind permission of Lady Darell.)

One of many grand fireplaces in the hall.
(Reproduced by kind permission of Lady Darell.)

Harrow. He took a commission in the Grenadier Guards in 1916, and won a Military Cross on active service during the First World War. He subsequently became an instructor at Sandhurst and, when war broke out again in 1939, he found himself in Belgium commanding the 3rd Btn Grenadier Guards. He was promoted to the rank of general and took over the command of the Guards Armoured Division. He was involved in a battle in Normandy, was at the liberation of Brussels and at the Battle of Arnhem.

He married Enid, the youngest daughter of the late Mr W.H. Dudley-Ward and the honourable Mrs Dudley-Ward, on 28 April 1919 at the Royal Military Chapel (now Guard's Chapel), Wellington Barracks. Gifts to the bride included, from Princess Mary, a Chippendale occasional table, made at Sandringham, Norfolk, while the bridegroom was given a motor car by his father.

Sir Allan and his wife had four children, Desmond, Bridget, Juliet and Annabel.

Sir Allan's successes in his military campaigns were marred by the loss of his only son, Desmond Allan Shafto Adair, a captain in the 2nd Btn Grenadier Guards, who lost his life on 10 November 1943 at the Battle of Monte Camino in Italy. It was some 18 months after he was reported missing that his death was confirmed, and his body was recovered from a communal grave in June 1945.

General Adair served in Greece after the war and retired in 1947, when his division was broken up. He then managed his parents' estate in Flixton until it was decided to sell most of it by auction. By then Sir Shafto and Lady Adair were quite elderly. The family retained only the hall, the park, the home farm and some woods. Messrs Bidwell & Sons prepared and

The grand staircase in the centre of the hall.

published an auction catalogue showing 85 lots, comprising 2,970 acres, including 21 farms, several smallholdings, three village Post Offices, two public houses, and numerous houses and cottages, as well as woodlands, marshlands and grazing rights. The rental value from all this property amounted to £3,000 annually. The sale was set for 13 July 1948, but local newspapers reported that the Metropolitan Railway Country Estates Ltd had purchased lots privately prior to the sale.

Not all the parish of Homersfield was included in the sale. Among the houses not in the auction catalogue were Swan Cottages and Nos 66–69 inclusive. Some of these appeared in a sale two years later.

Sir Allan was forced to sell what remained of his family's estate to pay death duties when his father died. Those contents of his former home not being kept were sold at auction in November 1950 – some 1,180 lots, including a library of 7,000 books; the sale lasted for five days and realised almost £16,000. Sir Allan and Lady Adair moved to nearby Raveningham, bringing to an end almost 200 years of Adair family occupation at the hall.

At the end of the 1950s Sir Allan and Lady Adair went to live at Strabane, where they spent the next 25 years. Lady Adair died in May 1984, Sir Allan in August 1990 at his home in Park Lane, London. The baronetcy died with him, there being no male heir to inherit the title.

THE ULTIMATE DEMISE OF FLIXTON HALL

Shortly after Sir Allan and Lady Adair had vacated Flixton Hall, it was put up for sale. Rumours circulated locally that it would become a police college or a mental institution came to nothing. Interest was expressed by East and West Suffolk County Councils in buying the hall and its surviving 250 acres as a joint farming venture, but this, too, came to nothing. It was eventually bought by Mr R.G. Lawrence of Colney Hall, Norfolk, a speculator, who literally took it apart, selling what he could and tearing down the rest. The gravel pits were sold off, as was the lead from the roof of the house. The demolition took almost a year, from the middle of June 1952, a sad end to what many regarded as one of the finest houses in Suffolk.

The land was farmed by Mr Seaman, who lived in the head groom's apartment in the courtyard. In

Victorian splendour at its finest, c.1925.
(REPRODUCED BY KIND PERMISSION OF LADY DARELL.)

1968 the estate was bought by Mr G. Clark, whose nephew, Adrian Sampson, farmed it. Two years later, the farm was rented to Mr F.W. Parsons until he subsequently bought it in 1984. When he died in 1988 it was taken over by his sons.

What remains today resembles the base of a multi-tiered cake, and is cut off at first-floor level. Almost all of the interior walls have been removed, along with the staircase and drawing-room. All the fireplaces have been closed up. There are now garage entrances for farm vehicles at what was the end of the east and west wings, and cows roam among the few crumbling walls. The offices added at the end of the 1880s have gone, although the stables and the buildings used to house carriages have survived, albeit minus their embellishments. The house now has a corrugated-iron roof.

Just one small part of the hall remains in its original state, and is now a listed building. The dovecote, dating from the Tasburgh family's first Flixton Hall of around 1615, when it housed birds destined for the dining table, stands alone, remarkably untouched by the desecration around it. Norwich once boasted the 'Samson and Hercules Ballroom', a room of which, known as the 'Flixton Room', was furnished with much of the oak panelling from the hall – panelling which has since been offered for sale. Other items reputed to be from the hall turn up locally from time to time; the author has seen for sale a large oak door and a fine two-drawer oak bedroom chest, the latter bearing the Adair coat of arms.

In its heyday, the estate comprised a little over 15,000 acres. Flixton Hall's park once extended to more than 500 acres and was famous for its deer herd, now all gone, as is much of the park, dug up for the sand and gravel beneath it, creating enormously ugly pits in the process. Gone, too, is the family, for two centuries fondly regarded as good landlords who treated their tenants well.

A dismal sight – the hall being demolished in 1952. (© EASTERN DAILY PRESS.)

❖ CHAPTER 8 ❖

The Best Days of Our Lives

THE BEGINNINGS OF SCHOOLING

Education for the children of ordinary working families was virtually non-existent until well into the nineteenth century. Only the boys born into better-off families received an education; prior to the eighteenth century it was considered unnecessary to educate girls, although a few schools, funded by charities, did admit girls. From around the middle of the eighteenth century many towns had an 'endowed' grammar school (such as Bungay) and often a 'commercial' school. Pupils at these schools were normally boys, the sons of well-off local businessmen, clergy and local gentry; their education was largely confined to classical subjects.

Girls attended such independently run schools as boarding-schools, day-schools (of which there were two in Homersfield in the early 1840s) or dame-schools, which some boys from poorer families also attended. Dame-schools were private enterprises provided for labouring families and run by educated, older (hence their name) women, who charged a few pennies a week for their services. In reality, a good many of them provided little more than a relatively expensive child-minding service with a rather poor level of teaching. Endowments funded charity schools, which also started to flourish, further income being raised from private donations and from

A delivery boy from Harleston outside the Dove, c.1912.

the children's parents. The village church, or a dwelling, were often used to hold classes. These schools provided only basic tuition in the three Rs, which was better than nothing, although children normally left school by the age of 12, often sooner. Illiteracy dominated the child's world until the appearance of Sunday schools from the 1780s onwards. These provided education, on Sundays only, which, although by definition including lessons of a religious flavour, were not of any particular Christian denomination.

A big step forward was taken in 1811, when the Anglican 'National Society for Promoting the Education of the Poor in the Principles of the Established Church' was founded, its aim being to provide a school in every parish. This body, together with the 'British and Foreign School Society' (which was principally supported by non-conformists) was especially responsible for providing elementary schools for boys and girls. Fairly early in the nineteenth century, a quarter of children were receiving education of one kind or another at a time when half the people in the country were illiterate. Another big step was taken when the government introduced an education grant in 1833. By the middle of the nineteenth century there were about 18,500 schools, of which around 17,000 were 'National' and the remainder 'British'. Boys and girls were taught in separate rooms in National schools, their parents paying 1d. a week for reading tuition and 2d. for writing and arithmetic. The government grant was increased a few times in the 1850s, when the concept of pupil teachers was introduced. These 'monitors' were intelligent older children who were paid to train as teachers for five years, teaching the younger children as they trained and gaining a certificate at the end of each successful year. By this time, matters had improved significantly, with three-quarters of all children attending a school.

SCHOOLING UNDER WAY

Forster's Elementary Education Act of 1870 saw the creation of school districts throughout England and Wales, each of which had its own elected school board. Each board had a responsibility to provide, at the public's expense, enough schools within its area of control if there were insufficient voluntary schools. However, many of these boards charged fees, so discouraging poorer parents from sending their children to school (even if at only a penny per week per

73

A schoolboy in uniform poses outside Swan Cottages, c.1905.

A charming group of Homersfield children on the green, c.1912.

child), since the family would also lose any money their children might otherwise be earning. School staff and the year-to-year upkeep of the buildings were the responsibility of the village community. Voluntary (existing) schools often resented the 'board schools' (which were secular but of no particular denomination), because they were obliged to provide satisfactory levels of schooling and were under threat of being taken over by the local school board if they failed to do so. Consequently, this Act resulted in many more schools being built, commonly with a house next to them for the accommodation of the schoolmaster or schoolmistress.

The minimum employment age was set at ten years by the 1873 Agricultural Children Act, but this did little to prevent children being absent from school at significant times in the farming calendar, especially at harvest time, when their presence in the fields was of great importance in rural communities.

When an Act of 1880 introduced compulsory education for the first time, by law, all children aged between five and ten years were required to attend school. Schools often took children younger than five years simply because it meant more income for the school from fee-paying parents, although the children of poor families were often allowed to attend the local school free of charge. Subjects taught included learning the alphabet, followed by some basic reading, the times tables, writing and history.

School fees were not abolished until 1891, although the impact that this had on absenteeism was minimal. Fees or not, children were still far more valuable as wage-earners at certain times of the year, and parents preferred, wherever possible, that their

A boy poses for the camera in Church Lane, c.1905.

Homersfield children in front of the pub, c.1908.

Two young boys by the bowling green enjoy the 1912 floods.

children earned precious money towards their keep. Child labour was also comparatively cheap, and farmers gladly employed them, especially at busy periods. Harvest, the most important time of the rural village year, took precedence over everything else, and attendance at many schools was always low at this time of year. Harvest holidays had to work around the harvest itself; if it was early, the holidays were brought forward, and if it was a late harvest, then the holidays were also late. Bird-keeping or bird-scaring was a common job for young boys, who were employed to walk around in the fields all day, alone and often cold, for a small sum at the end of the day. No doubt they would sooner have been at school on such days. From the fields they would also collect cartloads of stones which were sold on to the village highway surveyor and used to fill the many holes in parish roads caused by the constant passage of wheeled traffic throughout the year.

The school-leaving age was increased to 11 in 1893 and in 1899 was raised to 12 years.

MODERN SCHOOLING

Another milestone in the history of education was the passing of Balfour's Education Act of 1902. This resulted in the gradual replacement of school boards, responsibility being transferred to local education authorities under the control of county and borough councils. Education committees were established and several school managers elected in each parish to supervise the running of individual schools. The Act also made provision for secondary education.

The school-leaving age was raised to 14 in 1918. The 11-Plus examination came into being in 1944, and the same year the school-leaving age was raised to 15 (although, through special powers granted to the minister, this was deferred until 1947). The leaving age was raised again in 1972, to 16.

HOMERSFIELD EDUCATION

By and large, prior to the latter half of the eighteenth century, Homersfield children didn't go to school or receive any formal education. While the daughters of better-off families could attend a boarding school for 'young ladies' there was no schooling for the children of the labouring classes until the mid-Victorian era, and even then it was initially only for the boys, as daughters didn't need to be educated.

From 1862 onwards, all the children in Homersfield had a school to go to, and walked almost two miles to Flixton and back each day. In 1875 the younger children from Homersfield and St Cross left their older brothers, sisters and friends at Flixton and instead went to the newly built school in St Cross, just under a mile away. By 1895 Flixton school was serving the children from that village only, while those from Homersfield and St Cross went to St Cross School. In an exercise in economy, the older children at Flixton were transferred to St Cross School in 1921. It all went full circle 15 years later, when, in 1936, St Cross was closed and its children were transferred to Flixton. Here, Homersfield children continued to be educated until the end of July 1988, when more cutbacks resulted in the closure of Flixton School after 126 years. At the time of writing, it is a private dwelling.

Flixton School

Sir Robert Shafto Adair funded the building of a school in Flixton, an endowed school which opened its doors in 1862, serving Homersfield, St Cross and Flixton. Sir Robert and Lady Adair took a great interest in the school and visited it often. Lady Adair was particularly keen for the girls to learn needlework, and regularly sent supplies from the hall. The school was made free by order of Sir Hugh Adair in 1892. Much emphasis was placed on spiritual and religious learning, and the children regularly attended church on certain days of the year, including Ash Wednesday, the beginning of Passion Week (in early spring) and each Wednesday and Friday morning during Lent.

Teachers
Unlike St Cross School, Flixton staff were able to live in. One of its earlier teachers was Mrs Abigail Brooks, who was the mistress in 1869.

By 1872 she had left and Miss Alice French was the certificated teacher at the school. There were then four classes of local children to be taught.

Miss French left just before Christmas 1874 and was replaced by Miss Mary Elizabeth Osborne after the Christmas holidays. She stayed only until the following Christmas.

Miss Emily Dallastone then came to teach. It was at this time that the younger Homersfield and St Cross children started going to their own school. The following year, 1876, Emily's younger sister by six years, Caroline, aged 16, a pupil teacher at the school, took the youngest children for lessons. The sisters stayed more than a decade, both leaving during the school year 1888/89.

They were succeeded by sisters Martha and Eliza Harnden, who left three years later, at Christmas 1891, when two more sisters, Maude and Gertrude Grant, took over.

When Gertrude, the younger of the two, left at Christmas 1893, Lady Adair informed Maude that

Miss Adelaide Roff, of Beccles, was to replace Gertrude. Both Miss Grant and Miss Roff resigned just before the harvest holidays, in August 1895.

From the following year, only Flixton children went to the school, a situation which continued until 1936, when children from Homersfield and St Cross once again attended Flixton School until its closure.

Inspections
In March 1872 the school had its first visit from one of Her Majesty's Inspectors, who, in his summary, stated that:

The First Standard has not passed a good Examination – Reading is not more than passable in any part of the school. In other respects the Second and Third Standards have done their work fairly well, but the children presented in them ought by their age to be as a rule more advanced.

He went on to say: 'The Managers should take such steps as may be practicable to render the offices for the two sexes accessible by separate approaches from the School Room.'

The 1874 Inspector stated that: 'A very considerable number in classes 2 and 3 say no prayers at all at home, perhaps the schoolmistress may have an opportunity of pressing this on their attention.'

Curriculum
In addition to the three Rs, much emphasis was laid on religion. Children were taught about wild animals from around the world, and about different objects and everyday commodities. They also learned songs and read poetry. The history of major events in the world was also taught and, from 1891, drawing was introduced for the boys.

Holidays
Holidays at that time were very different from how they are now. The main holiday, then known as the

Flixton School, c.1930.

'harvest holidays' rather than the 'summer holidays', lasted for four weeks, from around the middle to the end of August, just before the most important event in the farming year. Two weeks were given for Easter and Christmas, and Valentine's Day, 14 February, was a school holiday until 1877, when it became a half-day holiday only (in the morning). It ceased to be a holiday altogether from around 1884.

Other, once-only holidays were sometimes given for such celebratory events as the installation of a new church organ, in February 1878.

Treats

Annual school treats regularly took place in summer, there being separate ones for the children of Flixton and those of Homersfield and St Cross combined. The Flixton children often visited the rectory, and Revd Smith, who ran a Sunday school in Homersfield, took those from the other two villages. These treats normally took the form of a day's holiday and commenced in the afternoon with a meal, no doubt with games afterwards. From year to year, 70 or more children would attend these treats.

Absence

Illness and the weather had a huge influence on attendance figures. On one day at the end of July 1871, very few children were at school on account of the extremely hot weather. There were none at all from Homersfield and only two from St Cross. The entry in the school log-book for 16 February 1888 shows few children present that day, nor for the following seven days, owing to deep snow. There were also low attendances during weeks at the beginning and end of March that same year due to bad weather. Snow prevented any of the children from going to school on two consecutive days at the end of November 1890.

In October, from 1873 to 1883, the school log-books often record significant numbers of children as absent gathering acorns, which were used to feed pigs; most families had one, which would be fattened in the weeks prior to Christmas.

Children were frequently kept away from school when the harvest commenced in August, in order to take their fathers' dinners out to the fields.

Bungay May Fair and Bungay Races (held in May, on the common) were consistently responsible for low school attendances, as were local flower shows.

Whitsun was also a time when children were regularly absent from school. Whit Monday was not a holiday until 1889, before which date children were often absent for a whole week, their parents needing them at home to help.

Closures

The school was closed not infrequently due to illness among the pupils. In 1875, after the harvest holidays, no Homersfield children were allowed to return to school due to an outbreak of fever in the village. Eight years later, when scarlet fever was rife in Homersfield and St Cross, children from both villages were barred from attending until the outbreak had subsided.

The weather also played a part in children having extra days at home. In January 1881 a particularly heavy snowfall resulted in the school being closed for a day.

It also closed for the funeral of the reigning monarch and for those of such prominent people as, in February 1886, Lord Waveney.

St Cross School

At a meeting of the ratepayers of Homersfield and St Cross held on 3 December 1875 in the new school-room, Lord Waveney was thanked for building the school at his own cost. The school stood adjacent to the road between Homersfield and St Cross, on a corner of a road which goes to Flixton, not far from the thatched School Cottage and what, to this day, is still known as School Corner. Sadly, the name is now all that remains to indicate its precise whereabouts.

At the same meeting, it was moved that the Revd George Smith of St Cross act as correspondent (secretary) and treasurer.

The school's income was derived from grants, donations and the school rate, paid by residents of Homersfield and St Cross. In addition, there were fund-raising activities – the occasional bazaar and the sale of children's work and of school desks that were being replaced, and so on.

Many smaller items were bought locally for the school from George Gower, at the Post Office in Homersfield, and from Henry Tidnam, who ran a general store next door, at what is now Waveney House. A clock purchased for the school was cleaned every few years.

A well and pump were installed, there were separate outside toilets, and a corrugated-iron coal shed was erected to accommodate the regular delivery of a ton of fuel for the winter months. The school also had its own gardens, where flowers and vegetables were grown, and a small orchard.

St Cross School after it had been enlarged, c.1912.

From the beginning, boys and girls were taught in separate groups, each group having its own gravelled playground.

In May 1888 the first officially appointed school managers were the Revd W. Morley Smith, acting as correspondent, Mr Thomas Poppy, Mr C. Smith and Mr Newham.

From 1888 to 1896 rooms were rented from Mrs Hadingham. The number of children to be taught had exceeded the capacity of the school until alterations began in 1895, when it was enlarged by the addition of another room. This was also to be used to teach the older children from Homersfield and St Cross, who were being transferred from Flixton. The cost of the work was estimated at £200. The classroom measured 20ft 3ins long by 14 feet wide by 10ft high, and the schoolroom 23ft 6ins by 18ft by 14ft. A maximum of 73 children could be accommodated, 31 in the classroom and 42 in the schoolroom, although in practice the average number of children on the school register at any one time was typically 50–55, but it did fill to capacity during the 1920s, when there was an influx of people into the area.

From 1892, prize books were given for high attendances at school, and a framed certificate of honour was given to any pupil who did not miss a single day at school throughout the year; there were no doubt few such certificates hanging on walls in Homersfield and St Cross!

From 1 April 1919 new registers were adapted in accordance with Board of Education regulations. These stipulated four school terms instead of three, ending on the last days of March, June, September and December.

The beginning of the school year after the harvest holidays in 1920 seems to be the time when the older Flixton children, aged 12 years and over, came to St Cross to be taught.

Just how poor some families were in the 1920s is ably demonstrated by an entry in the school log-book for September 1922, which records that on the morning following a very wet afternoon, during which the children got drenched going home, attendance suffered, 'some of them apparently not having a change of clothing and bad boots'.

A short Remembrance Service would take place at the school on Armistice Day, 11 November, and poppies would be sold in the school by ladies from the village. In 1935 the school log-book records such a visit from Miss Brock and Miss Skene, who returned the following day to help out with a jumble sale to raise money for the school, which was starting to experience financial difficulties.

On 21 November 1935, the 'Milk in Schools Scheme' started, and the school ordered 26 bottles, to be delivered each day.

By April 1936 it was being mooted that the school might have to close – money was running out and there was none forthcoming.

A final, poignant but to-the-point entry appears in the school log-book for 23 December 1936:

The school is to be closed from today. Mrs Rosen and Miss Reeder finish their duties today. Keys are handed to the Reverend Skene at the Rectory, St Cross. Stock has been checked, all property personal to the children or teachers has been removed.

Admissions

The admissions book for St Cross School shows that more than 20 children arrived on the first day, 17 January 1876. The first entry in the book is for Arthur Gowing, whose father, Samuel, the village thatcher in Homersfield, lived at No. 83. Several other children came from Homersfield that day, among them John and George Sampson, sons of Robert and Ellen Sampson, who lived in one half of No. 77 (St Mary's Cottage), and Rosa and Alice Gower, two of the three daughters of Mary Ann Gower, at the Post Office. Her other daughter, Ellen, started at the school in 1878. Children started at the age of four years or older and, at the age of eight or nine, usually went on to Flixton School for further education.

The last admission, No. 810, on 2 November 1936,

The first page of the admissions book for St Cross School.
(REPRODUCED BY KIND PERMISSION OF SUFFOLK RECORD OFFICE,
LOWESTOFT BRANCH, REF.: 291/5.)

Memorandum of Agreement made this 8th day of April 1899, between William Morley Smith Rector of S. Cross, David Hadingham Churchwarden of S. Cross, Charles Smith, Thomas Poppy, William Rufus Newham, and Robert Johnson, Managers of the National School at S. Cross in the County of Suffolk (herein-after called the Managers) of the one part, and Sarah Maria Hastings (hereinafter called the Teacher) of the other part.

An employment contract between Sally Hastings and the managers of St Cross School, 1899. (REPRODUCED BY KIND PERMISSION OF SUFFOLK RECORD OFFICE, LOWESTOFT BRANCH, REF.: 128/M3/1.)

relates to a St Cross child, Florence Potter, who left when the school closed a few weeks later, just before Christmas. The number of admissions entered in the book can be misleading when considering the number of children who attended during the school's life of a little over 60 years. A number of pupils were admitted more than once, several times in some cases, when the child was exempted for employment and was away for a few weeks at a time.

Teachers

At the initial ratepayers' meeting at the end of 1875, it was proposed that Miss Martha Hadingham, daughter of David and Hannah Hadingham of St Cross, be taken on as a teacher at a salary of £20 a year. She stayed for 11 years, leaving close to the end of 1886, her salary having increased by 50 per cent.

The school had many staff over the years, and there is space here to mention only a few. Most of those local to Homersfield are included.

Early in 1895 Miss Ellen Gower, a former pupil of the school, joined on a salary of £20 a year and taught the infants.

In 1899 Miss Sally Hastings came to teach at the school. She was born Sarah Maria early in 1866, the second of 13 or more children born to Richard and Sarah Hastings of Yarmouth. Her working life commenced when she was in her mid-teens, serving in her father's bakery shop at No. 53 Lancaster Road, Yarmouth. She worked there for well over ten years before going into teaching. A 'Teachers Agreement' for her post at the school in St Cross survives to this day and shows that she started working there on 1 May 1899 at a salary of £70 per year, paid quarterly, with a £5 bonus at the end of each school year. There being no schoolhouse, it was normal practice for teachers at the school to lodge at one of the farms in St Cross, and in 1901, Sally was lodging at Chestnut Tree Farm, home of William and Sophia Debenham.

Miss Amelia Poppy, of Heath Farm, Homersfield, also came to the school in 1899, to teach the infants temporarily. In 1902 she joined the staff as monitress, on a salary of £8 a year. Both she and Sally Hastings resigned at the end of June 1905, giving three months' notice. By this time Amelia had become an assistant mistress at the school. The two became lifelong friends and, later in their lives, both taught at schools in Yarmouth.

Miss Sally Hastings and Miss Amelia Poppy, c.1905.

A Norwich photographic studio portrait of the same two ladies, c.1910.

Following the departure of these two ladies, Miss Ellen Gower also resigned.

At the end of 1936 almost 51 years of teaching came to an end and the school closed.

Inspections

From the end of the First World War, a nurse visited the school every few months, principally to check the children's heads for lice. Outbreaks were frequent and pupils were not uncommonly excluded from attending school until the nurse had seen them again and pronounced them free of vermin. It often took more than one re-inspection.

From 1920, dental examinations were held twice yearly at the school, and children were sometimes sent to local towns to undergo treatment by gas.

Curriculum

Among the subjects taught, which were similar to those at Flixton, emphasis was placed on the importance of Empire Day, 25 May. A communication from the London Education Authority in 1907 expressed the wish that Empire Day be observed in all schools in East Suffolk by the hoisting of the Union Jack and the singing of the National Anthem, followed by lectures and games. The school log-book of 1934 shows the practice continuing. On Empire Day, the children marched into the playground, stood around the flag, saluted, and sang the National Anthem. Afterwards, there was a talk on the Empire. The usual timetabled subjects were suspended and the latter part of the afternoon was devoted to games.

By 1917 the girls were attending a cookery centre at the school in Mendham. Within five years this was being held at All Saints School.

There was also a gardening day for the boys, held at the school each week, with a visiting instructor. For many years a Mr White fulfilled this post, teaching the boys the art of growing vegetables and flowers from seeds and giving practical lessons in pruning and other aspects of garden work. The school had a good supply of gardening tools for these classes, and seeds were bought from such local suppliers as Notcutts at Ipswich and Green's of East Dereham. The vegetables resulting from the children's horticultural efforts were often sent to other schools in the area, notably to Sir John Leman School in Beccles, which not uncommonly received a hundredweight of potatoes at a time. 'Sir John Llewellyn' and 'Duke of York' were two of the varieties grown. Parsnips, onions, carrots and other produce were also sent to local schools; in turn, St Cross School received their own quota of vegetables from other schools. Manure, sent to the school by train, was delivered from Homersfield Station. However, it wasn't all plain sailing and there were some setbacks. In the spring of 1920, rats devoured three separate plantings of peas and beans.

From 1921 the boys attended a woodwork centre for one half-day a week at All Saints School.

From 1934 the children were taught swimming during two one-hour sessions, boys followed by girls, on Wednesday mornings at a place close to Mendham Mill.

Holidays

It appears that no holidays were granted for Easter until 1908, when a week was given. At the same time, the customary four-week harvest holiday was increased to five, although it seems that the additional week was short-lived; it was reintroduced in 1927. An additional week was granted in 1919 as part of the Peace Celebrations following the end of the First World War.

Half-term holidays did not come into being until 1923, and even then, it appears there was only one such holiday per year, despite there being more than one school term!

A holiday was given for the marriage of the Duke of York, on St George's Day, 1923.

From 1918 the children were allowed the odd day off in September to pick blackberries (some children were occasionally absent for a whole week), a practice which continued until the school closed. As much as a hundredweight of fruit, picked by the children, was then brought into school, from where it was usually sent to Ipswich, presumably to be made into jam.

On 18 July 1919, a holiday was granted to all schools in East Suffolk to celebrate peace.

Treats

Treats at St Cross were much as they were at Flixton, and were associated with the Church. Children who attended Wortwell Chapel had their own treat each year, and others were held at the rectory in St Cross, Mendham or Flixton Hall. Later on in the life of the school, it was sometimes closed for a half-day, in the afternoons, for treats.

For one day in July 1936 the school was closed for a school outing to Norwich by train. The party, including 21 children, left Homersfield Station at 9.34a.m., returning at 6.16p.m. It is recorded as having been a successful excursion, the children having visited the Cathedral, the Guildhall and the Castle Museum.

Homersfield and St Cross schoolchildren often went to the rectory for afternoon treats. This photo dates from around 1910.

Absence

Snow prevented any children from attending the school on one day in January 1918. Two days later, with many roads under water, 11 children still managed to get to school.

At the beginning of September 1922, a late harvest caused the harvest holidays to be a little later than usual and there was very poor attendance, many children being kept at home to carry dinner to their fathers in the fields.

There was an outbreak of whooping cough later that year, plus many colds and coughs, and children were occasionally absent with cattle ringworm.

On 12 March 1928, after a heavy snowfall, only four children arrived at school. Mr Dewing, the headmaster, unable to get his motorcycle through the snow, had to walk the last three miles.

Closures

As at Flixton, the school had to be closed occasionally due to illness. Such a closure took place in April 1902, when, during an outbreak of scarletina, the school was closed by order of the Medical Officer of Health.

In March 1918 there was an outbreak of measles, and more and more children were away over the next month. The headmistress also fell victim, and at the beginning of May, the School Medical Officer ordered the school to close until after the Whitsuntide holidays (27 May). The school was disinfected and scrubbed during the closure.

In June of the same year, the school was closed in the afternoon for a garden fête in aid of Suffolk Prisoners of War.

After the Christmas holidays in 1919, only six children turned up for school in the New Year, so the school was closed again. There were cases of scarlet fever and whooping-cough, but most of those absent were suffering from measles. The school was closed for two weeks.

In 1922, during an influenza epidemic, the school was closed for two weeks at the beginning of March.

Later that same month, the monitress, Miss Louie Hadingham, returned after four days' absence, stating that she had been away because she 'thought she was in for an attack of influenza'. Mr Simpson, the head teacher, was clearly unimpressed.

The school also closed for the annual Suffolk Show, which was held at a different town each year in the earlier years of the twentieth century. Flower shows, fêtes and the yearly races at Bungay and Flixton also resulted in the school being closed – so many children attended these events that there was little point in holding classes for the remaining few on such days.

The school also closed for funerals, such as, in 1928, that of Miss Aldous, a teacher at the school, and, in January 1936, of King George V.

CHAPTER 9

Only Two Things in Life are Certain...

... DEATH

Wills nowadays can be either very simple or very complicated, and, looking at Homersfield wills through the centuries, it is obvious that this has always been the case. Many Homersfield wills have survived the passage of time, some dating back to the early years of the fifteenth century. Here is presented a small selection associated with people from the eighteenth century.

The original spellings and contractions of words have been retained throughout. Where the meaning of a contracted word is not obvious, it is expressed in its expanded form in square brackets.

Thomas Breese, Carpenter, 1703

This example is typical of just how short and sweet a will can be.

In the Name of God Amen I Thomas Breese of Homersfeild in the county of Suff. carpenter doe by this my last Will and Testamt give and bequeath to my son Edmund his heirs and assignes All my landsholden of the Mannor of Lymborne Hom. I give to my son Thomas one Bed as it now stands in the Kitchin chamber. All the rest of my goods and chattels I give to Sarah my beloved wife wth sd [with said] Sarah I hereby nominate sole executive of this my last Will and Testamt. In witness whereof I have hereunto set my hand and seal this 17th day of Jan: Anno Dins [Dominus]. 1703.

Thomas Breese's name appears beneath this short will, together with his mark, indicating that he was illiterate, which was common in these times. Following this is a clause in Latin, a paragraph of standard text concerned with proving the will, dated 2 July 1709.

In the seventeenth century a bed was a much-coveted household item, and much importance was placed on it. Consequently, it is frequently mentioned in wills of this period and was always left to a close member of the family.

The Breese family were in Homersfield for more than 150 years. The first reference in the Homersfield Parish Registers is to the marriage of Christofer Breese and Susan More, on 24 January 1586. During the next 16 years, six of their children were baptised in the church where they had married. The last of these was John, baptised on 12 January 1602. He

married Honor Stonard (also spelt Stonner, later changing to Stannard) of Homersfield, one of the eight children of Henry and Francis, on the last day of May 1631. Between 1632 and 1645, they had five children of their own baptised, the second being Thomas, on 20 December 1635.

Thomas Breese married a girl by the name of Elizabeth and they had at least three children in the 1670s, Thomas, Edmund and Susanna. Their mother died young, as did Susanna, and in 1680 both were buried in woollen shrouds (required by law at this time) in Homersfield churchyard.

Six years later, Thomas was married again, to Sarah Piggett, who had lost her first partner on 28 September 1686. They were married for more than 20 years; Thomas was buried in Homersfield church-yard on 10 May 1709.

John Moor, Towdresser, 1762

This will is much more detailed than that of Thomas Breese; by comparison, those of 100 or more years earlier being generally much simpler in form. His will, dated 20 May 1762, begins:

In the Name of God Amen I John Moor of Homersfield in the County of Suffolk Tow Dresser being weak and Infirm of Body but of Sound Mind Memory and Understanding Do Make and Publish this my last Will and Testament in manner and form following (that is to say first I Give Devise and Bequeath unto my Son in Law Stephen Stannard All that my Messuage or Tenement wherein I now dwell with the Yard and Gardens Lands and Appurtenancies thereunto belonging Situate and lying in Homersfield aforesaid

Waterloo Farm, 2007.

and also all that my Water Grist Mill and Mills and Hemp Bunching Mill (being under One Roof commonly called or known by the name of Limbor Mill or Mills with the Appurtenancies in the Parish of Homersfield aforesaid now in the Occupation of the said Stephen Stannard and the Ground whereon the said Mill stands together who with all and Singular the Roads, Wares [weirs] and Mill Ponds and the Soil thereof to the said Mill or Mills belonging or appertaining and all Stanks, Banks, Ponds, Streams, Waters, Water Courses, Rivers, Fishing, fishing places, Ways, Paths, Passages, Easements, Profits, Comodities, Advantages, Emoluments and Appurtenancies to the said Mill or Mills and other the items or any of them or any part or Parcell thereof…)

A towdresser was someone who processed bundles of hemp *(Cannabis sativa)*, grown throughout East Anglia for cloth-making. It was certainly grown in Homersfield; on the 1839 Tithe Map a field close to Home Farm, and owned by William Adair, is called 'Hempland'.

In 1743 Stephen Stannard married John's daughter, Sarah, in the Redenhall area. Stephen was willed Limbourne Mill and all the soil and water that came with it – but only for a period of two years. After that, or if Stephen died before the two years were up, it passed to John's grandson, also called Stephen, who was left it 'forever'. All of this was subject to a clear annuity payment (one which is free of all deductions) of £6 annually to Sarah for the rest of her natural life. This was to be paid in two equal six-monthly payments, the first within six months of her father's death. If, for whatever reason, payment was not forthcoming, Sarah had the legal right to enter Limbourne Mill, remove whatever she wished and sell the item(s) to recover her due income.

John Moore's son, also named John and baptised in Homersfield at the end of 1742, was left 20s., to be paid to him by Stephen Stannard within one month of his father's death. This one-off payment may seem a trifling sum to leave to his son, when his daughter was left six times that amount every year until she died. One might think that father and son had fallen out, but this is not the case. It was standard practice at that time to leave a small sum to a very close relation in recognition of the fact that that same relation had already received a substantial sum (or equivalent) whilst the testator was still alive.

The last item in John Moore's will reads:

… and further I Give and Bequeath unto my said Grandson Stephen Stannard all my Household Goods and furniture and all other My Goods and Chattels whatsoever and wheresoever…

So his grandson was certainly well provided for. Debts and funeral and probate expenses were also to

Homersfield Lodge, 2007.

Homersfield rectory, 2007.

Valley Farm, 2007.

Valley Barn and outbuildings, which has been a local pottery business, in 2007.

be taken from John Moore's estate, so his family also were absolved of those responsibilities.

John had appointed two executors of his will, Thomas Good of Wortwell, and James Whiting, gentleman, of Homersfield. It was witnessed the following year, on 1 February 1763, by Thomas Blomfield, John Asten and R. Chandley.

At some point during his lifetime, John Moore

became an overseer of the poor; his name crops up in a bond dated 1744, which he witnessed in that capacity. Some of the Homersfield records relating to overseers have survived, but unfortunately not for the eighteenth century, so it is not possible to say when he first took up this post or for how long he held it. John wasn't baptised in Homersfield, didn't marry there, nor was he buried there, but clearly he lived in the village for a good many years, from 1742 at least, and was still living there over 20 years later, when he made his will.

Edward Cooper, Carpenter, 1841

John Cooper met Elizabeth Brown in Homersfield and married her there on 29 November 1768. They had several children, one of whom, Edward, was born on 6 June 1791 and baptised in Homersfield Church several weeks later, on 17 July 1791. Probably the last of their children, he became a carpenter and acquired property in villages besides Homersfield, so it would seem he became prosperous during his working life. However, it seems he never found anyone with whom to share his fairly short life, as there is no record of a marriage, nor are any children of his own mentioned in his will. He was buried on 3 June 1841 in the village where he was born, just a few days before his fiftieth birthday.

Despite never having fathered a child of his own, there was certainly no shortage of people to whom he could choose to leave his worldly acquisitions. His life teemed with nieces and nephews, the offspring of his surviving brothers and sisters (there might have been even more, but two of his siblings died very young). The executors of Edward's will were Edward Marsh, of Heath Farm, Homersfield, and his nephew Onesimus Edwards, a farmer by profession. The will is quite lengthy, so only the important details are included here.

He directed his executors to dispose of and sell all:

... messuages or tenements, cottages, land and heredita-ments with their appurtenances... lying in Wortwell in the county of Norfolk and in Homersfield aforesaid and St James Southelmham in the said county of Suffolk.

These were to be sold in one or several lots by public auction, private contract or partly by either. The money arising from the sale of this property was to be considered as part of his personal estate. Also to be converted into money were:

... all my household furniture and implements of house-hold, working tools, beds and all other my moveables and personal estate whatsoever and wheresoever of which I shall die possessed.

This was '... to pay thereout my just debts, funeral and testamentary expenses and the charge of the

One of the older twentieth-century dwellings in Church Lane, built c.1948, in 2007.

Mill Cottage, near the site of Homersfield Mill, in 2007.

A group of the Glebe Cottages at the top of Church Lane, built in 1952, photographed in 2007.

Cowslip Cottage, No. 2 Middleton Hall Cottages, 2007.

probate of this, my will'. Within 12 months of all the property and goods having been sold, the executors were instructed to make payments to his family and friends. Here, the extent of his family becomes quite plain to see. William, his brother, had already passed on eight years earlier, but to Elizabeth Cooper of Homersfield, his widow, he left 19 guineas. To his nephews and nieces, Elijah, Edward, Job, Eleanor and Agnes Cooper, the children of his brother, Robert Cooper, he also left 19 guineas each. Another of William's children, Mary Ann, married to James Walker of Homersfield, also received 19 guineas. At the time of Edward's passing, his sister, Hannah, was living with him as his housekeeper. She had previously married a man by the name of Edwards, presumably by then deceased. Her children, James, Robert, John, William, Edward and Onesimus Edwards (one of the executors), were also left 19 guineas each. Other nieces, Sarah, the wife of Henry Buckenham of St Margaret Ilketshall, Susan, the wife of William Reynolds of Gisleham, near Lowestoft, Mary, the wife of William Sayer of St George's Plain in Norwich, Charlotte, the wife of William Williams of Godderston in Surrey, and Hannah, the wife of

James Burleigh, also of Godderston (a daughter of his sister, Hannah Edwards), similarly all received 19 guineas each. To his nephew James and niece Susan, the children of another sister, widow Susan Cole of Keazley, in Essex, he left the same sum of 19 guineas each. The residue from the sale of his personal estate was to be paid:

... amongst my surviving brothers and sisters that is to say one third part thereof to my Sister the said Hannah Edwards for her own absolute use and benefit. One other third part thereof to my brother the said Robert Cooper for his own absolute use and benefit and the remaining third part thereof to my sister Susan Cole for her own absolute use and benefit. And I give to the said Edward Brunning Marsh for his care and trouble in the Execution of this my will the sum of Ten pounds.

For any nephews or nieces who had already died, their part was to be split amongst their issue, 'share and share alike' once they had reached the age of 21 years; the resulting interest and dividends were to be

Wood 'n' Wheels, No. 1 Middleton Hall Cottages, 2007.

Sunset Cottage in 2007. Now much enlarged, it retains the monogram 'RSA' of Sir Robert Shafto Adair, who died in 1869.

put towards the cost of their maintenance and education. If all the nieces and nephews had already died, then their part was to be given to 'the survivors or survivors of them my said brothers and sisters equally between them share and share alike'.

The last clause in the will reads:

And I lastly revoke all former wills by me at any time heretofore made and do declare this only to be my last Will and Testament in witness thereof. I the said Edward Cooper the Testator have to this my last Will and Testament contained in four sheets of paper to the first three sheets set my hand and to this the fourth and last sheet my hand and seal this seventh day of May one thousand eight hundred and forty one.

Edward Marsh and Onesimus Edwards no doubt spent a lot of time administering this will!

... AND TAXES

1327 Subsidy

Under Norman kings, taxation was based on the land owned by an individual. King Henry II changed the method of raising money during the second half of the twelfth century so that it was raised, for example, on rents, or on the value of animals and crops in rural areas, and of money and saleable goods in towns. These were known as 'moveables', and the rate charged could be applied to rents, moveables, or both; additionally, different items could be exempted from being classed as moveables at different times. The rate varied greatly depending on the purpose for which it was being applied and was expressed as a fraction, varying from as much as one fourth to as little as a fortieth. This taxation method was in use for about 150 years, until 1334.

In January 1327 Edward II was dethroned and imprisoned. He was succeeded by Edward III, a boy

Sunset House in 2007.

not far into his teenage years, who spent the summer of that year at the head of an Army fighting against Scotland. That war had to be paid for, and at a parliament held in the autumn at Lincoln, a grant was made such that the populace should pay one-twentieth of the value of their moveables towards the overall cost. Two commissioners appointed for each county in turn appointed a minimum of two freemen for each town or village, depending on its size. They were tasked with assessing the value of taxable goods for each household. The commissioners were then to go to each hundred, check that the assessments were correct and collect the money due from the head of the household. Lists were made of all the people from each hundred and the amount they paid. These lists therefore represent the names of the wealthier households in any given village or township, and probably a few of the not so wealthy. Exempted were those whose taxable goods fell below the threshold value of 5s.

On 5 May 1329 the Suffolk commissioners delivered to the Exchequer the parchment rolls containing

The Dell, one-time home of poet Elizabeth Smart and originally two cottages, in 2007.

the lists of names and the amounts paid. For the hundred of Wayneforde (Wangford), the householders' names for Homersfield are included under 'Southelmham'. This particular list therefore represents nine settlements and contains a total of a 112 names (Christian names were expressed in Latin), but as those relating to Homersfield cannot be separated from those relating to any other village in South Elmham, it is not appropriate to include the full list here. However, it is interesting to note that, approaching seven centuries later, some of the well-known local surnames in the list are still extant in the area today, names such as Noloth (Nolloth), Erl (Earl), Calwe (Calver, Carver) and Elmy. Of all the names mentioned, none of their houses is standing today. In the great rebuilding that took place in England in the sixteenth and seventeenth centuries, they were torn down and some of the timber reused.

1524 Subsidy

Cardinal Wolsey announced to the Commons in 1523 that King Francis I of France had broken many agreements made with King Henry VIII and his nephew, Charles, and as a result, the king and his nephew would be compelled to go to war the following year. A sum of at least £800,000 was needed, to be paid by the people at the rate of 4s. in the pound, levied on goods and land. There was subsequently much debate about this pronouncement.

Payments towards this subsidy could last for up to four years, depending on how well-off (or not) people were. Everybody paid for the first two years, but only the very well-off were required to pay for either or both of the third and fourth years of the subsidy. A shilling for each pound of their yearly value was required to be paid by everyone on their house and land for the first two years. Additionally, a sliding scale provided the means by which payments on moveable goods (defined in the relevant Parliamentary Act) were levied. Those whose

moveable goods were valued at more than £20 paid 1s. per pound. Those with goods valued at more than £2 and less than £20 paid 6d. per pound. A value of £1–£2 attracted 4d. per pound. The poorest, who did not even have goods worth as little as £1, still had to pay. Those aged 16 years or over, whose yearly wages were £1 or more, paid 4d. per pound. No one escaped payment, however poor, excepting those of 15 and under.

In the third year, 1s. per pound was paid by those who owned land totalling £50 or more in value. In the last year, 1s. per pound was paid by those who owned moveable goods valued at £50 or more.

This was a very unpopular subsidy, mainly because of the high rates applied. The number of people who paid during the third year was expectedly very small, and it is thought that no money was actually collected during the final year; there are no surviving records.

The assessments for these payments on each of the four years were made between Michaelmas (29 September) and Martinmas (11 November).

Shown below is an almost certainly complete list of householders in the Wayforth (Wangford) hundred for 'Homersfield in Elmham', who paid the subsidy in each of the first two years. Excluded from the list is the parson, who had the honour of being taxed separately.

	£	s	d
Richard Bery in goodes £5		2	6
Thomas Toft in goodes £7		3	6
John Hare in goodes £30	1	10	0
John Same in goodes £6		3	0
Nicholas Davy, Peter Freman, in goodes £8		8	0
William Bery in landes be yer £1		1	0
William Turnour in goodes £4		2	0
Robert Bery, Nicholas Ballys, in goodes £3		3	0
John Fulcher, Henry Palle, John Wodeward, in wages £1		1	0
Henry Bery, Robert Wegge, John Symon, in wages £1		1	0
Henry Wytnam in goodes £2		1	0
Margery Hare in goodes £2.13s.4d.		1	4
William Chapman in goodes £8		4	0
Johanne Salman in goodes £2.3s.4d.		1	1
Thomas Rechardson, William Hennale, in wages £1			8
	3	3	1

1568 Subsidy

In 1566 a grant of one-fifteenth and one-tenth was pledged for the purpose of supporting Crown expenses, which included paying the Armed Forces and the building of new ships. A subsidy was to follow. The fifteenth was to be paid by the rural areas, and the tenth by towns and cities, on moveable goods, cattle, crops, stock in hand and belongings. In fact, the stated fractions were commuted to payments of a fixed amount. The subsidy involved a payment of 2s.8d. in the pound on moveable goods and 4s. in the pound on the yearly land value; everyone was obliged to pay it.

The subsidy was paid in two consecutive years. In the first year, moveable goods attracted a payment of 1s. in the pound, and 10d. in the pound the following year. Land payments were 16d. in the pound for both years. This actually left a shortfall of 10d. in the pound for moveables and 16d. in the pound for land, implying that there should have been a third year's payment, but it seems never to have been imposed. The clergy were excluded from assessment by the commissioners, as were barons and those higher up the aristocratic ladder. Of the multitude included in the assessments, those with goods worth less than £3 or land worth less than £1 were exempt from payment. These would have constituted only a small part of the labour force.

A roll of 68 parchments joined together represents the returns for Suffolk and shows the names of everyone subject to the subsidy in March 1568.

Below are the names of those listed in the returns for the second year's payments for 'Homersfylde'.

Fisher's Green and Five Islands in 2007. Note the gravel-pit lake in the foreground.

Second and Corner Cottages in 1988.

	£	s	d
Margaret Ward, John Toste, each £3 in landes		8	0
Robert Chapman £10 in goodes		8	4
John Bury £8 in goodes		6	8
John Davye £5 in goodes		4	2
John Freman £7 in goodes		5	10
John Arnold £10 in goodes		8	4
John Skete £3 in goodes		2	6
John Love allien by the poll			4
	2	4	2

1674 Hearth Tax

In 1662, when King Charles II requested that Parliament raise money towards the costs incurred by the Civil War and the subsequent Cromwellian rule, from 1649 to 1660, the Hearth Tax was devised as a means to raise the funds. The Chimney Act of the same year required that an annual payment of 2s. be paid on every hearth and stove in England and Wales. It was to be paid by the occupier as from Michaelmas (29 September) 1662 in equal payments half-yearly at Lady Day (25 March, then the first day of the New Year) and Michaelmas. Within six days of the parish constable giving notice that the tax was to be collected, returns were to be submitted by parish-ioners showing the number of hearths and stoves in their homes. The constable was then to check that

each return was correct, by entering homes in the day-time to count the hearths and collect the tax due. This did not prove successful; in an Act the following year the king transferred the responsibility for collecting the money to high and petty constables, who would give occupiers ten days to provide the returns. Under the provisions of this Act heavy fines were to be imposed on anyone failing to provide the necessary returns or give true accounts, with £2 payable on each hearth or stove omitted. However, when the new constables proved reluctant to carry out their duties, due to sympathy for or fear of their fellow parishioners, yet another Act was passed in 1664 in which responsibility was passed to officers appointed by the king.

There were some allowable exceptions to the payment of the tax. Those who did not pay the Poor Rate (that is, those entitled to receive rather than those who paid it), or who lived in a house worth less than £1, were not obliged to pay the Hearth Tax. Such people held an exemption certificate and were described as 'certified' or 'those that take collection' (received money from the Poor Rate via the parish churchwardens). Also spared were those with

Nos 84–86, opposite the pub, in 1988.

Downs Farm in 1991.

furnaces, kilns or private ovens and the hearths in hospitals and almshouses, provided that their income was not in excess of £100 annually.

From the very beginning, this tax was detested and resisted nationally. Evasion was widespread; some returns showed fewer hearths than were actually present, some hearths were hidden and in, some cases, there were no returns at all. Violence also ensued, some 'chimney men' (as they were called) being bombarded with stones whilst going about their business. If anything, the appointment of officers by the king from 1664 onwards made the tax even more unpopular, as it meant complete strangers entering peoples' homes. Nevertheless, the tax remained in force throughout the reign of Charles II and beyond. It saw James II come and go and was eventually abolished in 1689, soon after William III came to the throne.

For Suffolk, the returns made for the year ending at Lady Day 1674 have survived and show the occupiers' names and the number of hearths; they also show the names of those certified as being exempt from payment due to being impoverished.

Bearing in mind the discrepancies between fact and fiction in the returns for this hated tax, it is not possible to tell with any degree of certainty those entries which are true and those which were falsified. Nevertheless, even allowing for the number of hearths to be lower than it should be, there were some big houses in Homersfield at this time, as can be seen from the figures below. Some of these houses are still to be seen in the village today. Note that those exempted are grouped together, suggesting that two or three families lived together in each dwelling; such tenements were common in seventeenth-century Suffolk.

Thomas Martin	6	**CERTIFIED**		
Mr Baxter	2	John Hudser	}	
William Pigit	2	James Piger	} 3	
Dan. Alexander	2	Widow Stevens	}	
William Whitinge	5	Edward Weells	}	
Robert Neech	6	Robert Flatman	} 3	
Edward Barker	1	Nath. Wills	}	
Thomas Chalcor	3	Mar. Bluter	}	
William Maninge	3	Widow Tillet	} 3	
William Spaldinge	2	James Fenn	}	
John Girlinge	2	Widow Claper	}	
John Bridges	1	Widow Wright	} 3	
Mr Fuller	4	Peter Wright	}	
Mr Cocke	5	Jo. Stuerd	}	
John Rushmer	4	Robert Rutland	} 3	
Thomas Barber	2	John Muly	}	
John Cotton	4	Jo. Walter	} 2	
Richard Nolloth	5	Richard Molocke	}	
	——			——
	59			17

CHAPTER 10

The Three Rs

In this chapter we look at the railway, the roads and the river.

THE TRAIN NOW STANDING...

The Coming of the Railways

The building of the railways began in the 1830s and, by the middle of the century, more goods were transported by rail than by road or river. People travelling any great distance also preferred to use the rail network, which gradually spread all over the country, and by the last quarter of the century cheap fares enabled men to seek work much further afield, often for better wages. This, in turn, allowed people to spend money on days out, especially after the institution of bank holidays in 1871, and trips by rail to the seaside became commonplace.

The railways had a sudden and significant impact on rural populations, providing local employment whilst they were built, and adding a healthy glow to the bank balances of those landowners who had sold off some of their land. Once the trains were running – still providing employment – they also brought a significant change to the basic way of life. Before steam trains added a new dimension to travel, in Homersfield the exact time of day was unimportant. Labourers in the fields knew when it was time to go home by the sound of the three church bells. Those same bells summoned worshippers to church at certain times, but otherwise there was little or no need to know the precise minute and hour of any day. With the railways came a need to be more precise, as the trains ran fairly accurately to a predetermined timetable. Whereas individual towns had always based time on the noon position of the sun, in 1840 one railway company began to set its clocks to the time in London; others quickly followed suit and it has been that way ever since. In 1849 Greenwich Observatory had an electric clock and within three years a signal (the Greenwich Time Signal) was being transmitted to the station at Lewisham and from there to other railway stations and Post Offices everywhere. The electric telegraph, first used by railway companies to exchange messages up and down the line, was increasingly used to send information in general, and stationmasters began to provide a postal telegram service, carried out on behalf of the Post Office.

The railways were not good news for everyone however, and were largely responsible for reduced road traffic, leading to the demise of coaching and toll roads. Such villages as Homersfield were not as quiet as they used to be, but by and large the difference was of no significance and the advantages afforded by the railways considerably outweighed the disadvantages.

Railway Mania

The principal investors in the building of railway lines were prominent bankers, the owners of cotton manufacturing businesses in the Midlands and north of England and those simply born wealthy. They would be persuaded to part with large sums of money, lured by the promise of high returns on their investments, all attractively presented in the prospectuses. The many schemes proposed for new lines to be built, together with the possibility that investors could make excellent returns on their money, resulted in all-out railway mania by the mid-1840s, with a brisk increase in the number of railway Acts passed from 1844 onwards. This lasted until the end of the decade, peaking in 1847.

THE WAVENEY VALLEY LINE

Setting the Scene

For more than 50 miles the River Waveney flows from its source at South Lopham eastwards to Breydon, the River Yare's estuary. River valleys were

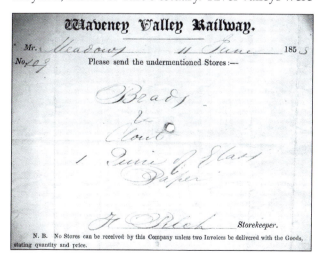

A very rare piece of Waveney Valley Line memorabilia – a stores request, dated 1855. The first section of line, from Tivetshall to Harleston, was not to open for another six months.

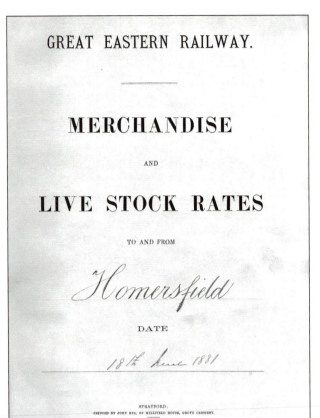

GREAT EASTERN RAILWAY.

MERCHANDISE

AND

LIVE STOCK RATES

TO AND FROM

Homersfield

DATE

18th June 1881

STRATFORD:
PRINTED BY JOHN REA, OF MILLFIELD HOUSE, GROVE CRESCENT.
1880.

The title page from the Homersfield Station rates book, dated 1881. This book was housed at the station and contains hand-written prices for carrying freight of varying weights to every other station in the British Isles.

always a popular location for railway lines because they are normally fairly flat, with only occasional slight rises and falls, and so ideal for steam engines – not keen supporters of gradients. The wide valley in which the Waveney flows would have made the building of a main line between Yarmouth, Lowestoft and London an attractive proposition, but much opposition to the idea in the 1840s resulted in other lines being built in the latter half of the same decade.

Beginnings

After several proposed schemes had come to nothing, the line that would be known as the Waveney Valley line was begun at the end of 1850. Close to Christmas of that year, local businessmen, meeting in Harleston to discuss a possible line from Tivetshall, decided to form the Waveney Valley Railway Co., which was officially incorporated in an Act of 3 July 1851. This gave the go-ahead for the building of just over 13 miles of railway from Tivetshall to Bungay within a stipulated time-frame of four years. A second Act, of 4 August 1853, authorised a six-mile extension from Bungay to Beccles.

A severe shortfall in available funding made for rather protracted progress, as did difficulties in acquiring the necessary land. Further delays were caused by a shortage of labour at certain times of the year, particularly around harvest time, when the men were needed to work in the fields. After four years, the line had been built only from Tivetshall to

A steam train with a mail coach, at least three carriages and a couple of goods trucks picks up passengers at Homersfield Station, c.1903.

Harleston, with additional stations at Pulham Market, Pulham St Mary and Starston, and was opened on 1 December 1855.

The building of the line continued slowly, and the second section of line, from Harleston to Bungay, with additional stations at Redenhall, Wortwell, Homersfield and Earsham, opened five years after the first, on 2 November 1860.

In the summer of 1862 the Great Eastern Railway (GER) was formed, incorporating the Waveney Valley Railway Co. in its entirety, on the day before the final section of line was opened, on 2 March 1863. Stations on this section, between Bungay and Beccles, were Ditchingham, Ellingham and Geldeston.

Although called the Waveney Valley Line, only about half of it was close to the river – at its western end, the line at Tivetshall was six miles north of it. The line ran eastwards, closely following a stream, the Beck, all the way to Homersfield, where it settled in the valley and then wound its way to Beccles. Almost all of the line was in Norfolk, crossing the river into Suffolk only at Bungay and Beccles.

Some 12 years after getting the initial go-ahead, involving several time extensions, endless problems with funding and shortages of labour, the line was finally complete and up and running. It had been very hard work; stations, buildings, bridges and level crossings all had to be built, in addition to many cuttings, and some architecturally fine Italianate station buildings were erected. For a line serving four market towns with no direct route to major cities such as London and Norwich, it is remarkable that it was in use for almost a century before the axe fell.

Passenger Services

When the first section of line opened between Tivetshall and Harleston in 1855, four trains a day

Homersfield Station, c.1906. (© EASTERN DAILY PRESS.)

A sleepy scene at the sleepy railway station, c.1911.

An excellent view of Homersfield Station, c.1910. Note the rather overloaded cart (middle right).

(REPRODUCED BY KIND PERMISSION OF GLEN EARL.)

93

Built at Stratford, Essex, in 1912, and restored by enthusiasts, locomotive 65462 is thought to be the only surviving steam train to have run on the Waveney Valley Line.

Another view of the 65462, showing the various controls. This and the top photograph were taken in 2006 at Weybourne in Norfolk, where the locomotive runs on the North Norfolk line.

ran each way along it. After the whole line was completed and opened in 1863, the number of trains each way varied over the next few decades, but didn't exceed eight each way. There were none on Sundays. By 1915 the line was busier than it would ever be, with eight trains a day between Tivetshall and Beccles, while a separate service took a few trains from Beccles to Harleston and back. Six trains each way was the order of the day around 1917, and this remained unchanged until the line closed, some 36 years later, in 1953. They ran essentially between 7a.m. and 9.30p.m. In any case, as the line was single track for its whole length, basically only one train could run on it at any one time, although it was possible for two trains to pass at some stations.

The time taken to travel all 14 stations, from one end of the line to the other, varied between 50 and 65 minutes. Trains did not stop at all stations along the way, the only definite intermediate stops being at Harleston, Homersfield and Bungay. Passengers who wished to get off at any other stop had to inform the guard before getting on the train. Whether the train stopped or not also depended on whether the train was subsequently given authorisation to do so at a particular station – despite the lack of traffic on the line it wasn't necessarily a foregone conclusion!

With the exception of the two world wars, throughout the entire life of the line Waveney Valley Sundays were only exceedingly rarely disturbed by the sound of steam engines. The very occasional Sunday excursion provided the rural population with an opportunity for a day out, but other than that, Sundays were designated sleepy.

Golden Days

The Waveney Valley line provided numerous local jobs in a region where a slump in agriculture had hit hard. The line employed many people, among them signalmen, stationmasters and all manner of station staff, including clerks, porters and crossing staff, who lived next to the level crossings (of which there were a couple of dozen) in gatehouses. Then there were the more mobile staff, train drivers, those who laid and maintained the track (platelayers) and those who maintained the engines and carriages in workshops. In addition to all of these, we must not forget that most important breed of employee, the manager, without whom nothing ever runs smoothly.

The goods conveyed along the line were many and varied. Horticultural items included roses and trees, and there were livestock aplenty – cattle, sheep, pigs, pigeons, chickens and new-born chicks. Trains carried game and poultry on their way to London, changing at Tivetshall for the capital. Fish came straight from Beccles via the daily Lowestoft catch. Unbelievably, wooden boxes packed with ice cream also travelled by train, as did such commodities as grain, sugar-beet and coal. In its twilight years, when

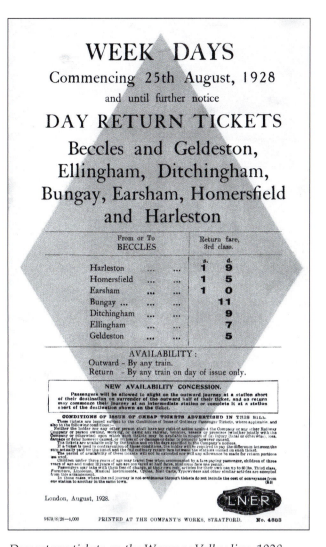

Day return tickets on the Waveney Valley line, 1928.

the line carried potatoes and eggs, it became affectionately known as the 'egg and chips line'.

The rule of no trains on Sundays was, understandably, not observed during the two world wars. Troops and much military equipment were moved on the Sabbath to avoid interfering with the normal day-to-day timetable. Traffic on the line was especially dense during the Second World War – the busiest period of its life, due in no small part to the number of airfields being built locally, mostly for the use of American allies. Flixton and Metfield airfields were close to Homersfield Station, and vast quantities of cement travelled through the Waveney Valley for their building.

Railway employees found themselves working for a new employer at the very beginning of 1923, when the Great Eastern was absorbed into the London & North Eastern Railway (LNER). The same happened on New Year's Day 1948, when the LNER was taken over by British Rail.

With the appearance of more and more motor cars, lorries and omnibuses came the start of the decline of the railway era. The number of passengers began to fall towards the end of the 1940s, when more and more people could afford their own motor car. Freight traffic declined similarly, goods being transported more frequently by road.

Homersfield Station

Being on the north side of the river, Homersfield Station was actually in Norfolk, and spanned the parish boundaries of Wortwell and Alburgh. Wortwell had its own station, and although Alburgh did not, it is thought to have taken the name of the village south of the river because the Adair family at Flixton Hall had contributed towards the building costs. As both Flixton and Homersfield are in Suffolk, the latter being the nearer of the two, the station was named Homersfield. Stationmasters were responsible for every aspect of the railway at their station, and many took a great pride in its appearance. At Homersfield many garden flowers were planted to full effect in the spring and summer months. In the autumn and winter, when there were often floods, footbridges enabled passengers to get to the station.

For a rural village station, Homersfield had superior facilities capable of handling all kinds of goods. The large goods shed was made accessible by a wagon turntable, which was still there in 1961, over 100 years later. The goods shed was rented by Woods, Sadd & Moore, local corn merchants. A large crane was also on site. A level crossing west of the station was operated from the signal box, from where the line passed over the Beck. The bridge here needed replacing after the 1912 floods.

Around the 1920s–40s, half-way up Dove Hill two redundant carriages, placed end to end, were being used as a residence.

The tracks were removed within two years of the line closing altogether in 1960, although the station was still there in 1969. The author can remember seeing the trackbed at this time and also the derelict blacksmith's premises at the foot of Dove Hill, where rusty horseshoes and a few tools could be seen, through the broken windows, lying on a straw-strewn floor.

The Demise

Although the line had been built in three separate sections, not every station shut its doors on the same day, nor was it closed in three distinct phases. The travelling public were affected first, and then freight.

A line such as this, with 14 stations on a track only 19 miles from end to end, was asking for trouble right from the start. It wasn't long in coming. There were simply too many stations in a relatively short stretch of line – not only that, some were very close to each other, very close to a town, or both. A lack of custom resulted in lack of use, rendering some of the village stations no longer viable, and a few closed to passen-

gers not long after opening. The first casualties, Starston and Redenhall, were closed on 1 August 1866. Wortwell closed next, on New Year's Day, 1878. The remaining 11 stations operated for more than 38 years before Earsham was closed, on 22 May 1916, due to a decision by the GER to close some stations during the war. It reopened on 1 August 1919. The railways were nationalised on New Year's Day, 1948, and reorganised soon after. One of many to suffer was the Waveney Valley Line, and all 11 stations were simultaneously closed to passengers on Saturday, 3 January 1953, never to reopen.

The line continued to carry freight for several years but gradually closed between 1960 and 1966. Some cost-cutting took place as a result of the line being designated a 'light railway' from 15 November 1954; this meant that the majority of level crossings no longer had gates or anyone to man them. Homersfield was the first station to be closed completely, on 1 February 1960. The next closures, on 13 July 1964, were of Geldeston, Ellingham, Pulham Market and Pulham St Mary. Bungay closed on 3 August 1964 and Ditchingham on 19 April 1965. This now meant that the section of line from Bungay to Beccles was fully closed. The closures of Harleston and Tivetshall on 18 April 1966, 111 years after the first part of the line was opened, signalled the end of all train services along the Waveney Valley.

Much of the railway line can still be followed; from Harleston to Ellingham the new road mirrors the line very well. Half of the 14 station buildings still stand, and are now either private or commercial residences. Tivetshall, Pulham St Mary, Redenhall, Wortwell, Homersfield, Bungay and Ditchingham are no more, although a goods shed, once part of the Homersfield Station complex, remains opposite the Wortwell Dove at the foot of Dove Hill. The upper floor has been converted into flats.

ARE WE THERE YET?

Ancient Trackways

Ever since man ceased to roam and settled in one spot, he began to make trackways by travelling the same routes in order to reach all sorts of destinations. As related previously, the fields in Homersfield may date from as early as the Bronze Age, or may be post-Roman, but however old they are, it is very likely (and very difficult to prove) that the trackways around them are of a similar age; however one thinks of them, they are ancient and have been with us for 1,000 years or more. The most widely used eventually became roads, whilst others in this intricate system of trackways survive in the form of public footpaths and bridle-ways. Typically, an ancient trackway, having had to circumnavigate obstacles, had several bends which, although such obstacles are long gone, have become permanent.

A very early 'fine weather only' motor car outside Homersfield's Black Swan, c.1900. (Reproduced by kind permission of Mrs Mary Rackham.)

By far the majority of settlements and outlying farms had at least one lane running past them. Many had other tracks and lanes that terminated in fields. Not every field could be reached via a lane; some could be approached only via other fields.

Roman

The Romans constructed many trunk roads, which were usually, though not always, straight, and connected two of their settlements together. They were built mostly during the first century AD for the purposes of local administration rather than for the use of native inhabitants. Troops were deployed along them, steadily extending the Roman Empire over a people newly brought under their control. The quality of their work was such that in the main, it needed no maintenance for several hundred years, and no new roads came into being until the enclosure laws and turnpikes of the eighteenth century.

Although a strong Roman presence is apparent from the many Roman artefacts discovered in Homersfield, there are no known Roman roads in the parish, the nearest example being Stone Street, in the Saints.

Medieval

In medieval times, the majority of roads had originated as ancient trackways, and progressed in relation to the times and the changing demands placed upon them. Every dwelling, farm building, field and wood in Homersfield was accessible by wheeled vehicles, and there were footpaths across most of the fields. Our village is typical of an ancient settlement; most of the roads here now were here 1,000 or more years ago, while a few have become hidden in the modern landscape.

During these times, larger goods (excluding animals) were transported by river. Drove roads (some of which passed through Homersfield) were travelled by a variety of people, not all of them by any means involved in moving animals from one place to another, although such roads were used primarily for that purpose.

Laws at this time were mostly concerned with a road's legal status as a highway – a right of way which anyone could use, whenever they wished. Manorial courts dealt with matters which might obstruct, prevent or cause irritation to those attempting to use a highway. Many of the goings-on in manorial courts were concerned with the abuse of common land and were called 'purprestures'. Commonly, these involved the dumping of rubbish on the highway, or a road having been made narrower, typically by farmland encroaching upon it. The courts often dealt with this by imposing an annual fine on the lord of the manor.

Drovers and Droving

For hundreds of years the most important travellers over long distances were those who drove herds of animals all over Britain, from early medieval times until the railways rendered them no longer necessary. They were well respected among farming communities, and earned more than the average farm worker. Responsible for many animals on the outward journey and much money on the return, drovers were generally honest, as well as reliable. In order to practise his profession, from 1552 each drover had to be registered and licensed annually by Quarter Sessions courts (compulsory until 1772), partly in order to circumvent problems with the country's vagrancy laws. To obtain a licence a drover had to be over 30 years old, married and a householder in his own right; holding a licence brought with it a good reputation and a degree of respectability. However, not every drover was trustworthy, and from around 1700 those with debts were prevented by law from becoming bankrupt.

Cattle were worth serious money and were seen as a fool-proof way of exchanging money. Drovers and those who purchased livestock commonly used promissory notes (a signed statement promising to pay to a particular person or to the bearer a specified sum of money on or by a fixed date, or on demand) or bills of exchange (orders from one person to another to pay a particular sum to a specified person or bearer on a particular date). These circulated throughout the country in exactly the same way as paper money does today, but were only accepted from reliable purchasers (or their representatives). They were therefore 'not worth the paper they were written on' if they were stolen or lost and later found by another party.

Some of the ancient trackways used by prehistoric communities to move livestock from one grazing area to another developed into droving routes. On one such route, from the Midlands, animals crossed the bridge in Homersfield on their way to their final destination, Dunwich. Towards the end of the 1300s this town became significantly smaller due to encroachment by the sea, and such traffic instead went to Walberswick.

The sixteenth century saw a significant expansion of towns and cities and, consequently, a number of livestock markets came into being to help feed the increased population; huge cattle herds, mostly black beasts, were transported along the country's roads from Scotland and Wales to the London markets and elsewhere over a number of distinct routes. One route took the animals to grazing pastures in East Anglia, where they were fattened up on the way to their ultimate destination. The journey took several months and progress was deliberately slow so that the cattle could feed on the roadside verges, greens and commons.

Some cattle droves, starting from Scotland and travelling down the Great North Road through Yorkshire, would digress from the north–south route to London and turn eastwards. These droves comprised long columns of up to 200 beasts, accompanied by one or more drovers and their dogs. There were several different routes to Norfolk, but the majority of animals passed through Wisbech, towards King's Lynn and then on to Norwich. From there, they travelled to the excellent East Anglian grazing meadows, where the cattle would put on weight quickly. The farmers in this area not only benefited from the income derived from renting land to graze animals, but also had their land well manured for free! Droving in the east of England was big business, upwards of 40,000 or more cattle being driven into Norfolk every year in the middle of the eighteenth century. The drovers would pay the farmer's fee and then move on towards London. They would stay overnight at an inn, of which there were plenty along the main roads, with meadows in which the cattle could be accommodated for the night. Homersfield's Swan was used as a regular overnight stopping place.

From Norwich, the drove would continue south to Suffolk, through Bungay, over Homersfield bridge, through Wortwell, Harleston, Needham, Brockdish, Hoxne, then Scole, Wortham, Botesdale, Walsham-le-Willows, Pakenham and Bury St Edmunds on their London-bound journey.

Travelling between villages, allowances had to be made for the avoidance of tolls on certain roads and for natural obstacles such as streams and difficult terrain, but the average distance travelled per day was approximately 15 miles. Onward travel could not have been helped by other animals travelling the same route, not to mention farm vehicles and public coaches; it was a skilled man indeed who could rise above all the confusion and retain his herd without losing either time or beasts along the way.

Cattle were by no means the only livestock transported. At times, roads in the area were filled with sheep and geese travelling short distances. Enormous numbers of turkeys, up to 500 at a time, and upwards of 300 droves, travelled from Norfolk in August along the route through Homersfield on their way to London. The birds roosted at night in trees by the roadside and the slow journey ensured they were well fattened by the time they reached market in time for Christmas dinner.

Tudor and Stuart

The enforced disappearance of the monasteries as a result of their dissolution in the second quarter of the sixteenth century had serious consequences for highways. Land tenure involved the obligatory maintenance of roads and bridges, and this was now under threat. Much of the land in England had new owners who didn't especially care for the duties they had inherited; they were more interested in the rights of highways than the fabric of roads and bridges. Road traffic increased gradually and a new kind of vehicle for carrying passengers and goods came into being, the wide-wheeled wagon. These traversed the country throughout Tudor times. Clearly, something had to be done to decide who was responsible for the state of the country's roads and, in 1555, something was.

The Highway Acts

The responsibility for maintaining the roads in Homersfield was passed on to the tenants of the lord of the manor, who made sure their obligations were complied with via the manorial courts. Those whose lands were rented from the lord and adjoined the highway were required to maintain it. Roads were primarily used by people and animals, but the increase in wheeled traffic in the sixteenth century, combined with the reluctance of tenants to carry out their duties and their lack of know-how, meant that the roads deteriorated. Vehicles often had to be prised out of axle-deep mud in winter, while in summer the roads were often watered to prevent huge dust clouds which formed during very dry periods. In 1555 the responsibility for looking after roads was transferred, via a Highway Act, to individual parishes. Homersfield churchwardens, together with the parish constable and other representatives of the parish, were required under this law to appoint a 'surveyor of the highways'. The

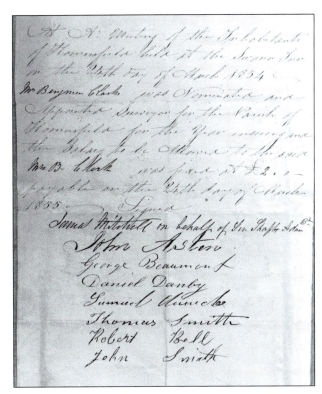

This document records a meeting of parishioners at the Swan Inn on 24 March 1854 to elect the Highways Surveyor. (REPRODUCED BY KIND PERMISSION OF SUFFOLK RECORD OFFICE, LOWESTOFT BRANCH, REF.: 128/A1/8.)

An invoice for expenses from Thomas Smith, the Homersfield Parish Constable in 1864/65 and authorised by a local JP.
(REPRODUCED BY KIND PERMISSION OF SUFFOLK RECORD OFFICE, LOWESTOFT BRANCH, REF.: 128/A1/15.)

appointment, made during Easter week, was initially not popular; the surveyor was unpaid, served for a year (and was often elected to serve for a further year), and could be fined for failing to carry out his duties or for refusing to accept the post.

The Highway Act of 1662 enabled the Homersfield church vestry to levy a highway rate on its parishioners to keep the roads in good order, to pay for labour and materials and also to pay the surveyor for services rendered. The parishioners alone chose the surveyor as a result of this Act, but in 1691 the law was changed, and a Justice of the Peace fulfilled the task, electing an eligible land-holder from a supplied list. From this date, the person fulfilling the role of surveyor changed each year. He was required to check the roads in his parish a minimum of three times a year and to organise the necessary labour force. He also had to keep the roads clear of obstructions and report anyone who refused to carry out the labour expected of them. Every capable householder or tenant had to provide four days' labour a year (later increased to six days), or could arrange for someone else to do the work. Refusal to do so resulted in a fine at the next Quarter Sessions, although, in prac-tice, the labour requirement could often be avoided by a one-off payment. Additionally, some individ-uals were obliged to provide a vehicle to assist with road repairs.

The office of surveyor declined rapidly and disap-peared when, under a Highway Act passed in 1835, accountability for highways was transferred to newly formed local authorities and district surveyors were responsible for several parishes, charging a highway rate. This rate coincided with the abolition of the statutory requirement to work on the roads. In the 1880s, responsibility moved again, to county coun-cils, and in 1894 the minor roads came under the control of local authorities.

Although the 1835 Highway Act resulted in surveyors of the highway becoming redundant, in many rural parishes they continued for a number of years. A 'Highway Surveyors Account Book' for Homersfield gives an interesting insight into the state of the roads and the costs of maintaining them between the years 1837 and 1846.

On the inside front cover of the book are the words: 'Measurement of Roads in this Parish taken April 7th 1836. Liable to be repaired at the Expense of the Parish. 4 miles 3 furlongs 25 poles.'

Listed are the surveyors' names for the period covered, all farmers in the village. In 1837/38 John Beaumont was elected, and in the following year, Edward Marsh, farmer at Heath Farm. For the next five years Horace Beaumont performed the surveyor's duties, while in the next (final) year covered, they were executed by Benjamin Clarke, who succeeded Horace at Holehouse Farm.

Date		Labourers Names	No Days	At Per Day	£	s	d	
1839								
Novbr	11	R Palmer	4	1s.6d.		6	0	Scraping roads
	25	Do.	6	1s.6d.		9	0	Do. Do. and Cleaning Sides
Decbr	2	Do.	5½	1s.6d.		8	3	Do. Do.
	"	W. Wince	4	1s.6d.		6	0	Do. Do.
	9	R. Palmer	3	1s.6d.		4	6	Cleaning Water Courses and Scraping
	16	W Wince	6	1s.6d.		9	0	Repairing Back Lane
	23	Do.	5½	1s.6d.		8	3	Mending footpaths and scraping
	"	R. Palmer	6	1s.6d.		9	0	Scraping and Cleaning roads
	30	Do.	5	1s.6d.		7	6	Barrowing and Breaking Stones Back Lane
	"	W. Wince	5	1s.6d.		7	6	Do. Do.
1840								
Janr	13	R. Palmer	5	1s.0d.		5	0	Scraping roads
	20	Do.	6	1s 0d		6	0	Do. Do.
	27	Do.	5	1s.0d.		5	0	Teaking of Bank and Scraping, Mendham Road
Febr	3	Do.	6	1s.0d.		6	0	Cleaning Water Courses and Scraping roads
	"	W. Swan	6	1s.0d.		6	0	Breaking Stones Flixton Road and Back Lane
	10	Do.	2½	1s.0d.		2	6	Do. Do Back Lane
	"	R. Palmer	6	1s.0d.		6	0	Scraping Roads

5 11 6

1840							
Febr	17	R. Palmer		1s.0d.	6	0	Screening Gravel and Breaking Stones St Cross Road
	17	W. Swan		1s.0d.	6	0	Picking and filling up Holes Flixton Road
1841							
Jan		J. Vince.		2s.0d.	2	0	Throwing Snow Different parts of Roads
Decbr	6	Do.		1s.2d.	7	0	Digin out Water Chanel
	20	W. Swan		1s.2d.	6	0	Making Chanel St Cross Hill
1842							
Febr	8	W. Swan		1s.2d.	7	0	Cleaning Water Courses Mendham Road
Mar	8	Do.		1s.2d.	7	0	Teaking of Bank Mendham Hill
	15	Do.		1s.2d.	5	3	Do. Removing Soil Stanfords Lane
	22	Do.		1s.2d.	7	0	Breaking Stones and Barrowing Flixton Road
1843							
April	29	Do.	6	1s.0d.	6	0	Cleaning Chanels in Homersfield
1844							
Mar	1	Swann	1	1/-	1	0	Picking in Ruts Back Lane
	16	Do.	3½	1/-	3	6	Breaking Stones Heath Road
1845							
Jan	11	Do.	6	1s.0d.	6	0	Cleaning Water Courses and Scraping Mendham Road
Febry	15	Vince	1	1/6d	1	6	Barrowing Silt on St Cross Hill
Mar	22	Swann	3¾	1s.0d.	3	9	Throwing Snow out of Church Lane
		Vince	2	1s.6d.	3	0	And the Back Lane
April	5	Swann	5	1s.0d.	5	0	Picking and Leving Back Lane and St Cross Road
May	24	Swann	2½	1s.0d.	2	6	Breaking Stones Spreading Gravil in the Street
		Barber	1½	1s.6d.	2	3	Digging of Well and Altering Water Course Street
	31	Barber	½	1s.6d.	1	0[!]	Laying of Pipes Road leading to Mendham
Dec	24	Swann	5½	10d.	4	7	Barrowing and Breaking Stones Back Road
1846							
Feb	14	Swann	5	10d.	5	0	Skirting the Road leading to the Down Farm
March	14	Swann	4	10d.	3	4	Laying Stones Great Road and Back Lane

The accounts are split into various sections, and some of the entries are reproduced here. Opposite is the first page of the book, which happens to be a typical page of labour costs; it gives the names of some Homersfield parishioners carrying out their statutory labour and divulges what they were paid for doing it (the name 'Wince' is actually 'Vince').

Some of the more interesting entries from the remaining years covered by the book are presented in the table above.

As can be seen, the majority of the work involved filling in holes caused by carts and other vehicles, levelling them once they'd been filled and cleaning out ditches. There was also the seasonal clearing of snow from the roads.

From 1841 onwards, William Swan[n] appears

				£	s	d
1839	March		Cash Church Bill New hammer etc.	-	2	8
	August	1	Paid to Mr Marsh for 35 loads of stones	3	10	0
1841	Novbr	4	Do. H. Beaumont 9 loads of stones	-	18	0
	Febr	27	Do. G. Borrett 1 load of stones 8 bushels	-	2	8
			Do. H. Beaumont 48 Loads of Gravel Carting	3	12	0
1844	Mar	5	By cash paid Mr Moore Cartd 38 Loads Gravel on Road leadg to St Cross	3	16	0
			Do. Mr Marsh Cartd 18 Loads Gravel on Broad road	-	18	-
			Do. Do. for 7 loads Stones and Cartd into Back Lane	-	17	6
			Do. Mr N. Squire for 7 loads Stones and Cartd towards Mendham Bounds	-	17	6
			Do. Horace Beaumont for 4 loads Stones and Cartd near Mill	-	10	-
1845	March		Paid Benjn Clarke for Carting 18 Loads of Gravel in the Broad Road	-	18	-
	May	17	Paid B Clarke for Carting 400 Brick from Redinghall [Redenhall]	-	5	-
1846	March	5	Journey to Bungay to have the Rate signed	-	3	-
			Mr Ashby for a Check Book	-	1	8

almost exclusively in the entries; no doubt he was paid by other parishioners to carrying out their obligations for them.

Stanfords Lane is part of the road from Homersfield to St Cross, immediately past the crossroads where it is crossed by Back Lane.

There are a great many other entries between December 1844 and March 1846, mostly concerning screening gravel, scraping and laying stones in the 'Great Road'; clearly a new road was being made.

The income for maintaining the roads was generally raised in the parish. A highway rate charged each year was occasionally bolstered by a fine imposed upon individuals. The surveyors' book shows a fine of 5s., imposed on 24 March 1840: 'Received of E. Mason for Riding with Team A fine'.

It was against the law to take a steam-powered agricultural vehicle on the roads on Sundays, and Mr Mason and his driving team were obviously caught doing so.

The money spent on repairing roads varied considerably from year to year. As can be seen from the entries above, many loads of gravel were bought (mostly from farmers in the parish) and barrowed by them to the site. The hammer referred to in the first entry was for breaking up large stones collected in buckets from the fields by poorly paid women, children and older men. The stones were sold on to the surveyor for improving the roads.

Turnpikes

The abject failure of many parishes to keep their roads in good order led to widespread complaints from the travelling public, particularly when traffic increased during the sixteenth century. Parishes were not uncommonly taken to court for neglecting to repair their roads.

In 1663 the first turnpike authority came into being, set up by an Act of Parliament to maintain a stretch of the Great North Road. Turnpikes were under the control of local justices, but this changed in 1706, when it became possible to establish separate turnpike trusts, initially for a period of 21 years. To begin with, trusts were slow in forming, but their numbers increased enormously in the eighteenth century. Trustees, commonly wealthy local businessmen with a professional interest in the state of the roads, were authorised to improve or build roads. Trusts were also empowered to erect tollgates and charge road users a toll to pay for maintenance and construction. Sanctioned road improvements included resurfacing and levelling, the rounding of sharp bends and the creation of cuttings on steep hills where horses could rest. Turnpikes tended to operate on the more important roads, whilst the minor ones were left to the parish to look after. Milestones were reintroduced on our roads as a result of the introduction of turnpike trusts.

The first turnpikes were bars made of iron or wood which tapered at one end. These rested on a central pillar, allowing them to pivot and turn. In

An agricultural steam engine at Homersfield Bridge, c.1890.

(REPRODUCED BY KIND PERMISSION OF MRS MARY RACKHAM.)

time these were replaced by gates, often double, with a separate gate for pedestrians, who were exempt from paying tolls – the charges were displayed on a board attached to the toll-house. Most vehicles were charged a toll, but farm vehicles were exempt, as were vehicles going to church, while animals were charged per head. Toll-houses, built immediately adjacent to the road, were often many-sided (commonly hexagonal or octagonal) so that approaching traffic could easily be seen. Tickets issued on payment of the required toll were valid for the whole day. Such roads, although improved and having a much better surface than the country lanes, were not popular with everyone, and drovers, for obvious reasons, avoided them.

The proposed creation of a turnpike road often met with resistance, particularly in the eighteenth century. There were frequent compromises, especially where exemptions and the exact placement of toll-gates were concerned. A common accusation was that the landowners involved had deliberately allowed the road to fall into a bad state in order that a turnpike trust could be created, so burdening road users with the cost of improving them.

Trusts started to wind down once parishes were allowed to group together and form highway boards under an Act passed in 1862; the roads were then handed over either to the new boards or, from 1888, to the newly created county councils. That the railways, in which vast capital sums were invested, also became so popular so quickly, also contributed to their demise, and road traffic declined as a result. The last turnpike took its final toll in 1895.

The first Suffolk trust covered the main road from Ipswich to Scole and was authorised in 1711/12. A turnpike road passed through Homersfield over the bridge on its way from Bungay to Scole.

Modern

The Bungay Bypass
After around 100 or so years of being a quiet, rural railway line, the stretch of disused trackbed between Harleston and Bungay was made into a road, known nationally as the A143 and locally as the Bungay Bypass. It follows the old railway line for almost the whole stretch, taking in the site of Homersfield Station along its route. Begun on 11 October 1982, it was completed 13 months later and officially opened on 9 November 1983.

Bridle-ways and Bridle-Paths
A bridle-way is a highway over which the public can walk, ride, or lead a horse and, in the past (but not necessarily now), has regularly been used for horse-riding. They are often ancient trackways or roads which have now fallen out of use. One such passes through Church Wood, from the road leading to St Cross into Church Lane.

Footpaths
A footpath is defined as a highway over which the public can pass on foot only. Like bridle-ways, they are often ancient trackways or roads which have become defunct. Some of the footpaths in Homersfield constitute part of the intricate group of walks collectively known as the Angles Way, which runs from the Brecklands to the Broads.

Footpaths have varying origins. Many are prehistoric, many link individual farmsteads or settlements or are part of a long-distance route once used by drovers. They commonly converge on bridges, and some were used to mark manor boundaries; others demarcated parish boundaries in Anglo-Saxon times.

Bridges

It is not known how many bridges may have been built over the Waveney on the site of the present Homersfield bridge, but there have been at least three, and no doubt the actual total is more than that. It is also not known when the first was contructed there, although the Romans built one more than 2,000 years ago. People were here long before we came under the control of Rome and may well have built a means of crossing the river without getting wet. We may never know.

Earlier Bridges
The Romans constructed many bridges during their occupation of our country. Those spanning the bigger rivers had stone piers supporting a wooden structure, whereas that in Homersfield, requiring a far less substantial construction, would have been made entirely of wood, with pillars driven into the river-bed.

One of Homersfield's bridges was very different from the Victorian construction we see there now. Remains of it are almost certainly the reddish bricks that can be seen today under its replacement, especially when the river is low, sometimes even sticking out of the water. This bridge, known as Wortwell Bridge, was late medieval in date, its five curved arches supported across the water on brick piers, with two much larger piers at either end on dry land. The top of each side was straight, slanting upwards towards a central apex, and the undersides were likely filled in with brick rubble to economise on building costs. Clearly, as the river is the dividing line between the counties of Norfolk and Suffolk, each half was in a different parish and the bridge had to take the name of one or the other! Its subsequent replacement, once it had seen better days, also changed its name.

Homersfield Bridge
Various dates have been quoted for the construction of this bridge, but it was built in 1870. Having a single curving arch, it is 48ft long with attractive

An early nineteenth-century print of a bridge where the Adair's replacement now stands.

wrought iron spandrels, and is the oldest pre-cast concrete bridge in Britain. Sir Robert Shafto Adair, also Lord Waveney and owner of the Flixton Estate, paid for it to be built and his family coat of arms, incorporating four bloody hands, can be seen on each side above the arch. It was designed by Ipswich architect Mr H.M. Eyton and built by T.&W. Phillips, of the Iron Department, Coal Exchange, London.

Being privately owned, and to prevent public highway rights being enforced upon it, it was closed one day a year from sunrise to sunset, when a member of the Flixton Hall staff would draw a chain across the road and loop it over two hooks, one on each side of the bridge. Invariably, a day was chosen when the river was in flood to prevent those wishing to travel from one county to the other from crossing the Waveney directly, thus avoiding the toll. For many years the price was a penny a wheel, later increased to twopence a wheel. Pedestrians could step over the chain and cross free of charge.

With rises in local rates and an increase in heavy traffic, including lorries and charabancs, which contributed nothing to local amenities, Sir Robert Shafto Adair was unwilling to continue to maintain the bridge and, in around 1921, offered it free of charge to Norfolk and Suffolk County Councils. The county councils apparently viewed the bridge as the responsibility of the district councils, who in turn considered it that of the county councils. The result, of course, was that the maintenance costs remained

Homersfield Bridge. c.1890.

Quite a crowd has gathered to see the Essex otter hounds enjoy a dip, c.1905. (Reproduced by kind permission of Glen Earl.)

with Sir Robert and no doubt this was how it stayed. The Flixton estate was sold in 1948 and from that point, ownership of the bridge became unclear. The bridge itself was not sold, but the land adjacent to it was. Quite possibly it was overlooked in the estate sale and quietly forgotten.

The old B1062 road, which crossed the bridge, was bypassed in 1971, when a new piece of road built included a concrete bridge over the river. The old bridge no longer took wheeled traffic, other than bicycles, and of course, pedestrians.

The bridge is considered an important and outstanding structure, as a result of which it was listed by the Department of the Environment in 1981 as a Grade II* building of special architectural and historic interest. In 1991 the bridge came under the newly extended conservation area of the village.

The question of ownership (or the lack of it) was not important until the bridge had seriously deteriorated; a few sections of the wrought iron had fallen over the side and were lying in the adjacent fields. A temporary wooden fence covered the absent sections for a few years, but it was decided that the authorities should repair it, and pressure was applied on them to do so. A scheme to restore the bridge to its former glory was estimated at £100,000. It was then that the underlying problem of who owned it became important. This unresolved situation dragged on for several years, and progress was made only when two people offered to accept ownership so that the relevant county councils could compulsorily purchase the bridge – which was bought for £1 in 1992. There was also the problem of an ugly bright yellow mains gas pipe which had been attached to the side of the

bridge during the period of unknown ownership. Two trusts opted to share responsibility for undertaking the repairs, funded by grants, if possible, although one had to subsequently withdraw. Extensive repairs were carried out, aided by grants from English Heritage and several councils. The work took four months and was completed in November 1995.

On 11 January 1996, an opening ceremony was held at 11.30a.m., when the chairmen of the seven councils involved in the restoration (Homersfield, Alburgh and Wortwell Parish Councils, Waveney and South Norfolk District Councils, Suffolk and Norfolk County Councils) cut a ribbon, and a horse-drawn carriage crossed the bridge at midday. Among those inside it were Lady Darell, one of the last of the Adair family, her husband, Sir Jeffrey, and the High Sheriff of Norfolk. A long list of invited guests, including representatives of English Heritage, the seven councils, Norfolk Historic Buildings Trust, MPs, British Gas, the Upper Waveney Valley Project and engineering companies, among others, then enjoyed a celebratory lunch at the Black Swan.

MESSING ABOUT ON THE RIVER

Navigation

In the seventeenth century, transporting goods via the highways was expensive compared to the cost of carrying them on the river, and so the Waveney was widely used for the purpose. Larger waterborne vessels need a correspondingly wider and deeper watercourse on which to travel, with locks to regulate

A carriage drives over the newly restored Homersfield Bridge at noon as part of the opening ceremony on 11 January 1996. Among those inside were Sir Jeffrey and Lady Darell. (© Eastern Daily Press.)

the flow of water. A few Acts of Parliament were passed with a view to improving the state of the river and to extend the limits of its navigation. The first of these, passed on 17 March 1670, authorised the widening and deepening of the Waveney inland as far as Bungay. The resulting increase in trade from wherries bringing various commodities (grain, malt, flour, timber and coal, amongst others) to the market towns along the river turned some merchants, and the owner of the navigation rights, into very wealthy people. Not only that, but surrounding villages, including Homersfield, also benefited directly from the increased trade in essential commodities.

It is possible that in much more distant times than have thus far been mentioned, vessels travelled further along the river, past Homersfield and at least as far as Harleston. If so, a great many years of silting-up and continuous lack of maintenance must eventually have significantly reduced the distance to which these goods were transportable. In the years immediately before the above-mentioned first Act, navigation was possible only as far as Beccles. In the seventeenth century, when trade was flourishing, a proposed scheme to extend navigation beyond Bungay did not come to fruition. Another Act, passed in the twenty-second year of the reign of King Charles II (1681), for making navigable parts of the River Waveney, installed commissioners for dealing with any problems that might arise in making it navigable, for maintaining the navigation once it was in place, for determining the rates to be levied for the carriage of goods, and for establishing the damage done to the river banks by vessels.

In 1749 an Act passed concerning the repair and maintenance of the Great Yarmouth Piers and Haven gave authorisation also for improving the rivers that flowed into Yarmouth by deepening them, thus making them further navigable. At this time the Commission of Sewers was responsible for the rivers, but those who lived locally considered the Commission expensive and thought it could be done more economically by a local business.

A small bundle of draft documents written in typical eighteenth-century hands survive to give an insight into one such proposed deepening of the river, which involved Homersfield directly.

Among the documents is a small map (if it can be called such), with names (interspersed with recognisable land references) against the line of a river – presumably the names of those who owned land immediately next to the Waveney. Among these two dozen names is that of William Adair of Flixton Hall. It appears he was instrumental in attempting to organise the necessary work, as two roughly written letters serve to outline the beginnings of a slow, protracted progression.

The first letter is from William Windham, a London solicitor who appears to be acting on behalf of William Adair, and was to be sent to Mr Van Kamp, a solicitor in Bungay:

St James Aug 7 1756

Sir,
When you was in London, I believe you found by the Conversation we then had about clearing the river, That we were determined to do some thing, but as a variety

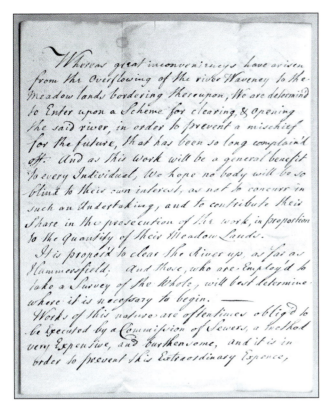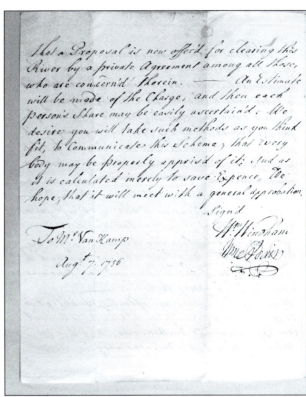

A letter concerning the deepening of the Waveney, dated 1756 and including the signature of William Adair.
(Reproduced by kind permission of Norfolk Record Office, ref.: MEA 8/2.)

of methods had been proposed, we were under some difficulty of coming to a Resolution. The more I hear of a Commission of Sewers, the more I am discouraged from entering upon that Plan, always altered with great Expenses and Delays. However if no thing else will do, we must have recourse to that. In the meantime, if People are properly appris'd of what is intended to be done, I shou'd think they wou'd concur in a Scheme that is calculated to save Expense in a Work, which they must allow is necessary to be done. Inclos'd is a letter to you sign'd by Mr Adair and me which you will make a proper use off, as you find opportunity. I am S[i]r Your most ob[e]d[ien]t Servant Wm Windham.

If this Scheme should be approved off, and that you find People are willing to contribute their Share in the Expense, a proper Instrument may then be drawn up for every body to sign. And as to the Work, I fancy we may find Stead and Hands amongst our own people capable of Undertaking and Executing it.

Next market day, you will have an opportunity of sounding People on this Project.

This letter clearly shows that financial support was needed from the relevant landowners so as to avoid the expense incurred in the Commission of Sewers carrying out the work. The second letter, referred to above and having the same date, shows the intention was to cleanse the river as far as Homersfield:

Whereas great inconveniencys have arisen from the overflowing of the river Waveney to the Meadow lands

bordering thereupon, We are determin'd to Enter upon a Scheme for clearing and opening the same river, in order to prevent a mischief for the future, that has so long been complain'd off. And as this work will be a general benefit to every Individual, We hope no body will be so blind to their own interest, as not to concur in such an Undertaking, and to contribute their Share in the prosecution of the work, in proportion to the Quantity of their Meadow lands.

It is proposed to clean the River up, as far as Hummersfield. And those, who are Employ'd to take a Survey of the whole, will best determine where it is necessary to begin.

Works of this nature are oftentimes oblig'd to be Execut'd by a Commission of Sewers, a method very Expensive, and burthensome, and it is in order to prevent this Extraordinary Expense, that a Proposal is now offer'd for cleaning this River by a private Agreement using all those, who are concern'd therein. An Estimate will be made of the Charge, and then each Person's Share may be easily ascertained. We desire you will take such methods as you think fit, to Communicate this Scheme, that Every body may be properly apprais'd of it; and as it is calculated merely to same Expense. We hope that it will meet with a general approbation.

Sign'd
Wm. Windham
Wm. Adair

To Mr Van Kamp
August 7 1756

Later, a draft 'Articles of Agreement' showed it was being proposed that the dykes and drains flowing into the river between Homersfield and Ditchingham were also to be cleaned. This agreement was originally dated 10 July 1756, but the year was subsequently changed to 1760; obviously the much needed financial supporters were dragging their heels:

Owners of Lands bordering upon or lying contiguous to the River Waveney between the several mills called Homersfield Mill and Ditchingham Mill...

Whereas the meadow lands bordering on or lying contiguous to the River Waveney between Homersfield Mill and Ditchingham Mill in the counties of Suffolk and Norfolk belonging chiefly to the parties who have executed these Presents have lately suffered great Damage by the frequent Overflowinge of the River and the Dykes and Drains emptying themselves therein for want of their having been depthened and cleansed for some time past and the s[ai]d Lands are in great Danger of being spoiled thereby unless some methods be taken to secure and prevent the same. And whereas the owners of these lands who have executed these presents being fully satisfied the s[ai]d Lands cannot be secured from the Damage or Loss frequently happening thereto otherwise than by the depthning and cleansing the s[ai]d River and of Dykes and Drains af[oresai]d. w[hi]ch cannot be done without a considerable expence that ought to be rais'd on the s[ai]d Lands ratably and in Proportion to the Quantity of Acres and Right of each respective Owner and the Damages or Loss he she or they shall or may be likely to sustain for want of the Doing thereof have caused a scheme and Estimate to be made thereof by skilful p'sons employ'd for that Purpose and hereunto annexed whereby it appears that it will cost at least the Sum of £340.18s.7³/₄d. to depthen and cleanse the said River Dykes and Drains in a proper manner so as to secure these Lands from the Damage and Loss frequently happening thereto for want of depthening and cleansing the same as aforesaid and for the Charge of surveying and overseeing the s[ai]d work.

No doubt many of those whose land adjoined the Waveney were reluctant to pay their share towards the proposed improvements to the river, despite the potential increase in trade it could bring; £340 (which would probably have been significantly more once it had been done) was a lot of money to contribute.

A year after this re-dated article had been drafted, another letter was prepared, dated 21 April 1761, to be sent from a Mr Black (possibly an employee in the same practice as Mr Windham) to Mr Van Kamp:

Flixton, April 21th 1761
Mr Le Grys sign'd without any trouble and I believe Mr Parry will also – only he declined until Thursday to consider of it when he comes to Bungay – and find that he is Mr Mathew's son in law therefore if your speaking to Mr Mathews would be of any service – I will call on Thursday.
I am S[i]r Y[ou]r H[umble] Serv[an]t.
Black

[Note 21th – dates in these times were expressed as the '1st and 20th', hence 21th rather than 21st, as now.]

It appears from this that money for the scheme was indeed slow in coming. Unless a document has been preserved confirming that the works were carried out, it is almost impossible to know whether the necessary money was raised, but it would seem that the slow progress in raising the funds had a direct bearing on the lack of direct evidence to show that the people of Homersfield saw a 'depthning' or 'cleansing' of their river in the eighteenth century.

Another scheme to extend the river navigation came about in the early years of the nineteenth century, during a further period of profitable and flourishing trade, when wherries operated by several businesses navigated the river on a regular basis. Great Yarmouth was the venue for a meeting held early in 1818 to discuss a proposal that, if successfully carried out, would result in vessels travelling further up the river, through Homersfield and on to Diss. Clearly, this proposal would have had a significant effect on the village. It involved deepening the riverbed, generally straightening it in the process, and creating a new channel, eliminating the need to negotiate the natural loop in the river around Bungay. Locals in and around Bungay were distinctly against this proposed plan, and a fight ensued; after much deliberation and campaigning, Bungay won the contest, and yet another plan came to nothing and was subsequently forgotten.

The use of the river to transport saleable goods declined rapidly once steam engines began to run from Tivetshall to Beccles in the 1860s; its demise as a means of transport was assured beyond doubt soon after motorised trucks came into being and roads were much improved by the application of tarmac in the early twentieth century. Navigation of the Waveney, so much a part of so many peoples' lives over the years, ceased altogether in 1933, having wound down to an almost complete halt; so ended a few centuries of river-borne trade from Great Yarmouth to Bungay.

CHAPTER 11

A Victorian Perambulation

The Parish Boundary

The annual custom of walking the parish boundary traditionally took place on Rogation Sunday, the fifth Sunday after Easter Sunday. Perambulation ceased during the twentieth century but 'beating the bounds' will be necessary again in order to leave no doubts about the precise boundaries. As far as the author has been able to determine, the Homersfield parish boundary has been unchanged for 1,000 or more years.

At Homersfield Bridge, the boundary is the Waveney, passing Limbourne (or Wortwell) Mill and turning eastwards along the Beck. At an old ford it takes the road leading to Middleton Hall, passes it and then turns north-east along a field boundary. It then turns north, intersecting a field, follows another field boundary and then crosses another field to rejoin the Beck. The boundary then travels northwards along a footpath, arriving at the road from Homersfield to St Cross. It then heads north-east towards Flixton, along a field boundary, through the middle of two fields and along two more field boundaries before following the field north-west. It turns westwards and passes between Home Farm and Flixton Hall, crosses the Homersfield to Flixton road, then runs through Long Plantation, where it rejoins the Waveney, forming the final part of the

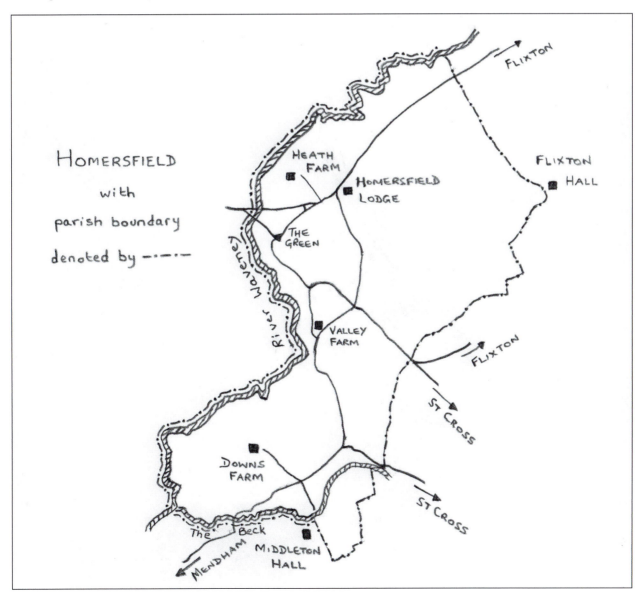

boundary to Homersfield Bridge. The boundary deviations through fields almost certainly represent evidence of much earlier field boundaries.

A TOTTER AROUND THE VILLAGE

The house numbers used in Homersfield addresses today originate in the numbering used by the Adair family to identify all their properties. By the time Homersfield had been reached with this numbering system, 60 properties had been numbered elsewhere; Homersfield numbers originally stopped at 91. This system came into being in the latter half of the nineteenth century, probably by 1880 (an estate survey of 1883 shows it to be in use), although it wasn't used by the enumerator when compiling census returns either before or just after the turn of the century. From the very beginning, these returns show only the most basic addresses (typically 'Homersfield Street') or none at all. The census commenced in 1811 and has been conducted every ten years since, although it wasn't until 1841 that individual households were included (previously they were concerned only with population, the number of males and females etc.), and as the law stipulates that the data must be at least 100 years old for the public to have access, currently the latest return that can be viewed is that from 1901. The effect of this is that it makes the task of individual house identification similar to that of attempting to complete a huge jigsaw puzzle, comparing the various ten-yearly returns in an attempt to identify patterns, where the overall number of pieces is known but some may be missing from one return (where houses have been demolished) and others added (new houses built) in another return, both of which serve to interrupt any determined patterns. A great many hours of research and patience are needed to reliably identify households and their occupiers.

The Adair family did not inherit all their property when the first of the family came to Flixton Hall, but gradually acquired farms, mills, public houses, cottages and land over a great many years. It has often been said that the Adairs owned every inch of Homersfield, and it will be seen from the details included here that they did indeed own most of it – but not all. Modern names for numbered estate properties are given under each dwelling for convenience of identification.

Many walks start from a church and end at a pub. So will this one.

The Church

Homersfield Church, dedicated to St Mary, is small in comparison to many other local churches, and is the oldest building in the village. That it is not the first church to stand on the site is indicated by a Norman lancet (slim and pointed) window in the south wall,

dating from the twelfth or late-eleventh century and retained from the previous structure, but it is almost certainly not the second church to stand there, either. It is very probable that, in Saxon times, after Christianity had come to Britain, there was a wooden church here which would have been built from the end of the seventh century onwards.

The Outside

The present church comprises a tower, nave, chancel and porch and represents work from a mixture of dates, the majority of it from the thirteenth century. At the west end, the square tower has lancet windows of the thirteenth century (the west-facing one having been replaced), above which is a line of projecting masonry known as a string course. Towards the top are bell openings containing tracery in the form of the letter 'Y', dating from around 1300. Another string course is present between the openings and the crenellated top. Churchwardens' accounts show that money was frequently paid to have ivy removed from the tower walls.

Next to the tower is the nave, which, until the Reformation in the sixteenth-century, was traditionally the domain and responsibility of the congregation. The nave windows are large and date from the thirteenth century.

In pre-Reformation times the chancel, at the east end of the church, was the domain and responsibility of the clergy. Its windows appear to be a little later than those of the nave. There is a south-facing door in the chancel, the priest's own entrance door, the stonework around which has been partly restored but nevertheless dates from the thirteenth century. The end wall, the gable, has a decorated fourteenth-century cross on top.

The porch is very probably not original to the present church building, but was likely added during the fifteenth century, from which time the now blocked-up windows date. The porch has been extensively restored and re-roofed, and the inner doorway has also seen some restoration. The outer doors were presented in 1971 by Miss Annie Welton, formerly of Plumtree Cottage. In earlier times the porch was a much-used part of the church and not merely a covered entrance to a House of God. Baptism services commenced there, part of the wedding service was conducted there and some of the words from the burial service were spoken there. It was also a stopping-place in regular parochial processions, and was traditionally the place where bread and other commodities were dispensed to the poor and where tithes, debts and other monetary payments were made.

The Inside

Stepping through the porch and into the nave, a relatively plain interior is viewed, it having been over-restored in the middle of the nineteenth century.

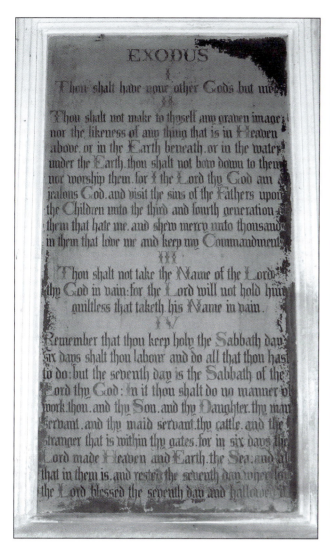
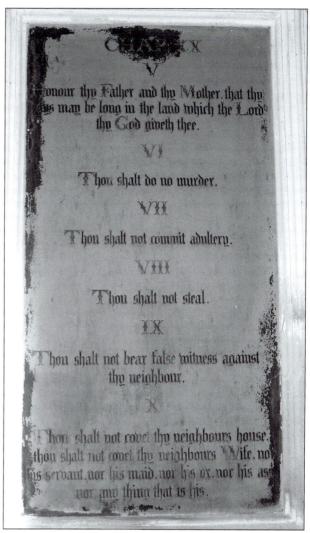

The decalogue panels in Homersfield Church. These are Victorian, but such panels started to appear in the reign of Elizabeth I, when it was ordered that churches rid themseles of decorations and adornments thought of as 'popish'.

At one time there were, no doubt, wall paintings, now probably lost forever. The floor is of pamments, common in East Anglia, with pine benches for the congregation.

A most unusual feature in the south wall is a double piscina (stone basin) with a central column and double moulded arches, originally from the thirteenth century but, with the exception of its shaft bases, the stonework has been completely replaced; no doubt it is identical to the original.

On a small diamond-shaped pane in the west window near the top of the tower are inscribed the words: 'This is to certify James Chappel glazed all of this church, May 1846, by order of Sir Robert Shafto Adair, Flixton Hall.'

The Victorian font is in a Norman style and its cover was presented in 1903 by the people of the village on King Edward VII's coronation; a brass font ewer was presented the following year.

In the chancel there would once have been a rood screen with a door and a large crucifix above, dividing it from the nave.

The Contents

On a wall is a large Nativity painting, probably Victorian, given in memory of Revd William Joseph Wilby, rector from 1904 to 1927.

Displayed on either side of the east gable window are stone (decalogue) panels dating from the nineteenth century and containing the Ten Commandments.

A small brass plate on the lectern holding the Bible gives the names of three Homersfield men who lost their lives in the First World War.

The first organ became worn out and was replaced in 1893; it needed tuning and repair the following year!

The chancel contains a ledger stone in memory of Revd Thomas Le Grys, rector of Homersfield and St Cross, who died on 10 June 1722 aged 58 years, and to his wife, Sarah, who had died more than ten years earlier, on 14 January 1712. Thomas had married Sarah Richards at St Margaret on 26 May 1696, and they subsequently lived and had children in St Cross.

The tulip-shaped chalice, part of the Homersfield Church silver.

The silver paten, or plate, dated on the underside 1567.

The Accoutrements

There are a few items of church silver. In the early 1800s there was a pewter flagon, replaced by one of silver in early Victorian times. Two other items are much older. A tulip-shaped chalice, engraved with the name HUMERSFYLDE, is thought to date from the reign of Edward VI (1547–53). An Elizabethan paten (plate) bears no wording but is dated 1567. It is a somewhat sad fact of modern times that in the interests of security, the silver is no longer kept in the church; nor for that matter, is anything else of value.

The Bells

One of the bells, cast by William and John Brend in the early part of the seventeenth century, bears the monogram 'W&A.B.', the 'A' referring to William's wife, Alice. The use of such trios of initials was standard practice during this period. The other two bells were cast by Braysyerl of Norwich in the fifteenth or sixteenth century, and both bear Latin inscriptions. On the second bell are the words '*Fac Margareta Nobis Dec Munera Leta*', which may be translated as 'Make Margaret, these offices joyful to us', and on the third bell '*Hac In Conclave Gabriel Nunc Pange Suave*', which means, 'In this chamber, Gabriel now sounds sweetly'. These three bells weigh about four, five and six hundred pounds respectively.

Having concluded our visit to Homersfield Church, we move on to the outlying farms, houses and cottages.

Hall Farm

This farm appears to have had a number of other names over the years. Prior to the 1840s it seems to have been known as Gooch's Farm, probably named after Bezaleel Gooch and his family. It was then known as Felmingham Farm, again, probably after the owner or occupier. The Fisher family lived here in the early 1840s.

A decade later, known as The Grove, it was occupied by Philip and Mary Pain, their four daughters and a servant. They were a much-travelled family.

A silver flagon, dating from the Victorian period.

Two very elegant ladies and a dapper young gentleman survey the damage at Homersfield Station after the storm of 26 August 1912.

The farm's name changed to Hall Farm during the 1850s and a few years later a Scottish family, James and Catherine Mitchell, their son, daughter and grandson were living there.

When James and Eliza Howlett and their two sons lived here in the 1870s it was known as Grove Farm.

In 1881, when the name had reverted to Hall Farm, James Vince was living here with his wife Pamala and their daughters, Maryann and Annie. He died in 1888 and was succeeded by John Danby, son of Daniel and Kezia Danby, who lived there with his wife, Emma, and six children. By 1901 they had moved and the farmhouse was temporarily empty.

Downs Farm

This building, dating from the sixteenth century and later, by 1810 had become part of the Flixton estate. William and Mary Squire were the first tenants. Their son, Nathan, born in 1803, was one of several children born in Homersfield and was the farmer in residence from 1835, together with his elderly mother and two servants.

A little more than ten years later Henry Websdale and his wife Theodosia were living here with three servants, one of whom was their niece.

In 1855 local man George Chambers came to the farm with his wife Sheba and their family. George and Sheba stayed until George's death in a Norwich hospital in 1894, aged 79. His daughter, Georgianna,

and son-in-law, Benjamin Smith, then came to live with George's wife, who died 11 years later, aged 91. Both were laid to rest in Homersfield churchyard.

Hole House/Valley Farm

Hole House Farm was quite a small building comprising six rooms, with many outbuildings, several of them thatched. It was integrated into the Flixton estate by 1803, having been bought from John Doggett. In 1839 it became the home of Horace and Sarah Beaumont, their three young sons and a servant, 13-year-old Anne Soanes.

Benjamin Clarke and his wife Mary Ann, their son Benjamin and a servant were living here two years later. The Clarke family lived here for more than 20 years before Benjamin and Mary Ann decided to move on, leaving their son to carry on farming. By 1881, son Benjamin had a wife, Kate, and two young daughters. Kate died young, aged only 32, in September 1885, which was possibly why Benjamin moved away.

Charles Pearce, his wife Emma and their son then came to work the farm, which by 1891 was called Valley Farm.

Within ten years the farm was in the hands of Page Hudson who, with his wife Anne and five children, previously lived at Middleton Hall Cottages.

The farmhouse, sold as part of the Flixton Hall estate in 1948, has since been incorporated within a modern building on the site.

Heath Farm

The earliest part of this farmhouse dates from the sixteenth century and has later additions. It was added to the Flixton estate in around 1779. An early tenant, from 1829 to 1838, was Job Sadd, succeeded by Edward Brunning Marsh, who married Esther Sadd in Homersfield in 1836.

In 1848 Daniel and Kezia Danby took over the farm, together with their three children and two servants. They farmed here for more than two decades until the early 1870s, after which date it was farmed by Edward and Mary Ann Brock, who arrived with three sons, two daughters, a sister, a mother-in-law and a servant. They handed over the farm some years later to Thomas Poppy.

Thomas was born in 1825 at Metfield, one of several children of Edward and Elizabeth Poppy. He decided to become a carpenter and in 1841 was lodging in Diss, as an apprentice, with an upholsterer and his family. However, he subsequently decided carpentry was not for him and by the early 1850s was back with his parents at the Huntsman and Hounds public house in Metfield, where his father also worked a small farm. In 1854 he married Emma Hatten in Metfield Church.

Emma had several children in Metfield. She and her husband took up farming in Weybread, where Emma gave birth to several more children, bringing

George Bryant Poppy, fifth son and seventh child of Thomas and Emma Poppy, born 1862 in Weybread, Norfolk. (Reproduced by kind permission of Ms Diane Poppy.)

Thomas Poppy with all his family at Heath Farm, c.1896. Left to right, back row: *George Bryant Poppy, George's wife Elizabeth, Ernest Frederick Poppy, Mary E. Poppy, Mary's husband William Hatten Poppy;* front row: *Emma Sarah Poppy, Elizabeth Poppy, Thomas Poppy, Emily Poppy, Amelia Poppy. In front of Thomas Poppy is his grandson, George, son of George Bryant and Elizabeth Poppy.* (Reproduced by kind permission of Ms Diane Poppy.)

William Hatten Poppy, c.1895.
(Reproduced by kind permission of Mrs Hilda Rowe.)

Top and above: *Heath Farm in 2007.*

The wedding of Robert Johnson and Emma Sarah Poppy towards the end of 1901, taken at Heath Farm.
(Reproduced by kind permission of Mrs Hilda Rowe.)

The sitting-room at Heath Farm, 2007.

A seventeenth-century game larder at Heath Farm, 2007.

Amelia and Emma Sarah Poppy photographed in a Norwich studio, c.1900.
(Reproduced by kind permission of Mrs Hilda Rowe.)

Heath Farm, c.1895.
(Reproduced by kind permission of Mrs Hilda Rowe.)

the total to 14. In 1878 Thomas and Emma came to Heath Farm, bringing with them most of their family: three sons, six daughters, Thomas' sister and niece were all living in the farmhouse in 1881. Emma passed away in 1885, aged just 49 years – no doubt bearing so many children took its toll on her health. Nevertheless, the family were still there 20 years later. None of Thomas and Emma's children was born in Homersfield, but one did marry there. In 1901 Emma Sarah married a farmer, Robert Johnson of St Cross, and Thomas gave them a cow for their wedding – a generous gift. Several of Thomas and Emma's children died very young, two at least (both in their teens) from tuberculosis, no doubt contracted from their own cattle. Rosalys Skene, who lived much of her life in Homersfield always said that 'they were just like poppies, they grew up, flowered and died', a reference to a few short-lived members of the family.

Thomas, very active in village life, was involved with Homersfield Church and acted as an overseer of the poor for some years, in addition to being one of the managers of the school in St Cross. He passed away in 1902 aged 77 years, and was much mourned. An entry in the St Cross School managers' meetings minute-book for 14 October 1902 sums up local feelings: 'Deep regret was expressed at the death of Mr Poppy who had been a respected and conscientious Manager of the School for fifteen years past.'

Thomas, his wife and six of their children are buried together in Homersfield churchyard, each with their own headstone.

Park Lodge

Two lodges, one in Homersfield, the other in Flixton, built when the Adair family decided to divert the road away from their home in 1869, stand at each end of the resulting unused highway. Homersfield Lodge was built in the early 1870s and the lodge-keeper's duties included letting the Adair family and their guests in and out of the hall grounds via a gate. Its first occupier seems to have been Robert Sampson, who previously lived in one half of No. 77. His sister, Eliza Jeffries, went to join him after No. 71 Homersfield was pulled down, probably in the 1870s.

By the early 1890s William Rouse and his wife Jane had moved here, with their daughter Elinor, from Flixton. William had joined the Royal Artillery whilst still a boy and, posted to Gibraltar, had met and married Jane Wink. Their children, Thomas and Mary, were born in Gibraltar, and when William was posted back to England another child, Sarah, was born in Woolwich. Aged about 38, Sergeant Rouse was discharged and joined the Suffolk Artillery in Ipswich. He became a Chelsea Pensioner upon his retirement in 1879 and came to Homersfield Lodge via his ex-commander, Sir Robert Alexander Shafto Adair. He passed away in 1902, probably at the Dove Inn, Wortwell, then being run by his son, Henry. His wife lived a further ten years.

Edward Jeffries, born in Homersfield in 1830, took up residence in his mother's old home after the Rouse family moved. His wife, Pamila, took on the responsibility of gatekeeper, while her husband continued in his trade as a carpenter.

Nos 61 & 62 (The Dell)

At some point prior to the 1870s it seems that these two cottages were one, lived in by Jonathan Vince, his wife Mary and seven children in the 1840s. All the children but one had flown the nest by 1851, while James, who later lived at Hall Farm, remained, but there were three grandchildren now living in the house. Within ten years Jonathan and Mary had the house to themselves.

From 1871 the two cottages underwent a few changes of name. Known as Grove Road in the early 1870s, they were known as Gas House Yard ten years later, when a gasometer was erected close by. By the 1890s, and certainly until the turn of the century, they were known as Sand Pit Cottages.

Now one dwelling, The Dell is famous for having been the home of poet Elizabeth Smart, who lived here from 1966 until her death 20 years later.

No. 61

In 1871, John Howell, a blacksmith, and his wife Eliza, lived here with an aunt and their son, Charly. Aunt Mary died in 1880, by which time there were three children in the house, two of them still at home

ten years later. The family moved away in the 1890s.

Probably in 1896, a shepherd, James Snowden, his wife Alice and six children moved into the cottage. They had previously lived at Stoke-by-Nayland, in Essex, and at Needham Market.

No. 62

In 1871, John Gowing, a gas maker by trade, his wife, two children and a granddaughter were living here, having previously lived in Yarmouth. Within ten years John had retired and all the children had gone. It seems the Gowings moved away not long after, as the cottage was empty in 1883.

By the early 1890s, a shepherd, William Riches, and his wife Esther had come to live in the cottage. A niece lived with them at this time.

In the latter part of the 1890s gardener Harry Gibbs, his wife Nellie and three children lived here.

No. 63 (Sunset Cottage)

This house was built during the 1850s. Around the end of the decade, George Howlett, an under-game-keeper, his wife Anne and their two sons moved here from Flixton. In the next ten years, Anne gave birth to seven more children; all nine children were living in this house, now called Wood Cottage, in 1871. They moved from the village some time afterwards and it was empty come 1881. It was also known as 'Sundown' and within two years Alfred Hunter and his wife Annie arrived. They had five children in the cottage and were still there at the turn of the century with two of their younger offspring.

Sunset House

Standing next to No. 63, this house was built in 1900 by William Cason, the Flixton Hall estate carpenter, who then moved into it with his wife Harriet and three children, born in Weybread and Norwich.

Wood 'n' Wheels and Cowslip Cottage

These two cottages (a single building) on Mendham Lane were built in 1874 as Middleton Hall Cottages. Census returns do not afford us the luxury of being able to distinguish between them, so the families detailed here could have lived in either of the two.

By the early 1880s Edward Hern, his wife and five children were living in one cottage, and Samuel Dunn, a widower, was living in the other. There had been at least one family living here before them.

Around 1883, William Flatt came from Mendham to live here with his wife Harriet and four children, one of whom died shortly afterwards They had had eight more children here by the end of 1892, one of whom died that same year.

In the other cottage Page Hudson, his wife Ann Maria and son moved in around 1890. They had five

A pretty Victorian resident of Homersfield, name unknown, c.1880.

more children up until 1900 and then moved elsewhere.

Robert and Elizabeth Elvin, a middle-aged couple, moved into the Hudson family's old home. Alfred Hall, his wife Alice and three children had moved into the other cottage by 1901.

Limbourne Mill

Fortunately, this lovely old mill is still standing and is said to date from the eighteenth century, although, as with Homersfield, there was a mill here in the time of Domesday. In older documents it is commonly called Limber Mill, and is also known as Wortwell Mill.

By the 1840s Henry Barber, his wife Elizabeth and six children were living here; Henry is described as an agricultural labourer.

In 1850 Henry Diggens, a journeyman miller (one paid by the day) was in residence, together with his wife Eliza and three children. They had a fourth child in Homersfield. During the 1850s it seems the adjoining dwelling was built, and subsequent census returns show two entries, which do not distinguish between the mill itself and the cottage.

In the early 1860s Robert Asten, a retired miller, lived here, as did James Vincent, a journeyman miller, his wife Eliza and three lodgers. Ten years later James had risen to be the foreman and the lodgers had gone.

Also here in 1871 were William Fisher, journeyman miller, his wife Mary Ann and their young son, born in Homersfield the previous year. They were still here ten years later, now with a second son; there was nobody living in the other dwelling.

By 1891 one dwelling was again empty and William Frost, listed as a labouring gardener, his wife Isabella and teenage son were living here.

Just after the turn of the century, James Smith, his wife Elisa, four adult children and a grandson were in residence.

Having visited all the peripheral buildings, the walk will continue into the village centre. The 1860s and 1870s were times of great change in Homersfield. During these decades, some 30 households disappeared from the village, representing a decrease of slightly more than half of the housing, while only a handful of new properties were built. These changes took place almost entirely around the village green.

Nos 1 & 2 Swan Cottages

The chimney stack of No. 2 Swan Cottages bears the date 1900, with the initials of Sir Hugh Alexander Adair beneath. This date denotes when building commenced, and the cottages were still being built during the census in March of the following year.

Nos 84–90

These cottages, probably among the older buildings in the village, were all bought by the Flixton estate and stood where there is now a playing-field. Among those living here in the 1830s were Elizabeth Burwood, John Garrod and Edward Cooper; one cottage was possibly a bakery, run by Lancelot Sadd. At the left-hand end of the playing-field Nos 84–87 stood joined together in more or less a reverse 'L' shape, the foot of the 'L' facing towards the Black Swan and the rest facing the green. The first to be demolished was No. 88, in 1871, followed in 1873 by Nos 84, 85 and 86. The demise of No. 87 appears to be unrecorded but it was there in 1871 and was probably pulled down in 1877 or 1878. The semi-detached Nos 89 and 90 survived into the twentieth century, but by the end of the 1940s were derelict and suffered the same fate as their near neighbours.

Although the exact tenants of these cottages have been difficult to identify, as they were often quoted in a seemingly random order in census returns, a reasonable amount of detail can be recorded.

No. 84

John Garrod, a carter, and his wife Mary came to live in this cottage in the early 1830s and, it seems, lived here until John's death in 1874, aged 90 years, after which Mary moved to Alburgh before joining her husband in Homersfield churchyard only nine months later.

No. 85

By the mid-1840s bricklayer Robert Todd, his wife Maria, three daughters and a son were living here.

Several years later Robert Sam[p]son (another bricklayer), his wife Ellen and three children were living in this cottage. They subsequently moved to another cottage in Homersfield.

At the end of the 1860s labourer George Read, his wife Sarah and their teenage daughter moved into the cottage.

No. 86

James and Mary Plumb had lived in Homersfield since the first decade of the nineteenth century. Together with their son and daughter they lived in No. 86 from at least the 1840s and very possibly before then. Mary died in 1856, after which it seems James moved elsewhere.

Henry and Phoebe Page then came to live here with their five children, and had two more in Homersfield. Henry drove agricultural machines for a living. They were here in the 1870s, and may have been the last family to live in the cottage.

No. 87

Samuel Howell appears to have lived here from at least the early 1840s for 30 years or more, after which the cottage was probably demolished. He married Mary Smith in 1831 and they had two children, a son and a daughter. Mary Ann died in 1835, aged three years, and her mother died three years later. In 1841 Samuel was living here with his mother and his son, George. He married Thirza Easter later the same year and together they had two sons and a daughter. Thirza died in 1877, followed, only six days later, by her husband.

No. 88

In 1841 John and Rachel Walker were living in this cottage with their son Job and grandson Job Howard. Ten years later their grandson was still with them, while their son was living in another cottage in Homersfield with his wife and two children. Job Howard continued to live in the cottage following the death of his grandparents (John in 1854 and Rachel in 1860) and was living there in 1861 with a wife and two young children. The family subsequently moved to another cottage in the village.

Shortly before it was pulled down, brickmaker Robert Isom, his wife and five children were living here. They moved from Wortwell and had previously lived in Alburgh and Essex.

No. 89

James Barber, a thatcher, his wife Matilda and their seven children were living here in the early 1840s and stayed for 30 years or more.

By 1881, Henry and Phoebe Page, who used to live at No. 86, were in residence with their son

Abraham. Other sons, Frederick and James, lived with their parents from time to time and the Page family were still living in the cottage in 1901.

No. 90

The names of the inhabitants of this cottage in the early years of Victoria's reign are uncertain, but by the early 1850s William Barber (no relation to James, living in the other half of the house), his wife Phoebe and family of three children were living here but had moved away by the end of the decade.

Charles Goodwin, who had lived in Homersfield two decades or more earlier, was living in this cottage in the early 1860s with his wife and daughter, both named Mary Ann, the latter a silk weaver. Mary passed away in 1866, and it seems that Charles moved over the road to another cottage a short distance away

In the early 1870s Samuel Calver, a woodman, his wife Charlotte and three children lived here.

James Butcher, his wife Susanna and children moved into the cottage towards the end of the 1870s and were to stay for more than 30 years.

No. 91 (Heath Cottage)

In the early 1840s, shoemaker Thomas Smith, his wife Sarah, and son Silvanus were living here, along with three others. Sarah died in 1846 and Silvanus married a few months later. His new wife came to live in the cottage and they had a daughter here, Mary Anne, born in 1848. In the following years Silvanus graduated from being a farm labourer to become a gardener. When Thomas passed away around Christmas 1862, aged 94 years, the family carried on living in the house for the rest of their lives. Silvanus died in 1893 and was buried next to his parents in Homersfield churchyard. His wife outlived him by nine days.

Arthur Gowing, son of Samuel, the village thatcher, then came to live here with his wife, Helen.

Having reached the end of the properties along this side of the road, we now turn around and walk back towards the green on the other side of the road, where we soon arrive at a small cottage.

Nos 71–73

These three dwellings were contained within two buildings that stood next to each other adjacent to the road. Very probably, No. 71 stood alone, while the second building contained the other two dwellings. The names of the families living in these properties are generally unclear from census returns prior to 1871.

Within ten years of this date all three residences had gone, probably pulled down around the same time as other properties in Homersfield during the late 1870s.

No. 71

In the late 1830s, a carpenter, Edward Cooper, probably lived here with his wife Elizabeth, a midwife. He died in 1841, and she lived here until her death in 1860. By 1871 Eliza Jeffries, who subsequently went to live in The Lodge after the cottage was pulled down, was living here alone.

No. 72

This cottage, together with its probable adjoining half, stood on the left-hand corner of Church Lane, and in the early 1870s, Charles Goodwin was living here alone. He subsequently lived in Wortwell, where he passed away in 1882, aged 82 years.

No. 73

The inhabitants of this cottage have yet to be identified, as it was empty when the census took place in 1871 and survived no more than a few years after.

In the early 1840s a tailor, Thomas Smith, his wife Hannah and five children were living at either No. 72 or No. 73. Thomas was one of the sons of his like-named father, who lived at No. 91.

We now walk a little way up Church Lane to where an old thatched cottage still stands, on the right-hand side of the road.

Nos 64–65 (Thatched Cottage)

Perhaps a little difficult to believe nowadays, but this little thatched house was two cottages until the early 1880s. The names of its occupants are unclear until the early 1870s.

No. 64

John Swan, an agricultural labourer, lived here in 1871 with his wife Sophia. John died three years later, aged 65 years. His widow, unable to support herself financially, ended her days in Shipmeadow Workhouse and died in 1879, aged 63 years.

No. 65

Daniel Stanton, a widower born in Leiston, lived here alone in 1871. He moved shortly after to Bedingham, where he died the following year, aged 79 years. The next occupiers' names are not known, and at some point during the years when No. 64 had also become empty, the two cottages were made into one.

In 1881 the house was unoccupied, but by 1885 Henry Fisk, an agricultural engine driver, his wife Eliza and their four children had moved into the house and were still there at the turn of the century.

We now come back down Church Lane to rejoin Heath Road. Prior to mid-Victorian times a huge mass of cottages arranged higgledy-piggledy stood between here and the church. Others stood beyond No. 70 and adjacent to Clare Cottage. Then owned by Edward Cooper the aforementioned carpenter, they had all disappeared by the end of the 1860s.

Nos 66–69

These two 'double houses', as they were called when they were built, were erected in 1869.

No. 66 (Second Cottage)

Standing just in Church Lane, this house was occupied in 1871 by George Cooper, his wife Sarah and five boarders.

Ten years later George and Sarah had just two boarders living with them; however this had risen to six by 1891. When George died in 1895 Sarah continued to live in the house and in 1901 was still there, with just a single boarder.

No. 67 (Corner Cottage)

Standing on the corner of Church Lane and Heath Road, this house was occupied by Job Howard in 1871, previously resident at No. 88. Living here with his wife Maria and their four children, he had moved back to Homersfield after living for a few years in Wortwell. The family subsequently moved to another cottage in the village.

John Gibbs, his wife Mary Ann and their four children were living here by 1881. In the next ten years, they had another son and daughter, although two others had left. In 1891 they also had a boarder living with them. They subsequently moved out of the village.

At the turn of the twentieth century, Abraham Page, who had previously lived with his parents at No. 89, his wife Louisa and their four children were living here.

No. 68

The 1856 County and Borough Police Act stipulated that all counties should employ their own police force. As there was no police presence in the village in the early 1860s, it is therefore likely that as soon as it was built, this house was occupied by the long arm of the law. The first officer here was probably Robert Pannifer, who, with his wife Hannah and their very young daughter, were occupying the house in 1871. Between then and 1876, they had four children baptised in the church.

By 1881 they had moved on and another constable, Thomas Elvish, was living here with his wife Susan.

William Milligan Smith was here by 1890, with his wife Margaret. They brought their five children with them and had another son, Reginald, baptised here. They did not stay long, however.

William and Sarah Franks moved into the house with their two sons. The elder, teenager Edward, had been part blind since childhood. A third child, Ellen, born blind, was baptised in Homersfield in 1893.

This family stayed until 1901, when Frederick and Rose Nolloth came to the village and had a son, Edward, baptised.

No. 69

Bricklayer Eli Baker, who had previously lived in two other houses in the village, quite possibly helped to build this one together with the other three dwellings erected in 1869. He, his wife Sarah and six children were living here in 1871. They had four more children whilst living in this house, the last in 1878, and moved out of the village not long afterwards. In all, they had 12 children, the first two in Wortwell and ten in Homersfield, four of whom died aged under six years.

John Page, an agricultural engine driver, and his wife Mary had moved in by 1881, with their two sons and two daughters. Within ten years they had nine children – 13 by 1901, although six of the 13 were no longer living at home.

No. 70

Here, again, the occupiers' names are difficult to determine prior to 1871, when George and Harriet Aldous were living here with their three children, all born in Wortwell. Ten years later, these three children had left home but living with George and Sarah was granddaughter Ellen, born in 1870 in Homersfield. They were living alone by 1891. George died in 1900, aged 84 years, and Harriet went to live in Belton. She died in 1902, joining her husband in Homersfield churchyard. Their old home was empty at the time of the 1901 census.

In more recent years the house has been known as Tamarisk Cottage, prior to which it was called Honeymoon Cottage.

Clare Cottage

This house was never owned by the Adair family. The building and the surrounding land feature on the 1851 and 1883 Flixton Hall estate surveys with the name 'Smith' next to them. Significantly, it is the only name to appear on the maps and the house was not sold in the 1948 estate sale or in the subsequent sale of 1950, when some of the houses that had been overlooked (Nos 66–69 inclusive) were sold. It also does not seem to appear in any estate records. For a great many years it was a shop, at least from the 1860s and almost certainly for a few decades before then.

Tailor Thomas Smith (one of the sons of Thomas and Sarah Smith), his wife Hannah and their children had at some point moved from No. 72 or 73 to live here. In 1861 Thomas and Hannah were running the shop as a grocer's and tailor's. Hannah passed away later the same year, aged 60, and Thomas was still in the house ten years later, selling groceries, with his daughter Mary Ann to help him. She had given birth to a daughter, baptised Rosa Smith in 1869. Strangely, Rosa was not with her mother on the night of the 1871 census, but was recorded as a one-year old (and sole) visitor at the Johnson household in Redenhall. In 1871 Mary Ann married George

Mrs Mary Ann Gower and daughters Rosa, Alice and Ellen, outside Homersfield Post Office, c.1910.

Gower, who came to live with her and her father. She gave birth to her second child, Alice, later that year. George was then a platelayer on the railway, and no doubt helped build the Waveney Valley line. When Thomas Smith died early in 1874, the village also lost a parish clerk. Born in Homersfield, Thomas had lived his whole life in the village, and was buried in the graveyard of the same church in which he had married Hannah Asten.

In 1875, shopkeeper George and Mary Ann had another child, Ellen. Her older sister, Rosa, took the name Gower and all three girls attended the school in St Cross. Probably during the mid-1880s the grocer's shop became the village Post Office. The first contracts for running Post Offices were issued in the 1840s but most village Post Offices did not come into existence until a few decades later and were run by unpaid sub-postmasters. A rural Post Office was therefore normally run from a shop, as was that in Homersfield. By the early years of the twentieth century there was a postal delivery twice each day of the year, including Christmas Day, when a letter or postcard posted to a local address in the morning would arrive that same day in the afternoon delivery.

George and Mary Ann continued to run the grocer's shop and Post Office until 1903, when George passed away.

The Post Office eventually closed on 30 June 1967. Letters were then posted in the box at Homersfield Station, probably until it was demolished at the end of the 1960s. In the early years of the twenty-first century, a postbox was moved from the village green to the bus shelter near Barnfield Cottages.

No. 74 (Waveney House)

In the early 1860s Henry Tidnam, a master tailor, and his wife Jane, a tailoress, were living in Homersfield, possibly in this house. They were certainly here at the beginning of the next decade, when they had three children, and Henry took the post of parish clerk, vacated when Thomas Smith passed on. In 1880 Jane died aged only 45 years, leaving her husband and two daughters to carry on running the shop, which was now a general stores as well as a tailor's. Ten years later Henry was there with just his youngest daughter, and at the turn of the century they were still running the shop. Henry later moved to Denton and died in 1931 at the ripe old age of 98.

Mill House

This appears to have been built in about 1870 and provided accommodation for the miller separate from the mill itself. Its first occupier was Charles Smith, whose sister, Mary Ann, had married George Gower and lived at the Post Office. A batchelor all his life, he served as miller until his death in 1901, aged 75 years. The house was then occupied by his niece, Rosa Gower.

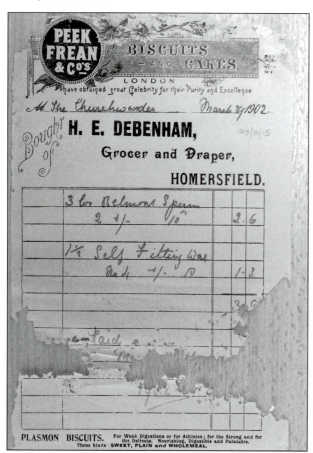

A very ragged, worm-eaten invoice from Henry Debenham's shop, dated 1902.

(REPRODUCED BY KIND PERMISSION OF SUFFOLK RECORD OFFICE, LOWESTOFT BRANCH, REF.: 128/A1/15.)

We now cross the road on our way back into the village and stop immediately at the mill.

Homersfield Mill

This beautiful building almost certainly dated from the sixteenth century and replaced an earlier mill on the same site. Exactly when the first mill was built is not known, but one existed here at the time of Domesday in 1086. It was an extremely important

A lovely old cart outside Homersfield Mill, c.1905.

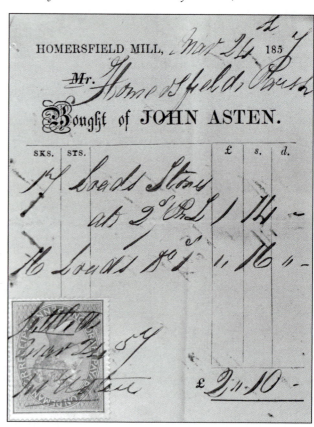

A bill from John Asten of Homersfield Mill to the church-wardens, dated 1857.

(REPRODUCED BY KIND PERMISSION OF SUFFOLK RECORD OFFICE, LOWESTOFT BRANCH, REF.: 128/A1/10.)

building in the village, for before the early 1800s, when there were no village shops and people were much more self-sufficient, corn would be taken to the miller to be ground into flour. Animal foodstuff was sold from the mill, in addition to flour.

Prior to around 1870, when a separate dwelling was built, the miller and his family lived in the left-hand end of Homersfield Mill. It is noted in 1871 that the 'Old Mill House' was uninhabited, and it is not mentioned in subsequent census returns.

By 1765 the mill had become part of the Adair estate. From 1828 to 1849 Robert Harvey junr is recorded as being there. In the early 1840s there were three other millers living in the village: Moses Caston, Edward Keable and Edward Barber. John Asten and his wife Anna then came to live at the mill. They were still there in 1870, when Anna died aged 58 years, and it is highly likely that John moved away as a result. He died in 1887 in Bungay, aged 77 years. Both are buried in Homersfield churchyard.

The mill ceased working in the early 1920s and, sadly, was demolished in around 1927.

Nos 75 & 76

Now demolished, these were a single building and stood between the mill and No. 77 (St Mary's Cottage), rather close to the river.

No. 75

In the early 1850s, Robert and Mary Palmer, a couple in their sixties, lived here. The seemingly random nature of entries in the first useful census means that they had possibly already lived in this cottage for more than ten years.

By 1861 bricklayer William Read, his wife Mary Ann and three daughters were living here

Ten years later a middle-aged couple, Thomas and Mary Ann Guyatt, occupied the cottage. They were there ten years later, but when Thomas died shortly afterwards, aged 77, Mary Ann's son-in-law, Samuel, a widower, and grandson, William Butcher, came to join her in the cottage. They were still there in 1901, and in 1903 Mary Ann also died at the age of 77.

No. 76

Jonathan Cock and his wife Jane, born in Ireland, who lived here in the 1850s and possibly earlier, had their daughter Mary living with them. They had moved away by the end of the decade.

In the early 1860s Eli Baker, his wife Sarah and two children were occupying the cottage. They later moved to No. 69.

Next to live here were James and Esther Aldous of Wortwell, who almost certainly arrived after Eli moved. Their daughter, Ellen, was born here in 1870.

By 1881, Robert and Maria Plumb, a couple in

Farm workers near Mendham Lane. c.1910. Note the binding at knee-height on the closer of the two men, worn to prevent rats running up trouser legs.

their seventies, had come to live in the cottage. They had two boarders living with them ten years later, but it seems the additional income wasn't enough to save Robert, at least, from the workhouse, for he died in Shipmeadow the following year. Maria, then living in Denton, passed away in 1906, aged 98 years.

They were followed by James and Ellen Warren, who brought two children from St Cross and had seven more in Homersfield; sadly, four of them never saw their second birthday.

No. 77 (St Mary's Cottage)

This house probably dates from the sixteenth century and appears to have been two cottages during the nineteenth century (and probably earlier), becoming one by the 1880s.

Robert and Susanna Sampson lived in one half of this house in the 1850s with their small family. They were in Homersfield ten years earlier, possibly in this cottage. By 1861 they had taken in a lodger. When Susannah died in 1865, Robert lived here alone for about six years, after which he moved to the newly built Park Lodge.

In the other half of the house in 1851 were James and Anne Plumb, together with Anne's son, William Todd. By 1861 James and William had both died, leaving Anne on her own.

Ten years later, Robert Sampson's son, also Robert, came to live next door to his widowed father along with his wife Ellen and six children, three boys and three girls, all born in Homersfield. One of these children, named after her mother, spent time in Norwich Prison at the turn of the century. It was in the years after Robert senr had moved, that the house was probably made into a single dwelling, a decision possibly prompted by having so many children in such a small cottage!

Job and Maria Howard, who had previously lived at No. 67, occupied the house in the early 1880s with their five children. Job died in 1889, aged 54 years. His wife continued to live in the cottage with part of her family and took in a boarder. She died in 1900.

William and Sarah Elliott then came to live in the cottage with their three children.

No. 78 (Waveney Cottage)

In the early 1850s, Zachariah Stannard, a pensioner, lived in this house with his wife Mary Ann and their three children. Also living with them was William Jeffries, Mary Ann's son from her previous marriage to Robert Jeffries, who died in 1834, aged 28 years. Possibly, Zachariah and Mary Ann were living here ten years earlier, when he was working as a sawyer. In 1861, living with his wife and son Frederick, Zachariah was described as a Chelsea Pensioner as well as an agricultural labourer! Mary Ann passed away in 1867.

Frederick then became head of the household and in 1871 was living in the house with his wife Rachel, three children and his father, who passed away three years later, aged 78 years. The family later moved out of the village.

Samuel Calver, a threshing-machine driver, his wife Charlotte, six children and his mother-in-law, Margaret Sampson, filled the house in the 1880s, having previously lived at No. 90. At the turn of the century the family were still there.

No. 79 (Greenview)

In 1841, it appears this cottage accommodated three households (tenements being common at this time). Zachariah Lanham, born in Homersfield in 1799, was living here with his wife Elizabeth and four children. Also here were Anne Thurston, an elderly widow, together with a presumed grandchild, as well as John and Anna Poole.

Ten years on, Zachariah and Elizabeth were still here with four children (not the same four as ten years previously) and Anne Thurston, recorded as a visitor. In all, there were nine Lanham children, born between 1831 and 1849, four of whom died young. By 1861 only one son was living with them. When Zachariah died in 1869, his wife lived alone in the cottage until she too passed away, in 1878.

From Wortwell, miller's carter David Page then came to live here with wife, Mary Ann, and two daughters. They had six more children, baptised in Homersfield between 1879 and 1887. In 1891 five children were living with their parents in this little cottage; two remained ten years later.

No. 80 (Plumtree Cottage)

In 1841 it appears that carpenter and joiner Charles Gibbs and his wife Mary were living in this cottage, together with another household, Esther Morris and her new baby, also named Esther.

By the 1850s they had moved and the cottage was occupied by Samuel and Rachel Smith, who came from Flixton with a son, daughter and granddaughter for company. By 1861, their daughter and granddaughter had left, leaving just their son, Charles. Samuel, who had become deaf in his old age, died the following year, aged 78 years. His wife's passing appears not to be recorded in Homersfield.

Charles married Mary Ann Stanton a few months after his father died and they had four children in the cottage in 1871. They moved to St Cross within a couple of years or so.

Robert and Sarah Botwright were living here by the early 1880s with their granddaughter Emma and a boarder. When Sarah passed away towards the end of 1883, aged 58 years, Robert married another Sarah early in 1885. They stayed in the cottage into the next decade before moving to Bungay.

Henry and Mary Debenham lived here next. When Henry died, early in 1901, his widow stayed on with her widowed sister-in-law, Louisa Botwright, who had married Mary's brother, John (apparently no relation to Robert). Also living here was Alice Debenham, Henry's daughter.

No. 81 (Stable Cottage)

In the early 1840s, an elderly couple, Thomas Saunders, a bricklayer, and his wife Jane were living in the cottage. She passed away in 1847, aged 79 years, and Thomas subsequently moved to Wortwell, where he died in 1865, aged 93 years.

David Baker, a master bricklayer, his wife Elizabeth and five children moved here from Rumburgh in 1850 and had another child baptised in 1853. By 1871 all the children had left home except for their youngest, and the family moved away during the 1870s.

In the early 1880s Job and Amy Sillett lived here with their two sons. Job was a journeyman miller and the family had previously lived in Wortwell and St Cross. Their son, William, followed in his father's footsteps and is shown as a miller living with his parents in 1891. He later moved out of the cottage, leaving his parents still there at the turn of the century. Job passed away at the end of 1915, aged 82 years; his wife died a year later at the same age.

No. 82 (Ivy Cottage)

Hannah Sampson, a pauper, was living here with her granddaughter, Emily, in 1841. Hannah died seven years later, aged 77 years.

By 1851 Simon Jeffreys, his wife Eliza, five children and elderly mother-in-law Susan had come to live here. Susan died in 1855, aged 91 years. Simon and Eliza had lived in Homersfield for at least 20 years previously, having had all their children in the village. It seems the family then left; Eliza returned later to live at No. 71.

Probably in 1860, Frederick Bunning, a journeyman carpenter, his wife Charlotte and their three sons came from Bungay to live in the cottage. Four sons and finally a daughter were born in the next ten years; all eight of them were living in the cottage with their parents in 1871. Another daughter was born the following year.

Sadly, Frederick died in 1879, aged 54 years, and was buried two days before Christmas Day. The rest of the family stayed on, and by 1881 there were six children living in the cottage with Charlotte's father, Stephen Earl.

Ten years later, all the children had left and Charlotte had three boarders, a railway porter, a plasterer and a miller. In another ten years Charlotte was living in the house alone. She died in 1902, aged 70 years.

No. 83

Grocer George Borrett lived here in the early 1840s with his wife Sarah and five children. They were all still here ten years later, when George and Sarah's three sons had commenced their working lives, one as a plumber and glazier, another as an apprentice shoesmith and the other as an apprentice carpenter. George was by now a master saddler. By 1861 all but the youngest had left, the one remaining daughter being a dressmaker. George had changed profession again and was now a cordwainer (shoemaker) and kiddier (one who made gloves, shoes, etc. from goatskin). The family moved away during the 1860s.

By 1865 Samuel Gowing, a thatcher, and his wife Sarah came to live here. They had two sons, who both died in infancy. In 1871 George's brother and sister, William and Elizabeth, were also living in the cottage. Two more sons and a daughter followed during the 1870s. By the beginning of the 1880s William and Elizabeth had departed. Ten years later, the three children were still at home, son Arthur, a thatcher's assistant, probably working with his father, while the other son, William, had taken up gardening. In 1898, Sarah died in Shipmeadow Workhouse, aged 57 years. At the turn of the century Samuel was still in the cottage, with servant Emma Parker. He died in 1910, aged 69 years.

The Black Swan

This public house became part of the Flixton Hall estate when it was purchased from John Kerrich in 1828. The external brickwork seen today is clearly of

A delivery from Gordon Barratt, ale, wine and spirit merchant of Broad Street, Bungay, to John Borrett's Swan Inn, c.1905.

Mr and Mrs Miles' wedding, in front of the Swan bowling green, c.1908.

(REPRODUCED BY KIND PERMISSION OF MRS MARY RACKHAM.)

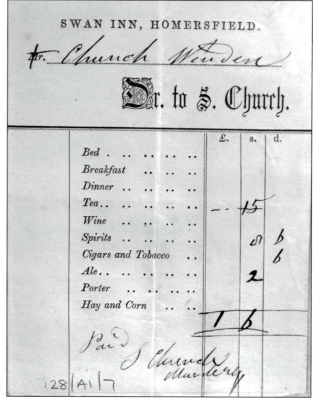

An undated invoice from 1864/65 from Samuel Church, landlord of the Swan, to the Homersfield churchwardens. Note that the cost of the tea was almost twice that of the spirits! (REPRODUCED BY KIND PERMISSION OF SUFFOLK RECORD OFFICE, LOWESTOFT BRANCH, REF.: 128/A1/7.)

a later date and masks its true date of construction. The author has come across references to the Swan or Black Swan (the names have been interchangeable throughout much of its history) going back to 1783. Many public houses were rebuilt in Victorian times and this is possibly true of the one remaining pub in the village.

A legal document concerning this pub mentions another in Homersfield, the King's Head, but frustratingly (as is all too common), gives no precise details as to its location. Another pub, the Cock, dating from at least the early years of the sixteenth century, is mentioned elsewhere; it was still in existence in 1679, when it was referred to in a legal document. An alehouse in the village in the early years of the seventeenth century was run by William Mosse, and in the 1830s James Lanham was running a beerhouse. These had sprung up all over the country after the 1830 Beer Act, which enabled anyone to sell beer, ale and cider (but not spirits), without a licence from local justices, on payment of a one-off fee of two guineas. These were frequented by the labouring residents of a parish, and no doubt there were several other such houses in Homersfield over the years.

In 1828 Samuel Church was the landlord of the pub, Elizabeth Church being recorded as landlady in 1841. Samuel having died two years earlier, she lived here with daughters Elizabeth and Maria and a grandson. Also in residence were a male servant, an agricultural labourer and a retired man. Elizabeth passed away in 1842 and when her mother followed six years later, her son Samuel, a blacksmith, and his wife Betsy, came from Wortwell to run the pub. Samuel continued blacksmithing – it was common

practice for innkeepers to carry on a second trade. They had eight children altogether, one of whom died in infancy. In the early 1850s five of their children were living at the pub, together with a female servant. Four were still there ten years later. When Samuel passed away in 1865 the family moved away.

John Borrett, possibly a brother of George, who once lived at No. 83, came to run the pub with his wife, Mary Ann. With them in 1871 were a son, two daughters and two granddaughters. The parish registers show that one of these granddaughters was born to Mary Ann, John and Mary Ann's unmarried daughter. The father's name, Abraham, has been crossed out, but there is a clue as to his possible identity. The register states he was the stationmaster, then Abraham Kilbourn. In the early 1880s John and Mary Ann were still running the pub, with just one daughter at home, a dressmaker. In 1885 John's wife died, aged 74 years. His eldest son, also John, took over the running of the pub and continued to farm the land that came with it, including the Barn Field. Two adult children, two young ones and John's father were at the pub in 1891, with John and his wife, Mary Ann. At the turn of the century, three of John and Mary Ann's offspring were still living at home, together with Harold Brice, their grandson, and a lodger.

CHAPTER 12

Acts of God

BRING OUT YOUR DEAD

The Black Death

The plague is known to have been present in the Middle East and North Africa in around 350BC – probably 800 years before that date. The outbreak of 1346 probably originated in an area of land stretching from the north-west side of the Caspian Sea into Russia, towards the Crimea. In 1347 Italian cargo ships transported the disease, known centuries later as the Black Death, from a port on the Black Sea to those on the Mediterranean. This incident was paramount in the spreading of the disease.

It is almost certain that in the following year, this terrible disease came by boat to Weymouth in Dorset, around the end of the first week of May 1348. By the end of the year, the Black Death had made itself extremely unwelcome along the whole of the south coast and on the east coast of England as far as Suffolk. From here, it spread further, carried by boats inland throughout Suffolk and Norfolk. By then, it was spreading to other parts of England by whatever transport was available. That this is how it was spread was not understood until centuries later.

At the time, there was no knowledge of the existence of bacteria or the causes of disease. Most were convinced that God was punishing them for their wrongdoings. The origin of the name 'Black Death' is not entirely clear, but is thought to be traceable to an incorrect translation of a Latin phrase more commonly interpreted as 'terrible death'. Doctors used the word 'pestilence' from the Latin *pestis* or *pestilentia*, which translates as 'epidemic'. It was also known as the 'Great Mortality'.

Most of those infected developed the tell-tale buboes, or swellings, in the armpits, groin or thigh after an incubation period of between three and five days. These could be as small as a pea or as big as a small apple; whatever their size, they were excruciatingly tender and invariably developed in the lymph-nodes. These are part of the body's natural defences, and the swelling was the result of the disease being concentrated at a point where it could be dealt with. That was the principle, but within three to five days of the buboes appearing, purple spots on most parts of the body, varying in both number and size, heralded impending death. The disease was highly contagious, and to visit dwellings where people were ill or had died was to put one's life seriously at risk.

More than 500 years passed before the cause of these deaths was understood. It had been noticed that where people caught the plague, there were black rats, often dead and often covered in fleas. A connection was suspected, the theory being that when the rats died of starvation, their fleas were forced to find another host. There was a medical breakthrough in around 1870, when it was discovered that contagious diseases were caused by micro-organisms. After a serious hunt for the culprit in the last decade of the nineteenth century, the same bacteria, named *Yersinia pestis* after their discoverer, bacteriologist Alexandre Yersin, were found in rats as were found in humans infected with the plague. The black rat was named as the primary, albeit indirect, cause, when it was found that their fleas inflicted bites into which they regurgitated plague-infected blood. The bloodstream then transported the bacteria to the lymph-nodes, resulting in the painful swellings, which normally appeared between two and three weeks after the infected fleas had infested a house.

When the Black Death appeared in England and Wales, the population in England, about six million at that time, was decimated by approximately 60 per cent. The rural population had increased greatly in the thirteenth and the first half of the fourteenth centuries, greatly increasing the demand for land. In turn, lords of the manors were not only able to charge high rents but could demand heavy labour commitments from their tenants. Consequently, the rural population, those at or near the bottom of the social scale found themselves under pressure in a crowded labour market, and had to work extremely hard for relatively little remuneration. Prior to the Black Death there was a surplus of people seeking a tenement who were often denied the opportunity. The plague changed all that; numerous tenements became vacant and many people's dreams were realised. There was also a significant labour shortage, and tenants were able to earn much more for the same work their predecessors had done only a year or so before. Needless to say, the Black Death changed the country economically as well as socially. The standard of living of the lower classes improved enormously, whilst that of the upper classes declined due to a reduction in their incomes.

Registers kept by the Bishop's Registrar for a diocese (diocesan institution-books) contain details of new incumbents in every parish. Though there are some vacancies due to resignations, most are because of the death of the incumbent priest. These registers contain useful information on the deaths and resignations of clergy in normal times that can then be compared with those during the period of the Black Death. They also provide evidence of the spread of the disease and the time taken for it to broaden its territory. Those clergy in Norfolk and Suffolk under the Diocese of Norwich were reduced by almost half.

During the five years immediately preceding the outbreak, the average number of new incumbents to all kind of benefices throughout the Norwich diocese was 81 per year. During the 12 months from 25 March 1349 (then the first day of the new year, Lady's Day), these institutions increased by a factor of more than ten, to 831.

By the spring of 1349 the epidemic had reached Norwich, the headquarters of the diocese, and some of the clergy within a few miles of the city had already succumbed. Spreading quickly and relentlessly, by June the plague had arrived at the Benedictine nunnery of Bungay, one of its victims being the prioress herself. In a period of just 20 days, 100 clergymen were admitted to vacant benefices. The Bishop of Norwich fled and took up residence at Hoxne. In June, July and August things were at their worst. In July alone there were 209 appointments of clergy to vacant benefices. During the year ending March 1350, considerably more than two-thirds of the benefices of the diocese had become vacant at one time or another, and more than 800 clergy had perished of the disease. Allowance must also be made for the curates, chaplains, vicars of parishes whose endowments were insufficient to keep a parson in residence under ordinary circumstances, and members of monastic orders. These increased the number of deaths well into four figures. However, it seems that the incumbent of Homersfield Church was spared, as there appear to be no new incumbents during these times and, although this in itself is not indisputable proof, it is likely that his parishioners also avoided the ravages of the disease.

The Black Death was the first serious outbreak in Britain of the bubonic plague, and in the following centuries there were others. There were serious outbreaks in 1361/62 and 1377; lesser ones in 1369 and 1374. The last major outbreak was the Great Plague of London, in 1665. None diminished the population as seriously as had the Black Death, but nevertheless its virulence remained strong and communities were in constant fear of an outbreak in their parish.

Smallpox

This highly infectious disease appears to have originated in China or the Far East at least 2,000 years ago. The cause is the *Variola* virus, most commonly contracted simply by inhaling in the vicinity of an infected individual. Symptoms, which may take between one and two and a half weeks to appear, include fever, headache, nausea, aching muscles and fatigue; this is the time when the disease is most infectious. Between 24 and 48 hours later a characteristic rash appears all over the body. These distinctive pocks, fluid-filled blisters, are present mainly on the face, arms and legs, but can also form in the mouth and throat. After the best part of a month, these form a crust and then fall off.

Smallpox had reached Europe by the early years of the eighth century and 1,000 years later had reached plague proportions; understandably, the thought of contracting it instilled fear in everyone. It first arrived in England during the sixteenth century. Contrary to popular belief, it wasn't the killer disease that people think it was, with, on average, only about three in 20 succumbing. Mortality was high among children, and higher still among infants. Surprisingly, perhaps, the elderly had a far better survival rate. Those who did survive were invariably scarred for life. The cure came in the form of cowpox, first injected in 1796, and vaccination against the disease became compulsory in 1853.

The disease was commonly spread in this country by infected travellers staying overnight at inns, and by the end of the seventeenth century smallpox was a common cause of death. The lack of proper sanitation did not help; waste pits were often dug near water supplies, and household waste was thrown over hedges and into ditches, or buried nearby.

From the 1760s to the end of the eighteenth century, smallpox outbreaks were common in northeast Suffolk, and in several especially bad years, particularly 1774, the disease raged locally for over a year. In 1798 there was a particularly bad outbreak in Homersfield and the surrounding villages, probably caused by a certain Mr Coan, who travelled around the country with a puppet show. On June 11 of that year he arrived by carriage in Homersfield intending to perform at the fair in the village that same day. He said nothing about the sick family he had brought with him; when they left Homersfield after a few days the disease stayed behind, causing mayhem in its wake. It spread through the area like wildfire, infecting hundreds of people. Inevitably, there were some deaths, although possibly only one in Homersfield. In 1778 John Lark(e) and Susanna Spratt married in Homersfield and had seven children baptised there between 1783 and 1798. The last of these, Robert, born on 25 March that year, was baptised in his parents' home the following day. He was buried a few months later on 11 July. In the Parish Register there is no mention of smallpox in his burial details but it remains a possibility, even considering infant deaths were extremely common during these times. Elizabeth Patrick, a widow of Alburgh, who died in August 1873, aged 92 years, remembered the outbreak, and Mr Coan, well. She recalled that, when confronted with the probability that he was responsible for bringing the disease to Homersfield and, subsequently, for the untimely deaths in the surrounding parishes, his arrogant response was: 'They got it without paying for it and they may keep it.'

RUMBLINGS IN THE NIGHT

Earthquakes are not common in England by any means but they do occur occasionally and a few would have been experienced by the parishioners of Homersfield. These are detailed below.

Just after everyone had celebrated Christmas, a great earthquake, on 28 December 1480, affected almost the whole of England. In Norwich, which was particularly hard hit, buildings fell to the ground and there was an enormous amount of damage.

During the afternoon of 8 September 1692 a violent earthquake, the epicentre of which was probably in Brabant, was felt in several European countries. In East Anglia, it was felt in Norwich, Ipswich and Colchester, among other places.

In East Anglia, on a Monday in early March 1757, in the early hours of the morning, a slight shock was felt followed by a rumbling noise. As most people were asleep, it was not heard by many, but was felt and heard by some in Bungay and South Elmham and clearly would have been audible in Homersfield.

A possible earthquake took place on 11 June 1760, in the late afternoon, when a loud noise, appearing to originate west of Diss, travelled eastwards. It was heard in several places, among them Diss, Norwich, Bungay and Beccles.

East Anglia was mildly shaken by a minor shock on 18 February 1884, and, as is common with earthquakes, there was much worse to come. Around 9.20a.m. on Tuesday, 22 April 1884, East Anglia experienced the biggest earthquake since the one four centuries earlier. The epicentre was very close to the village of Abberton, in Essex, just a few miles south of Colchester, and it was felt as far north as Brigg, in Lincolnshire. Its effects were felt within a radius of about 135 miles – an area of well over 50,000 square miles – where a rumbling noise was followed by gusts of wind. These were followed by more than one shock, probably two, lasting between three and ten seconds. The shocks were described by some as being more violent than any felt since a similar event in the Midlands in 1863.

Understandably, Essex fared worst, with more than 1,200 buildings in need of repair of one sort or another. This figure included some 20 churches and 11 chapels. The spire of a Congregational church in Colchester, 150ft high, crashed to the ground. Chimney stacks, walls and tiles were damaged, floors vibrated and windows rattled. In Norfolk and Suffolk the shocks were felt in many places. In Bungay walls shook slightly and a longcase clock in Mettingham was stopped at 9.20a.m. by the tremor. In Diss houses shook briefly, while in Harleston, Ditchingham, Shipmeadow, Beccles and undoubtedly Homersfield, all felt the earthquake.

WATER, WATER EVERYWHERE

Unlike earthquakes, flooding and, in winter months, expanses of frozen water, have no doubt been commonplace since the Waveney Valley was formed. Invariably, the more elderly long-standing inhabitants of villages along the valley will have many memories of the river bursting its banks and flooding the surrounding land, whether it be spring, summer, autumn or winter. The persistent rain commonly experienced in the winter months, combined with masses of melting snow, often cause the Homersfield marshes to become submerged, creating a large lake. In years gone by, this would have frozen over and the villagers and their children were not slow in making the most of the temporary change in the landscape. It was not just the marshes that flooded; the roads were sometimes inundated to the point where, often for some days, motor vehicles could get neither into nor out of Homersfield.

In 1828, during harvest time, 3 July was very hot indeed, and towards the end of it, rain started to fall. It rained on and off for several weeks, for 47 days in all, delaying the harvest greatly, and in the middle of August there was flooding the length of the valley when the Waveney rose by more than 4ft.

In the summer of 1877, after very heavy rain on three consecutive days, the river level rose so much that some local houses were under a few feet of water.

The most serious floods in the last 100 years occurred not long before harvest-time, in August 1912. The summer had been very damp, and during a gale on the night of Sunday, 25 August, torrential rain poured down on the whole of East Anglia, continuing into Monday morning. By mid-morning, many roads and fields were under water. There hadn't been such a storm in living memory, but worse was to come. The rain eased off, which served only to lull people into a false sense of security. Anyone who thought this a short, albeit very wet, outburst was soon proved very wrong. In the early afternoon, the wind got up even more and another downpour continued for the rest of the day and throughout Tuesday, eventually ceasing in the early evening, around six o'clock. The regions close to rivers were worst affected and the Waveney Valley was particularly hard hit. Some houses in rural areas were surrounded by $2^1/_2$ft of water; cattle in the fields were up to their bellies and cornfields were completely flattened. Bridges either disappeared or, like those at Mendham and Shotford, were seriously damaged, although that in Homersfield survived intact. The railway escaped nowhere near so lightly, and long stretches of the Waveney Valley line suffered. Enormous damage was sustained, the worst of it at Homersfield, where, along with the Waveney, the Beck (the little stream running from Tivetshall through Homersfield and beyond) also flooded. The Beck ran very close to the station plat-

Above and opposite page: *Crowds of people view the storm damage from the night of 26 August 1912 at Homersfield Station. Nothing quite like it had ever been seen before.*

REPRODUCED BY KIND PERMISSION OF MRS MARY RACKHAM

REPRODUCED BY KIND PERMISSION OF LADY DARELL

REPRODUCED BY KIND PERMISSION OF LADY DARELL

form, which disappeared under water, while some of the embankment was swept away. Part of the roadway also vanished under the onslaught of so much water and the track was badly twisted, sticking up into the air in places. A replacement bus service ran between Harleston and Beccles.

There had been so much rain that, just as vast numbers of fields became lakes, town roads became rivers. In Norwich, the Wensum rose more than 16ft. Incredibly, over $7^{1}/_{4}$ ins of rain fell in the first 24 hours of the deluge.

The worst floods since those of 1912 came in the last week of January 1939, when several hundred thousand acres of East Anglia were flooded. Rivers rose rapidly, completely halting rail and road traffic in the two counties and leaving many villages along the Waveney Valley totally stranded. Many local roads were under 2ft or more of water, some flooded to a depth of 5ft.

The winter of 1947/48 is well documented as being particularly bad in East Anglia, where the melting of over 6ft of snow caused serious problems.

In April 1951 there was major flooding in the southern half of England, particularly in the eastern counties, the greatest depth of water, 3ft, being recorded at Homersfield.

In March 1954 the problems for drivers caused by snow and ice were made worse by strong winds, sleet and hail along the East Anglian coast. Melting snow made the Waveney rise, causing localised flooding in the area around Bungay, covering several miles of fields between there and Mendham. A 200yd stretch of road 15ins deep in water was observed in Homersfield.

Eight months later, when much of the country suffered torrential rain, Homersfield was flooded to a depth of 18ins.

In torrential rain at the very beginning of August 1968, the Waveney Valley was seriously flooded. At the time the author was on holiday in Homersfield with his parents and aunt. The rising water level resulted in all three roads in and out of the village being flooded and impassable. We, along with many others, no doubt, were marooned for a full three days. The Homersfield village shop had closed the previous year and, when eventually able to get out of the village, the author remembers a visit to the shop and Post Office in nearby St Cross to buy a loaf of bread. It was an unsuccessful trip, the lady behind the counter apologising that she only had two loaves, one of them already promised to a regular customer in St Cross, which left one spare loaf for the whole of the rest of the village! It was a serious situation, of course, but we all found it very amusing.

In more recent times, there was bad flooding in the winters of 1993/94 and 2002/03.

Skating

In 1813, a great many hard frosts having resulted in a lot of thick ice, skating was enjoyed in the Waveney Valley during the Christmas celebrations. Towards the end of the century the Waveney froze over and in 1895 a skating carnival was held locally. Hard frosts, lasting for many days at a time during the winters of the 1920s and 1930s, created several opportunities for this seasonal pastime on the ideal skating surface of the marshes. People ventured from their homes to take advantage of the situation and at Earsham ice-hockey drew large crowds of spectators!

BLOWIN' UP A STORM

The winter of 1885/86 was one to remember; it was indeed a cold one, and on 1 March 1886 a terrible snowstorm covered the whole country. Railway lines were deep in drifts of snow , and road traffic could go nowhere, the snow being 5ft deep in places, double that in some parts of the countryside. Some cottages were in snow right up to their roofs.

A tornado hit the local area on 24 March 1895, a Sunday, and was never forgotten by those who witnessed its vast capability for destruction.

On Saturday, 22 February 1908, a severe storm, lasting just ten minutes or so, caused damage that had to be seen to be believed. Roofs were stripped of their tiles, chimney stacks seriously damaged and many trees completely uprooted. In churchyards, headstones were broken or blown horizontal, and in Bungay three chapels were damaged, one of them, built in 1855, being almost completely flattened.

Within living memory, the storm of all storms is the so-called hurricane which hit Britain on the night of 15–16 October 1987, immortalised in the words of a television weatherman:

Earlier today a woman phoned in to say she had heard that there was a hurricane on the way. Well, if you're watching, don't worry, there isn't, but having said that, actually the weather will become rather windy.

Unfortunately, the reference was to a storm over the western part of the North Atlantic which wasn't expected to make contact with Britain. It didn't, but it did get very windy. Nevertheless, the weather forecast left a lot to be desired on this occasion. With heavy rain forecast, rather than wind, people went to bed largely oblivious of what was to come during the night. The greatest damage was done in south-east England, which suffered repeated gusts of 35mph hour for several hours. The fiercest winds were between 2a.m. and 6a.m., the highest wind speed recorded in the UK being 51mph, at Shoreham, Sussex. A hurricane is defined as a wind of 64 knots (a little over 73mph) sustained over a period of ten minutes, which, in fact, didn't happen. Gusts of wind are excluded when defining a hurricane. So the 1987 storm, though not a hurricane, is remembered as such; exceptional it undoubtedly was. On the

The willow trees by a disintegrating Homersfield Bridge after the storm of 1987.

morning of 16 October the people of England woke to a scene of unprecedented destruction. Gusts may be short-lived, but it was these that had caused the majority of the damage. In the order of 15 million trees were uprooted, the cost of the damage amounted to around £1,500 million and 18 people lost their lives. The greater part of the damage occurred south-east of a line running from Southampton through London to Norwich. Falling trees damaged or destroyed all manner of objects in their path, including cars and buildings. Similarly, road and rail traffic was severely impeded; fallen trees were everywhere, and homes were without electricity for 24 hours or more. It could have been a lot worse; had the storm taken place during the day instead of at night then doubtless more lives would

Photographed in 1993, this is the closest the author has seen the river get to the underside of the bridge.

have been lost. Heavy rain in the days prior to the storm had saturated the soil; had it been dry, and had the trees already shed their leaves, then a lot more of them would have stayed upright.

As might be expected, there was much damage in the Waveney Valley. In Homersfield, a line of willow trees planted close to the river bank several years before were blown flat, as if a passing giant had pushed them down with his hand.

Storms like the one in 1987 happen here on average once every 200 years or so. Others affected England on the night of 7/8 December 1703, 28 February 1662 and 23 January 1362.

ACCIDENTS WILL HAPPEN

Mr Meadows

In the early 1800s the mineral water business in Harleston, owned by a prominent family in the town, was very well known. Eventually it was taken over by one Edgar Everson, in whose service a drayman suffered a memorable and unpleasant accident.

A dray pulled by two horses and loaded with mineral water and other goods from the warehouse at Framlingham customarily delivered to businesses in the local area. On a day when the river was in flood, the Adairs of Flixton Hall decided to exercise their right of ownership by closing the bridge in order to collect a toll. The customary chain was in place, preventing drayman Mr Meadows, his horses and the dray from crossing and making a delivery to the Black Swan in Homersfield. Meadows declined to pay the toll, with disastrous results. He tried to go through the ford at the side of the bridge, not realising that the water was too high to attempt a crossing. The dray was swept away and the two horses drowned in the fast-flowing torrent.

Frederick William White

William John White, a farm labourer, and Mary Ann Debenham, a housemaid, both lived in St Peter. They met in their teens, married in the summer of 1884 and had a baby, Frederick William, born on the last day of August the following year.

Some years later, in 1901, when Frederick was living with William and Sophia Debenham, his aunt and uncle, at Chestnut Tree Farm in St Cross, he decided to join the Forces and met a very untimely end. Gunner White was attached to the Fifth Heavy Battery and, on 26 March 1904, was driving a team of inexperienced horses pulling an ammunition wagon on a march from Weybread through Harleston. At the end of The Thoroughfare, at a junction with the main road, the horses were startled and bolted. A number of children narrowly escaped injury; two were actually knocked down, the wagon miraculously passing harmlessly over them.

Galloping along Station Road, the horses ran past Haddiscoe Lodge and made straight for a lamppost, the leading horses passing one on each side. The impact threw Gunner White out of his seat directly into the lamppost, smashing one side of his face and breaking his jaw and neck. Though still breathing when taken to a local doctor, he succumbed very quickly. An inquest into the accident was held at the Railway Hotel.

On 31 March 1904, after a full military funeral attended by many hundreds of people, the Last Post was played and Frederick White was buried in Homersfield churchyard.

Although the family moved to Mendham, another child of William and Mary Ann is buried next to Frederick. a little brother whom he never knew, Charles Frederick, who passed away in 1913, aged just seven years.

The graves of Gunner Frederick White and his little brother, Charles, in Homersfield churchyard, 2007.

CHAPTER 13

The Swinging Sixties

This chapter offers an insight into a very few of the people who lived in Homersfield in the 1960s.

Annie Eliza Welton

Annie Welton came to Homersfield in the early 1950s and enjoyed almost two decades living in her cottage. She was a very popular, delightful, kind and caring person whom everyone admired and respected greatly.

Family Background
John Welton, a farm labourer born in Heveningham, married Caroline Barber in the late spring of 1854. They lived in Peasenhall and their first child, Ann, was born in the summer of 1859, followed by Harry in early 1862 and Margaret in 1864. David, the last of their children, was born the following year.

The children grew up in Peasenhall. Ann became a dressmaker, David a shoemaker, and Harry, preferring farm work, followed in his father's footsteps. As a boy he would help drive the cattle to market in Halesworth, and later worked in the orangery at Heveningham Hall. Margaret went into service.

In the summer of 1890 Harry became the last of the children to marry. His bride was Lucy Minnie Dale, daughter of Daniel and Eliza Dale, of Plum Tree Farm, Heveningham. Harry and Lucy Welton first lived in Heveningham but subsequently moved to Little Haven, on the outskirts of Horsham, in Sussex. Here, they had two daughters, Minnie Caroline, born on Christmas Eve 1895 and Annie Eliza, born on 12 November 1898. The family then moved to Roffey, a nearby village, and had a third daughter, Doris Grace, on 21 October 1901.

Early Years
Some years later the Welton family moved to Christchurch, in Dorset, where the two older girls attended All Saints School. At Christchurch level-crossing gates Harry and his two little girls, Minnie and Annie, watched the royal train taking the body of Queen Victoria from Osborne on the Isle of Wight to London. In about 1909 the family moved again, to Picketts Farm, a Victorian farmhouse in Eastwood, Essex, where they stayed for around 20 years. Annie attended the little Victorian school in the village, about half a mile from home. She loved children and so it was a natural progression for her, when she left school a couple of years later, to go into service as nanny to a family who lived above a shop near the

church in Leigh-on-Sea. Subsequently, she went to work for the Croome-Johnson family at Hampstead as a nanny and lady's companion. The head of this family was a High Court judge and Annie would occasionally help serve at table at their grand dinner parties. She stayed with this family for many years, eventually leaving to work in Golders Green for the Heron family, of whom she became very fond. As a lady's companion she travelled with them whenever they were away from home. Miss Heron was head-mistress of an exclusive girls' school.

Annie, aged ten, at Picketts Farm, Eastwood, Essex, 1909.
(Reproduced by kind permission of Brenda Meachen.)

Annie's mother, Lucy, at Picketts Farm, c.1910.
(Reproduced by kind permission of Brenda Meachen.)

Annie in her early teens, c.1912.
(Reproduced by kind permission of Brenda Meachen.)

A lovely picture of Annie in her early twenties, c.1920.
(Reproduced by kind permission of Brenda Meachen.)

Minnie, Annie's elder sister, c.1916.
(Reproduced by kind permission of Brenda Meachen.)

Annie's sister, Minnie, became engaged to Reg Grant, but Reg was killed while serving in the Army during the First World War. She later married Reginald Wadland at the Wesleyan Methodist Chapel in Leigh-on-Sea on 31 March 1923, and in the years following gave birth to twins Jean and Basil and later, Bryan.

Annie's other sister, Doris, married Sidney Wallace and also had three children, Ronald, Brenda and Bernard.

Annie became engaged to Bob Hatt, a railway worker, but they never wed. Sadly, marriage was not to be for Annie, so she never had the children she undoubtedly wished for, although she did have six nieces and nephews on whom to lavish her affection.

Annie at Daws Heath, Essex, c.1930.
(Reproduced by kind permission of Brenda Meachen.)

Annie with her younger sister, Doris, at Clacton, c.1935.

Annie's mother, Lucy, ill throughout the winter of 1928, died on 5 March 1929, aged 61, and was buried in Eastwood churchyard. Her husband, Harry, now on his own, lost interest in farming and sold up, going to live with his daughter Doris and her husband in Daws Heath, Essex. In 1933 they moved to Thundersley, and in around 1941 Harry moved to Bocking Churchstreet to live with his younger brother and second wife. After the war he spent four months of every year with each of his daughters in turn. Towards the end of his life he lived alternately with daughters Minnie and Annie, and, with Doris' husband so ill, spent just a month or so with them in the summer. He died on 18 August 1951, aged 89, and was buried with Lucy in Eastwood.

Middle Years

When the Second World War interrupted Annie's working life she moved to the basement flat of a house in Cavendish Road, Brondesbury, north-west London. She was drafted into war work at the Heinz soup factory and also acted as a kind of warden, supervising those going into shelters during air raids.

After the war, Annie started to look for a home of her own, and saw a cottage advertised for sale in a newspaper. One weekend she came up on the train from her home in Brondesbury to see it, and decided she had to have it. On 23 October 1951 she signed a contract to buy No. 80 Homersfield from the Metropolitan Railway Country Estates. She paid £500 for it and named it 'Plumtree Cottage' because it

Annie's father, Harry Welton, c.1948.

reminded her so much of her grandparents' farm-house in Heveningham. The locals told her it used to be the village beerhouse.

She settled into the slow pace of village life with her beloved black and white spaniel, Lal, and was a

137

popular figure in the community. A regular church-goer, Annie was a member of the Parochial Church Council and, with the village children in mind, was keen on providing a play area for them. She also ran the village library! For several years she kept the books for the village on her windowsill overlooking the green. She chose them when the travelling library van called, accommodating any requests for particular titles. On Friday mornings the front door would be opened for the villagers to come and change their books.

On summer afternoons she could often be seen in conversation in the village or sitting in her cottage garden reading a book. Like her father, she was a very contented person and most enjoyed the simple things in life; nothing much bothered or worried her. There were several fruit trees in her garden in the 1960s, mainly apple and pear, but also damson, Annie's favourite – she loved damson jam, and the shelves of her pantry under the stairs often had jars of it, home-made from fruit picked from the tree in her garden. Cottage garden flowers and roses, which she particularly loved, filled her garden.

Plumtree Cottage came with rights to the osiers in the river at the bottom of the garden, and a basket-maker came once a year to cut the reeds, which were then made into chair seats and baskets. One year, Annie had a chair made for herself.

To help boost her income, Annie decided to offer overnight accommodation, and her cottage was recommended by a cycling organisation. She took in cyclists for a while and then started to let the cottage to friends and family during the summer, moving into a green caravan half-way down the garden when she had guests. Torrential rain in the first week of August 1968 caused the river to flood alarmingly during the night, and the caravan was quickly under a few feet of water, with Annie asleep in it. Deciding to leave before it got any worse, she opened the door in the moonlight to see her pension book floating on the water! She waded through it and walked down to the Mill House, where she stayed for the next few days, returning to her cottage once her guests (in this instance the author and his family) had left the following weekend.

In the summer of 1966 Annie was able to buy the cottage next door, No. 81 (now Stable Cottage). Throughout the time she owned it, the cottage had the same tenants, Mr and Mrs Calver. The following year, she decided to have another dog, and Tessa, a friendly brown and white Jack Russell terrier, shared her life for many years.

Later Years

In 1970, Annie's cousin's husband, Cecil Harris, died, and although Annie loved Homersfield dearly, with her advancing years and the village shop having closed three years earlier, she very reluctantly decided to sell her beloved cottage and move to

Annie at Plumtree Cottage, Homersfield, with her beloved spaniel, Lal, not long after she had come to live there, c.1952. (REPRODUCED BY KIND PERMISSION OF BRENDA MEACHEN.)

Miss Welton's garden in June 1964, with her favourite flowers, roses, arching over the path.

(PHOTO TAKEN BY THE AUTHOR'S FATHER.)

Cecil's house in Bridge Street, Bungay, where she could be close to the shops and local amenities. She left Homersfield at the very end of 1970, having lived in the village for 19 years. She once told the author in a letter: 'I think so much of my happy years at Homersfield', and also told his parents that Homersfield was 'my first love'.

Although not able to return to the village often, Annie kept up an active interest in it and in 1971 presented the gates to the church porch. In the closing years of her life she and her two sisters took holidays together, and Annie usually spent

St Cross rectory in 1878.

Annie in the garden of her last home, 30 Bridge Street, Bungay, c.1971.

Christmas with one of her six nieces and nephews and their families.

The three sisters passed on to the next world in the reverse order in which they had come into it. Doris, the youngest, passed away in Southend Hospital in the early summer of 1986, aged 84. She was laid to rest in Thundersley churchyard alongside her husband, Sidney, who had died in 1958, aged 63.

Annie lived in Bridge Street until her death whilst walking near Ditchingham Dam, on 15 April 1988. She was 89. Her funeral service took place at Holy Trinity Church in Bungay on 29 April 1988 and she was buried where her family knew she would want to be – in Homersfield. In her will she remembered the children of the village and left some money for the playing field.

Minnie, the eldest of the three sisters, and her husband, Reg, spent the final years of their lives in Poole, Dorset, with their daughter and son-in-law. Reg died in November 1989, aged 96, and Minnie three months later, in February 1990. She was 94.

Rosalys Christabel Skene

So much could be said about Rosalys, so varied, interesting and entertaining was her life. Here, space permits only hints at a very fulfilled life.

Family Background

George Smith, born in Langley, Derbyshire in the mid-1820s, came from a farming family. In the summer of 1854 he married Anne Rachel Mackie in Wakefield, Yorkshire, and their first child, Annie Gertrude, was born in autumn the following year.

When George felt he didn't want to be a farmer and chose to be a clergyman, the Smiths moved to Westminster, London, where he took a curacy at St Peter's (the actors' church) in Great Windmill Street. Here, George and Anne had five more children, Herbert Mackie, Selina Constance Eliza, Edith Mary, Wilfrid Edward and George Alwyne.

A postcard sent by Revd William Morley Smith and his wife Edith to a friend in Luton, Christmas Eve, 1903.

As George's health deteriorated the family decided to move out of London for some country air, and in 1867 George took the living at St Cross and bought nearby Spring Farm, with 30 acres of land. At the rectory he fathered two more children, Fannie Mackie and Ernestine Georgiana. A nephew, William Morley Smith, took up a curacy there, but with all the unmarried girls at the rectory, had to live at Spring Farm instead! When George passed away in 1887, William took up the living and a few months later, in early 1888, married George and Anne's fourth child, his cousin Edith.

After George died, the family moved to Albemarle Road in Norwich, then to Beech Bank, a large house off the Unthank Road, where George's wife lived until her death in 1911.

Fanny trained as a nurse in Middlesex and also learnt midwifery. Her first job was at Greenwich Seamen's Hospital. Returning to St Cross rectory to live with her cousin and sister, she worked as a district nurse whilst waiting for a posting overseas, eventually travelling by ship from Tilbury to Malta.

Samuel and Charlotte Skene had three children, two daughters and a son. Robert Ernest Skene, born in 1870 in Dublin, Ireland, became a chaplain and was also posted to Malta. At garden parties there, among other entertainers, Robert would sing. Fanny Smith, who was nursing the wives of soldiers and

Revd Robert Skene with Fanny and Nigel at Hevingham, 1907. (REPRODUCED BY KIND PERMISSION OF CHARMIAN SMY.)

Mrs Fanny Skene with Nigel at Hevingham, 1907.
(REPRODUCED BY KIND PERMISSION OF CHARMIAN SMY.)

sailors, attended these parties and fell for the man with the golden beard and the lovely baritone voice. Clearly, Robert was very taken with Fanny, as he proposed on only their third meeting.

Cowes, Hevingham, St James, Swainsthorpe and Raveningham

Robert and Fanny were married at the church in Fanny's home parish, Christ Church, Norwich, in the summer of 1905. Their married life began with Robert taking a curacy at Cowes, on the Isle of Wight.

Revd Robert Skene with his wife and children at Raveningham, c.1914.
(REPRODUCED BY KIND PERMISSION OF CHARMIAN SMY.)

Rosalys, probably at Raveningham, c.1914.
(REPRODUCED BY KIND PERMISSION OF CHARMIAN SMY.)

A studio portrait of Nigel, Rosalys and Maisie, c.1916.
(REPRODUCED BY KIND PERMISSION OF CHARMIAN SMY.)

Rosalys, Nigel and Maisie, probably in 1916.   (REPRODUCED BY KIND PERMISSION OF CHARMIAN SMY.)

Less than two years later he obtained his first living, and he and Fanny came back to Norfolk. Whilst living at the rectory in Hevingham, near Aylsham, Fanny gave birth to a son, Nigel Robert Mackie, on 2 March 1907, at a nursing home in Surrey Street, Norwich. Soon after, they moved to take up another living at the rectory in St James and, in the same nursing home on 23 October 1908, their daughter, Rosalys Christabel, was born. The family moved again, to a living at Swainsthorpe, where they stayed for a few years before going to Raveningham. Here, their last child, Maisie Meriel, was born at home in the parsonage on 8 March 1912.

Robert and Fanny taught their two elder children at home, after which they were taught for a year or so by Mr Ferrell, the vicar at Heckingham.

Then came the First World War. Robert signed up as a private (despite being over age) and went to the Dardanelles. With no resident rector, his family had to vacate the rectory and moved to Norwich, where Rosalys went to a nearby private school. Maisie underwent three operations to cure a chronic ear infection, but on 3 May 1917 sadly died, at just five years old, and was buried in Eaton cemetery, Earlham Road.

Robert was promoted to lance-corporal but was later invalided out of the Army due to bouts of dysentery. Keen to continue serving his country, he became a chaplain, and was stationed at Felixstowe, where his family travelled from Norwich to see him.

Sutton

The family was reunited with Robert in 1917, when he was offered the living at Sutton, near Woodbridge. Rosalys absolutely adored it there, swimming at Shingle Street and Methersgate, and tearing around the heath on her bicycle with the dogs, dodging the keepers (who didn't want the birds disturbed).

Every day for three years she attended Sutton Hall, where she was taught by a governess. Aged 12, she went as a weekly boarder to a school in Felixstowe, run by two Miss Lasts, the headmistress and her sister, Miss B. Last. Not seeing her family all week meant that she lived for Fridays, when she could go home for the weekend.

After a year she moved to a Canon Woodward school, St Michael's, in Bognor, a beautiful country house with lovely gardens. Unable to see her parents at weekends, she didn't like it there and was very homesick at first. She loved the gym and games though, and played hockey, tennis and lacrosse. She also loved English and writing essays, didn't mind French but hated maths. She used to swim in the sea at Bognor, and remembered walking the promenade.

Rosalys would sometimes stay with her Auntie Corner (her mother's sister, Constance) at the top of Unthank Road, and shop in Norwich. She was there in the era of trams and her ambition then was to be a tram conductress!

Revd Skene with Fanny, Nigel and Rosalys at Sutton, c.1918. (REPRODUCED BY KIND PERMISSION OF CHARMIAN SMY.)

She left school at 16, and then went to her head-mistress, in Kent, where she spent a few terms 'finishing' before her schooling concluded.

After finishing she went to a women's agricultural college, Studley Castle, in Warwickshire. There a group of eight girls called themselves 'The Family'. Nobody told them what they were supposed to do – they were just thrown in at the deep end.

In a two-year course in general agriculture, a month at a time was spent learning ploughing, hay-making and working with cattle, pigs, poultry, and horses. She also studied crops and dairying, and learned about cheese and butter-making, which involved milking short-horn cows by hand.

The Family had transport – Rosalys had a Francis-Barnett motorbike – and on Sundays, their day off, they would go to the Malvern Hills for picnics and swim in the river there. They would also cycle to Stratford-on-Avon to see matinée and evening performances, then cycle back the 12 or so miles at around midnight. The salt-water baths at Droitwich were also visited. Rosalys kept in touch with four of the Family throughout her life. Compared to school, the Agricultural College was heaven, there being so much more liberty.

After returning home, Rosalys took holiday jobs for a couple of weeks at a time until the beginning of the Second World War. Her first was at an old dairy farm, New Bells, in Haughley, near Stowmarket, run by Miss Eve Balfour (later Lady Eve Balfour, a pioneer of organic farming), and her sister Mary.

Rosalys, c.1929.

(Reproduced by kind permission of Charmian Smy.)

They had a herd of Guernsey cows and Rosalys did the five o'clock milking and filled the bottles for the door-to-door delivery rounds.

When the motorbike started misbehaving Rosalys' father bought his daughter her first car, an old brown Citroen Cloverleaf, for £30.

Rosalys had always longed for a donkey and in the 1920s saw one advertised at Ipswich; the donkey carried her home in a four-wheeled cart, all bought for £3. Tabitha, as Rosalys named her, walked slower and slower and became more and more tired on the way back, and it took ages to get home.

Nigel joined the Marines when he was 18. When he was home on leave, he would often motor down to Tor Royal, near Princetown, Devon, with his sister. Their Uncle Wilfred and Aunt Florrie lived in a lovely old farmhouse, and kept beef cattle, with chickens and dogs running around. Rosalys rode horses all over the surrounding moor with her aunt, and loved it. Their visits stopped when war broke out in 1939, as there was no petrol.

St Cross (1)

Rosalys and her parents had been at Sutton for 17 years when Mr Macaulay, the Melton vicar, told them that the living at St Cross had become vacant. Sir Shafto and Lady Adair of Flixton Hall subsequently invited Robert and Fanny to lunch and offered them the living. They moved to St Cross rectory on 1 October 1934, together with Tabitha the donkey and their dog. For Fanny, it was the third time that she had lived there. In those days, there were no tractors on the farms and theirs was the only car.

Sutton was where Rosalys first acquired her love of wild flowers, animals and the sea, and, though she felt heartbroken at leaving there, she loved St Cross right from the start.

The rectory was a big house with nine bedrooms, and two maids came in once a week, Annie Clarke on Sundays to prepare and serve supper. Robert once said to Annie: 'You know, Annie, Mrs Skene was born in this house.' 'Oh, yes?' she replied. He continued, 'And now I've brought her back to die here!' (Rosalys said he could be quite naughty like that.) Annie replied, 'Oh, that will be nice,' and they all fell about laughing.

The family settled into St Cross very quickly, and Robert gave scripture lessons to the St Cross school-children. When war broke out in 1939, Rosalys was working for Henry Debenham at Chestnut Tree Farm. For the first harvest of the war he indulged himself in a tractor, which Rosalys had great fun driving at harvest time. One of her many jobs there was to ride carthorses to the blacksmith at St James to be shod. In harvest time she took food with her and was out all day until late.

On one of her occasional holidays, Rosalys was invited to go on a cruise and visited Tehran for a day and Lisbon for a day before sailing on to Madeira. She also had a couple of other short trips abroad, on cargo boats, first to Finland and then to Norway, sailing from Harwich via the Hook of Holland. She arrived back at the end of August and war was declared on 3 September.

A group of evacuees were taken from Homersfield Station to the Iron Room, the little hall in St Cross, from where Rosalys drove them to their temporary homes. The Skene family took in two boys aged about five, Ray and Norman, Ray's elder sister, and a teacher, but they didn't stay very long.

When a branch of the Red Cross was started in St Cross, Rosalys joined it as second-in-command. She worked a shift at Denton House, a sort of hospital, and did night duty at All Hallows, which she enjoyed immensely.

Rosalys' brother, Nigel, posted to Fife, Scotland, met and married Diana Erskine in August 1941 at Pittenweem, a small fishing village. Rosalys and her mother travelled to Edinburgh by train for the wedding and the newlyweds went to live in the seaside town of Elie. Sadly, their happiness was to be short-lived. Nigel, keen to join the Fleet Air Arm, was sent to a training centre at Leuchars, near St Andrews. Having risen to the rank of major, he was subsequently posted to HMS *Avenger*, which, at 4.15a.m. on 15 November 1942, was torpedoed off the coast of northern Africa. In the explosion the bow and stern rose high into the air and the ship sank within a couple of minutes. Of the 526 on board, there were only 12 survivors.

When Rosalys' father, whose health had been deteriorating for some time, suffered a heart attack

Revd E.P. Whalley (Rosalys' cousin), Mrs Fanny Skene (Rosalys' mother), Mrs Ernestine Whalley (Fanny's sister) and Rosalys, c.1944.
(REPRODUCED BY KIND PERMISSION OF CHARMIAN SMY.)

A studio portrait of Rosalys, c.1950.
(REPRODUCED BY KIND PERMISSION OF CHARMIAN SMY.)

Outside Sunset House, 1959. Left to right, back row: Mrs Elizabeth Jones (Rosalys' cousin), Rosalys and Mrs Mavin Shulver (Mrs Jones' daughter); front row: Rosalys' daughters, Stephanie and Charmian.
(REPRODUCED BY KIND PERMISSION OF CHARMIAN SMY.)

and died just three months later, on 16 February 1943, Rosalys and her mother were again devastated by this second tragic loss.

Homersfield

Rosalys and her mother had three months in which to leave the rectory and find other accommodation, so ending a long association between St Cross and her family dating back to 1867. One day, Lady Adair rang and offered them Sunset House in Homersfield. On seeing it, Rosalys decided it was for them. Sunset House, built in 1900, was originally the Flixton Hall estate carpenter's house. Mrs Greswolde-Williams, who had been living there, had died in June 1942, aged 98, and the house had been empty for nearly a year when, in May 1943, Rosalys and her mother moved in. Shortly after, there was a heavy snowfall! The inside walls were a shade of yellow, having been painted with brown distemper, but the rent was £30 a year and the rates were very little. For the first time in her life, Rosalys had neighbours, as there was a cottage next door. Also for the first time, Rosalys had to do the housework and learn to cook, her parents having had servants all her life.

Rosalys continued to work for Henry Debenham – she would make her mum breakfast in the morning and then go off to work. She did mainly manual work, such as chopping out sugar-beet, hoeing and hedging in the winter. Five people were employed, herself, the horseman, the cowman, Mrs Plumb and Freddie the boy, who came straight from school. In harvest and haysel (hay harvest) times they worked as a team and Rosalys loved every minute of it.

There were only a few incidents in St Cross to remind everyone that the war was really happening. Other than rationing, everyday life was rarely directly affected. Rosalys watched a German plane come down in flames near College Farm, where it set a stack on fire. The crew bailed out and were taken prisoner. Once, when she was shopping in Harleston, there was a dog-fight over the town and she rushed to shelter in the back yard of the Magpie. She also had a close shave when, alone except for her dachshund, she was machine-gunned while working in a field of sugar-beet. The pilot came straight at her, and with bullets flying all around, she jumped into a ditch with the dog under her arm. She recalled: 'I was furious, I stood up, shook my fist and shouted at him, how dare he do that to me in my country!'

She did get very run down at one point and went

to stay with friends in Sturminster Newton, Dorset. She cycled to Homersfield, caught the train to London, biked across London, caught another train to Dorset and cycled the last nine miles to her friends. She thoroughly enjoyed the holiday, although it wasn't as peaceful as she might have wished; while there, a German plane fired at people in the town. She saw the plane from her bedroom window and at one point was staring straight at the pilot. The plane went all round the market square but fortunately nobody was hurt.

Her mother would collect sticks in the woods, a pastime in which Rosalys joined. There were no keepers in wartime and they enjoyed having the woods to themselves. Her mother's health gradually deteriorated and like her husband, she had several minor heart attacks before succumbing to a major one. She died on 29 May 1946.

Rosalys had always wanted children and, having never found the right man for herself and having lost all her family, her thoughts turned to adoption. Rosalys named her ten-day-old daughter Stephanie Jane. Nearly two years later she adopted another girl, just seven weeks old, and named her Charmian. Both were baptised in St Cross by Revd Ted Whalley, Rosalys' cousin. She slipped into motherhood easily, and ran the local branch of the Mothers' Union for a number of years. Later in life, Stephanie and Charmian were to make her an 'illegitimate grandmother' (as she put it) seven times over!

When the Adairs died in the years following the war, the majority of estate tenants had the chance to buy the property they were renting. Rosalys bought Sunset House for £1,000 and lived there for 37 years.

St Cross (2)

Rosalys returned to St Cross in 1980, taking up residence with her parrot, Sidney, and later, her labrador, Bracken, in her final home, Innisfree, a bungalow enjoying lovely views over the surrounding fields, and from where St Cross rectory can clearly be seen. At all times of the year she regularly travelled with Bracken to Dunwich, a place she adored, staying at Cliff House for holidays or sometimes just meeting a

Charmian and Stephanie on the step of their mum's home, July 1995.

The plaque in St Cross churchyard in memory of Rosalys.

friend for lunch and an afternoon walk on the heath or in the woods, or to see the snowdrops in February. Blessed with good health, she enjoyed life to the full right to the end. She was so busy that to see her at all required an appointment, and her diary was so full that there was often a wait of two or three weeks.

Her strong faith and endless enthusiasm for the countryside, wild flowers, animals and, above all, life itself, showed no bounds. She entertained the young and the elderly alike, with endless stories from her past. She was one of a dying breed, although dying she certainly wasn't. She always had such a positive outlook and left an indelible impression on those who knew her well. When the end finally came, on 19 July 1995, she was doing what she enjoyed most, walking with friends in the countryside. She wouldn't have wanted it any other way.

A celebration of Rosalys' life was held on 16 August in St Cross. The church was full, and a good number of people had to stand wherever they could find a space. More than 200 attended, such was her

Innisfree, St Cross, Rosalys' last home, taken two days after she passed away in July 1995.

145

popularity. More than ten years after her passing, she is still much talked about and still greatly missed, a compliment in itself to a very remarkable lady. A flagpole and brass plaque at the entrance to the churchyard provide reminders of her life.

Harry Bedborough, a friend, wrote the paragraphs below shortly after Rosalys passed away.

Charmian told me her mother always hoped she would die whilst on one of her walks. St Cross Minster was a special place for Rosalys and I feel extremely privileged that I was with her when she took her last walk. She embodied so many things of which I admire, and I would dearly like to be. On the walk, she stopped, bent down, cupped a tiny little wild flower in her hand, named it, enthused over its beauty and said, 'I do so love wild flowers'. Never once did I find anything about her pretentious. She'd had the background, family, presumably education and that wonderful accent, yet was down to earth and real. Alongside all this earthiness was the most incredible simple faith. Like a schoolgirl really. Also, despite her Victorian clergy background she had learned the lesson of modern life. She seemed to accept fully things like people living together, not being married, divorce and so on, and to declare that it was for the good because if there was anything in it which was wrong we would all see good come from it because that is how God works. Her faith I envy. She was positive that in some place (it was not for her to question where) she would be reunited with all her family and loved ones. I always put so much credence on Rosalys. I feel her very close, not far off – but just out of sight.

She made an impact on my life like no one else. I just cannot believe that all that influence and personality is for nothing. She enriched my life and no doubt will continue to influence what's left of my future. I do consider that there was some kind of irony and privilege also that I took the last earthly walk with her. Me – the most insignificant of her friends. It's become a kind of blessing on my life and a warning not to be so cynical in the future. She was a girl – never an old lady. Working her age back she would have been about 57 when I first met her, but her liveliness, charm and fun never diminished. One could be given many gifts in life – money, property, position etc., but no gift could be more meaningful than having known people like Rosalys.

Harry Bedborough

Harry was born in Twickenham in 1931. He went to school during the Second World War and subsequently had a wide variety of jobs, but the majority of his working life was spent as an undertaker. From a young age, he yearned to move away from suburbia to a cottage in the country. In coming to live in Homersfield, he came from a London back-street to a place he'd never heard of.

When the opportunity arose, he took early retire-

Harry on his tricycle in Lion Road, Twickenham, 1936. He remembers waking up on Christmas Day and seeing the chrome handlebars gleaming by his bed.
(REPRODUCED BY KIND PERMISSION OF HARRY BEDBOROUGH.)

The shop on Christmas Day, 1964.
(REPRODUCED BY KIND PERMISSION OF HARRY BEDBOROUGH.)

The back of the Post Office, Christmas Day, 1964.
(REPRODUCED BY KIND PERMISSION OF HARRY BEDBOROUGH.)

Harry with his mum, c.1965.
(REPRODUCED BY KIND PERMISSION OF HARRY BEDBOROUGH.)

Harry's dog, Flash, c.1965.
(REPRODUCED BY KIND PERMISSION OF HARRY BEDBOROUGH.)

ment and now lives in Derbyshire. He enjoys cooking, socialising and likes to express the way he feels by writing poetry, some of which was published at Christmas 1996 in *The Years Between*. Harry considers his greatest achievement in life to be that of having become a father. Tim was born at the West Norfolk Hospital on 9 February 1966. He and his wife, Yvonne, made Harry a very proud grandfather in July 2001, when grandson Tommy was born.

At the time of writing Harry is 76. He says he has no regrets about life and now sees any hiccups just as part of a very interesting journey. His son, daughter-in-law and grandson still live in Norfolk. When he visits them he still goes with them to Horsey.

He says if he could choose one thing in his life as having been most important to him, it would be having had the good fortune to live to Homersfield;

to have met all those he did meet, and to feel as he does that Norfolk and Suffolk are home.

The words below are entirely Harry's.

My wife and I bought the house opposite Plumtree Cottage in 1964. It was then the shop and Post Office. We were only there for three years yet those three years made more impact on my life than almost anything before or since. I was born in a little run-down back street in London. All I dreamed of as a little boy was one day having a little cottage and shop in the country. I wanted a big garden and when we bought the shop it had two-thirds of an acre. This seemed massive to me. We had room for a dog (Flash) to roam and I suppose all the daft sentimental things which can so often prove impractical.

I remember us passing the removal van on its way to Norfolk. We were in our little Morris 1000 complete with Wimsey the cat. I also remember us singing our heads off – 'On the Road to Mandalay' – as we turned in over the little bridge to Homersfield. We found this rather damp, dirty little house, with brick floor and porch. I don't really know why but the porch was so important to me and I eventually had a 'Lady Sylvia' rose climbing all over it.

The previous shop owner to me was a Mr Cantrell. He did let it all go, house, shop and garden. I suspect that is why I was able to afford to buy it. The owners before him were Mr and Mrs Reynolds, I think. They were very progressive and made it work well. There was a deed or scrappy bits of paper I seem to recall when I bought it. A Mr Gower had renovated it during Victorian times, having bought it rather run down then. We found several Victorian coins in between the bricks on the floor in the sitting room. I used to hear someone walk up the gravel drive at night sometimes and hear a tapping on the window-pane. When I opened the door, there was no one there. I always thought it was Mr Gower, revisiting.

Clare Cottage has hardly changed in a century. I've walked through the same doors, trodden on the same oak doorstep with the crack in it. There was a pump. The excitement of having a brick floor and feeling I had a dwelling which was nothing like any other because mass products had not started. The two modern things were electricity and a phone. Even the phone was old-fashioned.

We thought we were in heaven, but there was much heartache at Clare Cottage – we gave it that name. I was totally in love with it all. It was for me the impossible dream, but not for my wife.

We were able to sell the house in London and buy the cottage and shop outright. Someone sympathetic to cottages lent me £500 to re-stock the shop. A lot of money in 1964. We started broke with a Post Office income of £3.10s. a week and I did a post round for a fiver. I've always been an early bird and that's why I coped so well with the early mornings at Homersfield when I had to be up at 5a.m. to let the two postmen and

Homersfield Post Office, 1965.

(REPRODUCED BY KIND PERMISSION OF HARRY BEDBOROUGH.)

Harry with Rosalys Skene at Calke Abbey, Derbyshire, in 1991.

one postwoman from Wortwell in at 5.30. The shop turnover was £40 a week – £4 to us. So there we were, £12.10s. a week coming in. I took down a wall at the back of the shop and included the store room in the shop area. Working on the premise that what people see, they may buy. I put the Post Office counter up the back and I made this with old bits of oak or mahogany and the grille was made from old brass stair rods. The idea was that when people came for a 2d. stamp they might see something on the way out which they would buy. By the time we closed the shop about two and a half years later our income was £28 per week. We grew much of our own veg and of course shopped in our own shop whenever possible. We introduced frozen foods to the village but by the time we'd bought the fridge and used the electricity there was hardly a profit to be made on that. I did sell postcards, which were rather good ones that were photos my then brother-in-law took for us. We had them done in small quantities to sell in the shop.

Mrs Plumb was my best customer and I got on with her very well. She was the only one who had a regular weekly order. She'd spend 30 bob [shillings]. A lot then. Because of her loyalty I gave her two and a half per cent discount. I used up all the left-over loaves in the shop, stayed up half the night making bread pudding and sold it for half a crown [2s.6d.] a pound. Mrs Plumb used to ask me to save her some. With the fruit and spice, eggs and margarine, sugar and cooking, I doubt if we made a profit. I loved it – the doing of it and the pudding. Much to my surprise so did the girls in the village. I thought they'd all be making their own. But they preferred mine. What a laugh.

I eventually got so hard up I had to wash and collect eggs on that farm which was Rosalys' [Rosalys Skene] childhood vicarage home and then cleaned someone's house. A schoolteacher who lived up the Alburgh Hill somewhere. She paid me four bob an hour and for the egg cleaning I got 3s.6d. an hour. Eventually I took a job on a mushroom farm doing the wages. I think I got about £15 a week over at Eye. The laugh was that I suspect the villagers thought we were rich people from

London. In fact we were probably far less well off than the farm labourers. Hey ho.

Elizabeth Smart, an author, used to come to the shop. My knowledge is not all first hand. She was when I first met her, editor of Queen magazine. One day, one Sunday, a posh car drew up and she and a current man friend came into our garden and asked if we were open. There was no Sunday trading then. She had apparently bought a cottage on a farm near Flixton. She wanted to use it for holidays and weekends. The Dell! She became my best customer when she did come and live there permanently for she would walk around my shop piling everything up and sometimes almost clean me out. I'd have to go to cash and carry the next day because stocks were so low. The current boyfriend usually wrote the cheque. She eventually retired to the cottage and there were sometimes streams of the loveliest-looking young people who came to stay or to visit for the day, presumably from London. She and they looked like hippies or artistic people. She died after I left Homersfield and although I wasn't there, I heard that coachloads of people came to her funeral. She had some beautiful children.

Flash is buried in the garden. It will be in the right-hand corner – which is now next door's garden joining Thorpe House [the Mill House, where Major Thorpe lived]. We wanted Flash as near to the river as we could get him. He used to play there so often.

We had a son, Tim. We are mates, there is no other way of describing our relationship. My wife and I separated and six years later, divorced.

I kept the cottage on and took a job and a flat in Cambridge. I intended to pick up the baby, come home

Harry's son, Tim, daughter-in-law Yvonne and grandson, Tommy, at Dovedale, 2002. (Reproduced by kind permission of Harry Bedborough.)

to Homersfield, re-open the shop and bring Tim up myself. Working from home would have made it easier and Tim, I imagined, would go eventually to the local school. Tim moved in with me when he was 13. We only went our different ways in 1994, when I was made redundant, took early retirement and he bought his little cottage near Wymondham. I came to Derbyshire simply because the houses there were much cheaper and I was able to raise a sum to invest to enable me to live more comfortably. I'd been staying with my son and came to Homersfield to see Nan's [Annie Welton's] grave and say goodbye to her. My move to Homersfield enabled me to appreciate green fields, trees, rivers, wildlife and to link with real life – and being somehow nearer to God.

Sunday mornings, Tim, the dog and I used to go to Dunwich – whatever the weather. In 1971 I moved from Cambridge to a house in College Road, Norwich, near enough to visit Homersfield and it took 15 years before I could do so without crying. Tim and I adopted Horsey in place of Dunwich for our weekend runs.

Despite all the sadness which seemed to come to a head at Homersfield – that village was one of those wonderful interludes in my life which has given me so much depth spiritually. I was only there for three years yet it remains the most significant move I ever made. I still think of it all with very fond memories. I wouldn't have missed it. Homersfield was the place that changed

my life. Coming from the back streets of London to a cottage in the country and a garden (then) said to be two-thirds of an acre. I walked across fields with the dog. Listened to the ghostly wind in Church Wood. In three years we never really made a profit but broke even when selling the property, which in those three years had doubled in price. I hated being postmaster for £3.10s. a week but loved having that tiny shop. Open spaces. That's what I liked most.

We were probably seen as just another couple of brash Londoners who had come and eventually taken away their Post Office. We called the house Clare Cottage because we had a Franciscan connection and decided to call it after St Clare.

The shop closed in 1967 and the people who bought the place from me as a private house were Major and Mrs Gledhill.

Nan and Rosalys both did so much for me, although I've no doubt Rosalys would think nothing of it – just her natural way of living the Christian lifestyle. When Tim was 18, I invited them both to join Tim's friends at a dinner party at the Nelson Hotel in Norwich. I remember trying to say thankyou to Rosalys. She just laughed it off and said something about me being an old smoothy who always said the things I thought people needed to hear! Maybe there is some of that in me, but not so on that occasion. Without her and Nan Welton I just don't know where Tim and I might now be.

The roofs of the white-painted Barnfield Cottages being tidied up in the summer of 1966.

Thatched Cottage in a still unmade Church Lane, 1984. The road was made up within a couple of years.

Large beasts on the green, a common sight in medieval times but unusual nowadays! Note the spelling of a local town – magnificent!

The pump near the shop door at Homersfield Post Office, c.1937.

The official opening of the playing-field, 25 April 1959. (REPRODUCED BY KIND PERMISSION OF CHARMIAN SMY, POSSIBLY A NEWSPAPER PHOTOGRAPH BUT PROVENANCE UNKNOWN.)
1. Mr Les Riches; 2. Janet Riches; 3. Mr Ernest Hadingham; 4. ?; 5. Miss Rosalys Skene and Prudence; 6. Stephanie Skene; 7. Charmian Skene; 8. ?; 9. ?; 10. Dr Dinn; 11. ?; 12. Linda Pointer; 13. Mr Rowland Debenham; 14. Mrs Ruby Burford; 15. Mr Alfred 'Tubby' Lawton; 16. Revd E.P. Whalley; 17. Miss Annie Welton; 18. ?; 19. Judith Cantrell ?; 20. Michael Debenham.

Right: The Iron Room, meeting-place for Homersfield and St Cross residents, founded by Revd W.M. Smith in 1892.

CHAPTER 14

The Twentieth Century and Beyond

POPULATION

The village population can be conveniently ascertained at regular intervals from the national census, which has taken place every ten years since 1801 (with the exception of 1941, when other unwelcome events took priority). The population figures for Homersfield are shown below.

These figures show there were nearly 300 people in Homersfield in 1841, a figure which has not been approached since; within 30 years the population had dropped below 200 and has remained below it to this day. The 40 years after 1841 saw a marked decline in the population, due largely to the introduction of agricultural steam engines. A direct consequence of this was that the number of local employment opportunities fell dramatically and people moved away to seek employment elsewhere, particularly to the cities. For the last 120 years the population has remained reasonably constant, staying within at most a 20 per cent variation of the 1881 figure.

HOUSING AND ROADS

Barnfield Cottages

These six cottages, designed by M. Chesterton, were built in 1922 for retired Flixton estate workers and in around 1961 were bought by Wainford District Council. Numbered 93–98 inclusive, these thatched almshouses present an attractive on entering the village from Harleston or Bungay. The walls, originally painted pink, were white by the mid-1960s and have since returned to their original colour.

Church Lane

The group of four houses built here not long after the Second World War, followed by a further 14 in 1952, are known as Glebe Cottages. Previously there were allotments here. The lane was originally an unmade road and remained so for around 40 years after the

first four dwellings were built, not being finally made up until towards the end of the 1980s.

The Rectory

In relatively recent times, the incumbent of Homersfield also served St Cross and lived in the rectory there. When Homersfield rectory was built in 1948, its first inhabitant was the Revd E.P. Whalley. It is now a private house.

Nos 84–86, The Green

The holdings of the Black Swan included the piece of land opposite. The maltings that was here towards the end of the eighteenth century was later demolished, and by the first decade of the twentieth century it was the pub's bowling green, entered through a well-kept topiary archway. Some decades later the land was gravelled over and a pair of petrol pumps stood on it, part of a motor repair business run by Mr John Bunting ('Bunny' to everyone who knew him) from No. 83. When the business closed down, the land was sold and these three houses, built towards the end of the 1980s, use some of the old Flixton Hall estate numbers.

Others

Additionally other single dwellings have come into being, among them Five Islands on the corner of Church Lane (where Nos 72–73 previously stood), Fishers Green House, Waterloo Farm, Valley Farm (incorporating the much older farmstead), Valley Barn, Walnut Tree Barn, Dove Barn, Home Farm and Mill Cottage.

PRESERVATION

Listed Buildings

The listing of buildings was introduced as a means of

Year	Population	Year	Population	Year	Population	Year	Population
1801	147	1851	248	1901	139	1961	168
1811	153	1861	208	1911	144	1971	170
1821	201	1871	178	1921	143	1981	144
1831	233	1881	144	1931	140	1991	156
1841	291	1891	160	1951	125	2001	163

preserving the country's more important architecture. Those listed as Grade I are the most important structures, Grade II being of lesser importance. There was also a Grade III, but this has been dispensed with. Grade II* structures fall between Grade I and II in significance.

The majority of ancient churches are listed, and in 1953 Homersfield Church was listed Grade II*. Homersfield Bridge, Grade II listed in 1981, was subsequently upgraded to Grade II*.

As well as initial listings made in 1953, a survey undertaken by the Department of the Environment in 1987 resulted in the listing of buildings still current today. Grade II listings apply to No. 74 (Waveney House), No. 77 (St Mary's Cottage), No. 79 (Greenview), No. 80 (Plumtree Cottage), No. 81 (Stable Cottage), No. 82 (Ivy Cottage), No. 83, Wortwell Mill, Wortwell Mill House, Heath Farm and Downs Farm.

The most recent addition is the telephone box, listed Grade II in 1990. The telephone boxes introduced in the early years of the twentieth century resembled wooden sentry boxes. There were numerous other designs and the boxes changed considerably over the years. In 1935 a GPO committee investigated the possibility of mass producing a box for the whole country, the resulting design being introduced the following year. Known as the 'Jubilee' or 'K6', and designed by Sir Charles Gilbert Scott, more than 35,000 had been produced by the Second World War. By far the most successful box, the Jubilee remained in production into the 1960s, and was only superseded in 1968. Standing just over 8ft tall and weighing 13½cwt, the Homersfield box stood at the end of the Post Office garden until it was moved to the green in 1967.

Conservation Areas

In conjunction with the concept of listed buildings, conservation areas were introduced to prevent indiscriminate building and to preserve areas of land. The part of the village where housing is most concentrated, designated a conservation area in 1976, was extended in 1992.

MAINS SERVICES

Water and Sewerage

For hundreds of years water was drawn from wells (excavated down to the water table) in gardens, until eighteenth-century engineers developed a means of pumping water. Initially however, pumps were generally used in towns and were uncommon in rural areas until at least the middle of the following century, and often not until the 1880s.

There were several wells and pumps in Homersfield. Each of the farms had its own, as did

Nos 69, 89/90 (on the playing-field), the Black Swan, Barnfield Cottages and Mill House. The pump for Heath Cottage is still there to this day. Others had the right to draw water from pumps in the village; for example, Nos 77–83 inclusive drew their water from the pump in the garden of Nos 89–90, No. 74 (Waveney House) drew its water from the Mill House pump, while Nos 65 and 70 drew their water from the pump at No. 69.

These pumps were still in use when the Flixton Hall estate was sold in the summer of 1948, but within a few years mains water came to the village, as did mains sewerage, although some houses, where outside toilets remained in use, were not connected to the new sewer until several years later.

Gas

A natural byproduct of coal, gas was in use to light even remote rural parishes by the 1840s, having been introduced around 50 years earlier. It was another 20 years before gas was available for heating water and for cooking. Initially, many gas companies supplied the nation, but by the end of the century most of the smaller ones had amalgamated.

Gas lighting was certainly used in Homersfield, though mains gas did not arrive until well into the second half of the twentieth century.

Electricity

There was electric lighting in some streets and buildings as early as the 1870s. Household lighting developed following the invention of the light bulb in the next decade. Electricity gradually appeared in towns from the 1880s, although it wasn't common in workplaces until at least the 1920s. As usual, rural parishes had to wait rather longer.

Mains electricity came to parishes in north Suffolk over a period of some years; Homersfield was supplied just prior to the Second World War, but other villagers, such as those at St Cross, had to wait for the war to end before they could enjoy its benefits.

FISHING

The River Waveney

The water dividing Norfolk and Suffolk has long been known for the quality of its fishing. The Waveney contains a good variety of fish, primarily roach, chub, dace and pike, with some perch, tench, eel, gudgeon and the occasional trout (one was caught by the author's grandfather in the 1960s). In more recent years 'foreigners' infiltrating the river include the zander and the American crayfish.

Pike Fishing Competition
The Homersfield Pike Fishing Competition was inau-

gurated by a few regular customers of the Black Swan. Its rules require fishing to take place from 10–12a.m. between Homersfield Bridge and Mendham Bridge, the winner being the one who has landed the heaviest pike and returned to the Black Swan by noon. Held every Boxing Day, it first took place in 1995, when the winner was Mr Tim Savile. Though in some years a good many pike have been caught, in others not a single fish has been landed!

The Gravel Pit

The Homersfield gravel pit is to be seen on maps dating from the 1870s. During the Second World War gravel extracted here was used in the construction of local airfields, among them Flixton and Metfield. Later filled with water, it was used initially for water-skiing and by speedboats, and subsequently became a private fishing club. A British record-breaking catfish caught in the lake in 1993 weighed 4 ounces short of 50lbs; the record has since been broken again.

THE VILLAGE HALL, PLAYING-FIELD AND CHURCH

A village hall was mooted a few years after the end of the Second World War. Some while later a committee, chaired by Revd Ted Whalley, was set up, and the chosen site, next to Barnfield Cottages, was given to the village by the landowner. Although the foundations for a hall were laid, it was never built. A building was purchased from Garboldisham, Norfolk, but when no one could be found to erect it at a reasonable price, it was eventually sold.

Instead, a village playing-field came into existence in around 1957, with a Playing Field Association to manage its welfare and the installation of children's equipment. It was officially opened on 25 April 1959 by Dr Dinn, a Harleston GP.

As well as new gates at the church porch in 1971, a pair of wrought-iron gates costing more than £1,000 were installed in the summer of 2003 at the entrance to the churchyard. These gates replaced wooden ones and were the culmination of much work, carried out principally by two residents of the village. The graveyard was improved over a period of more than a year, a car park was created and many trees were

The new gates, installed 2003, in February 2007.

cut back, resulting in the transformation of a dark and overgrown area into a noticeably brighter and tidier one. The new gates were officially opened by the churchwarden, Mr Bill Holdridge.

SIGNS

The Village Sign

The idea of a village sign for Homersfield first came about in 1983. It depicts a Roman centurion standing on the Adair family's bridge, reminders of the Roman artefacts found here and of the village's more recent history – a period of more than 2,000 years. Early in November 1986 the sign was officially unveiled by Mr Ernest Hadingham, the first Homersfield Parish Council chairman and a former resident of Middleton Hall, on the very outskirts of the village. He subsequently became chairman of Wainford Rural District Council.

The official opening of the village sign, November 1986.
1. Mrs Joy Hadingham; 2. Mrs Pansy Riches; 3. Mrs Etheridge; 4. Mrs Ruby Burford; 5. Mr Leslie Burford; 6. Mr Bill Holdridge; 7. Miss Rosalys Skene and Bracken; 8. Mr Lawrence Hammond; 9. Mrs Stephanie Hammond; 10. Mr Les Riches; 11. Alexander Hammond; 12 Toby Hammond; 13. Adam Pretty; 14. Mr Jonathan Riches; 15. Mr Andrew Vickers; 16. Megan Edwards ?; 17. Mrs Betty Gooch; 18. Mr Ernest Hadingham; 19. Samantha Welch; 20. Anna Welch; 21. Mr Leslie Speed; 22. Mrs Julia Speed; 23. Jenny Speed. (© EASTERN DAILY PRESS.)

'River Story', carved by Mark Goldsworthy of Bungay, photographed February 2007.

The Millennium Sign

Waveney District Council commissioned a local man to sculpt the 'River Story' in Homersfield as part of the millennium celebrations. Capturing the feel of the river, his carving of a man in a boat can be seen on top of a large tree trunk when entering the village from the Homersfield to Flixton road. This sculpture was the work of Mark Goldsworthy, who had a studio in Bungay, and the tree from which it was carved was a cedar of Lebanon from the Blickling Hall estate. It was carved in situ, with the medieval name of the village, 'Humersfylde', around its circumference, and Mr Goldsworthy could be seen at work for several weeks in the summer of 2000.

THE COMMUNITY BUS

Homersfield and nearby villages have enjoyed the benefits of a community bus since 1979, when there was little other public transport. Since then, the number of villages covered has doubled from seven to 14. Self-funding, the majority of income is from fares charged, which are the same regardless of one's destination along the route; other income is derived from fund-raising activities. The bus provides a daily service locally, as well as round trips to Norwich and Lowestoft on certain Saturdays during the month.

The Waveney Community Bus is administered by, and driven by, volunteers from the villages concerned, and provides a most useful facility to local parishioners.

THE WOMEN'S INSTITUTE

A branch of this sterling organisation was founded here in 1950 and enjoyed more than 40 years of existence. The members had their last Christmas meal in 1992, shortly after which the Homersfield and St

The taking down of the sycamore tree on the green after it had succumbed to honey fungus, 2001.

A view of the pub and Nos 81–83, 1977. The notices attached to the tree forbid cycling and car parking on the green. (Reproduced by kind permission of Frank Honeywood.)

Cross WI disbanded. At the time of writing, seven of the 12 members still have monthly lunches together.

THE PARISH COUNCIL

The Local Government Act of 1894 was responsible for the introduction of Parish Councils, elected bodies of local administrators responsible for minor matters arising in the parish. Homersfield did not have a Parish Council until more than 60 years later, but had parish meetings from 1910. The initial meeting of Homersfield Parish Council took place at the end of March 1959.

When the author first came to the village, in the summer of 1964, there were three mature trees, two chestnuts and a sycamore, on the green, one at each of its three corners. The Parish Council, deeming one tree dangerous, had it felled in 1975 and replaced it the following year. The sycamore had to be felled in 2001, having succumbed to the deadly honey fungus.

The Parish Council has secured the playing-field and village green for the village. Towards the end of 1998, the council purchased Church Wood, which was officially opened on 12 June the following year.

THE TWO WORLD WARS

It'll be Over by Christmas

When war was declared on 4 August 1914, huge numbers of men joined the Forces, some of them under-age, some regarded as too old. Amid much patriotism, the general feeling among the people of Britain was that a war would have little real effect on their lives and wouldn't last very long, and volunteers across the country were sent off to rousing cheers. People were proved very wrong; Germany eventually surrendered on 11 November 1918, the war having lasted more than four years.

Tragically, three Homersfield men were not to see

Horses taken to water during the First World War.

another Christmas. The names of J.E. Bedwell, J.W. Page and W. Butcher, who all died serving their country, are engraved on the brass lectern in Homersfield Church.

We'll Fight Them on the Beaches

War raised its ugly head again when Germany invaded Poland on 1 September 1939. Two days later Prime Minister Neville Chamberlain famously announced that Britain was at war. Conscription for 20-year-olds had already been introduced, but as a result of the war, all men between the ages of 18 and 41 were eligible to be called up. Many airfields were built in East Anglia, two close to Homersfield, one in the grounds of Flixton Hall and another at Metfield. Britain suffered the worst of the bombing towards the end of autumn 1940 and over the ensuing winter. In October 1940 bombs were dropped nearby at Bungay and in May 1941 high explosive bombs were dropped at the roadside near Homersfield Lodge. Damage was limited to a few trees being uprooted.

The very unpopular measure of double summer time, introduced in March 1942, meant that children were sent to bed with the sun still high in the sky! More bombs fell locally later the same year. Germany again eventually surrendered, Britain having been much helped by American forces, and VE (Victory in Europe) Day was celebrated on 8 May 1945; VJ (Victory in Japan) Day followed three months later, on 15 August 1945.

Fortunately, no one from Homersfield was killed during this war.

COMMUNITY NEWS

After Homersfield Parish Council produced a few newsletters, the *South Elmham Community News* was conceived in the mid-1980s. Residents of Homersfield, Flixton, St Cross, St James, St Margaret and St Peter receive the magazine, which gives details of local parish news and events. Approximately eight issues are produced each year.

Members of RNAS (Royal Naval Air Station) by the Dove during the First World War. This branch was based at Pulham, where the airships known as the 'Pulham Pigs' were made.

Events

Fêtes

Fêtes were taking place in Homersfield in the 1950s and 1960s and included a tug o'war across the river. These were revived in 1995 by Wing Commander Ball and his family, partly to celebrate ten years of their being at the Black Swan.

Celebrations

Homersfield committees arranged over-60s outings and a children's Christmas party during the 1960s, both of which events ran for 21 years. On one occasion there were as many as 60 children at the Christmas party.

The Queen's Silver Jubilee celebrations, on 7 June 1977, included a 'Miss Homersfield' competition (which had been held once or twice before), the winner of which wore the traditional sash. Mugs were presented to all village children under five years old and a great many daffodils were planted on the green.

In the summer of 1995, the fiftieth anniversary of VE Day was celebrated at the Black Swan, those who had served in the war wearing their uniforms for the occasion.

A scarce tree, a chequer (also known as the wild

service), was planted in the centre of the green to mark the millennium. Its bark tends to peel off in rectangular shapes, leaving a chequered effect, hence its name, and in times gone by its berries were eaten as a cure for colic and dysentery. They were also used to make a kind of ale, explaining the chequers pub sign often seen in England.

After a church service on 1 January 2000 a yew tree given by Waveney District Council was planted to mark the millennium.

Her Majesty's Golden Jubilee celebrations, on 3 June 2002, comprised a day of festivities and games on the playing-field; additionally, a number of men dressed as women could be seen playing ball games on the green! Again, ceramic mugs were presented to the village children.

Best Kept Village

This competition, in existence during the 1960s, had become much more widespread two decades later. A bi-annual event, Homersfield was the outright winner in 1987, runner-up in 1989 and winner again two years later. The success was repeated in 1999, the competition then being known as the 'Village of the Year', and Homersfield won yet again in 2003. Trees were planted in the village to mark these successes.

Homersfield village fête under way in the summer of 1967.
(Photo taken by the author's father.)

The tug o'war over the river, 1969.
(Photo taken by the author's father.)

Top and above: *Houses around the green adorned with patriotic flags for Her Majesty the Queen's Golden Jubilee, 3 June 2002.*

Sources

Chapter 1 – Once Upon A Time...
Fairclough, John and Hardy, Mike (2004), *Thornham and the Waveney Valley*.

Chapter 2 – Foreigners
Fairclough, John and Hardy, Mike (2004), *Thornham and the Waveney Valley*.
'Village Appraisal with Stories Relating to Life in Wortwell', material contributed by Mr Michael Hardy, 2002.
Smedley, Norman and Owles, Elizabeth (1960), Proceedings of the Suffolk Institute of Archaeology: vol. 28, pt 2: 'Some Suffolk Kilns: A Romano British Pottery Kiln at Homersfield'.
Smedley, Norman and Owles, Elizabeth (1960), vol. 30, pt 2: 'A Face Mould from the Romano-British Kiln Site at Homersfield'.

Chapter 3 – Domesday is Coming
Morris, John (General Ed.) and Rumble, Alex (Vol. Ed.) (1986), *Domesday Book: Suffolk*, Phillimore & Co

Chapter 4 – Church Matters
NRO DCN 126/5/1: Disagreement between Vincent Freeman and Henry Starlinge, 1641
NRO MC 1842/2: Registration Certificate for Non-conformist Meeting House, Homersfield, John Larke, 1798
SRO(L) 128/A1/10: Homersfield, bills and receipts, James Chappell, 1857
SRO(L) 128/A1/13: Homersfield, bills and receipts, John Brock, 1775
SRO(L) 128/A1/15: Homersfield, bills and receipts, Vino Sacro, 1901
SRO(L) 128/A3/1: Homersfield, Church Vestry Book, 1865–1936
SRO(L) 128/C5/1: Homersfield, Church Terrier, 1801
SRO(L) 128/E1/1: Homersfield, Churchwardens Accounts, 1843–94
SRO(L) 128/E1/2: Homersfield, Churchwardens Accounts, 1748–1843
SRO(L) 128/G6/1: Homersfield, Overseers' Accounts 1838–52
SRO(L) 128/G6/2: Homersfield, Overseers' Accounts 1848–67
SRO(L) 947/A/10/1: Homersfield, Apportionment, 1839
SRO(L) 947/A/10/2: Homersfield, Tithe Map, 1839
Redstone, V.B. (1912), Proceedings of the Suffolk Institute of Archaeology, vol. 14, pt 3: 'South Elmham Deanery'.

Chapter 5 – From Pillar to Post
SRO(L) 128/G3/5: Homersfield, Removal Order for Mary Bullock alias Rust, 1760
SRO(L) 128/G3/6: Homersfield, Removal Order for Thomas Leman, 1762
SRO(L) 128/G4/1: Homersfield, Settlement Examination for Mary Mayes, 1755
SRO(L) 128/G4/2: Homersfield, Settlement Examination for Mary Bullock alias Rust, 1760
SRO(L) 128/G4/3: Homersfield, Settlement Examination for Thomas Leman, 1761
SRO(L) 128/G4/5: Homersfield, Settlement Examination for Mary Jessup, 1764

Chapter 6 – Christmas Day in the Workhouse
SRO(L) 36: Wangford Union collection
SRO(L) 36/AB1/1: Wangford Union Minute-book, 1764–68
SRO(L) 36/AB1/21: Wangford Union Minute-book, 1795–96
SRO(L) 36/AB1/23: Wangford Union Minute-book, 1797–98
SRO(L) 36/AB1/24: Wangford Union Minute-book, 1798–99
SRO(L) 36/AB1/25: Wangford Union Minute-book, 1799–1800
SRO(L) 36/AB1/38: Wangford Union Minute-book, 1815–16
SRO(L) 36/AB1/39: Wangford Union Minute-book, 1816–17
SRO(L) 36/AB1/40: Wangford Union Minute-book, 1817–18
SRO(L): Shipmeadow Bastardy Book, 1770–1823

Chapter 7 – The Big House
SRO(L) 613/1: Roll of Maps of Deanery and Manor of South Elmham, 1838–40
SRO(L) 947/A/1: Flixton Hall estate map, c.1800

Chapter 8 – The Best Days of Our Lives
County directories (various)
SRO(L) 128/M1/1: St Cross, School Managers' Meetings Book, 1895–1936
SRO(L) 128/M3/1: Teacher's Agreement between Sarah Hastings and St Cross National School, 1899
SRO(L) 290/2: Flixton, School Log-book, 1871–1900
SRO(L) 291/1: St Cross, School Accounts Book, 1875–1898
SRO(L) 291/5: St Cross, School Admissions Book, 1876–1936
SRO(L) 291/6: St Cross, School Log-book, 1916–36

Chapter 9 – Only Two Things in Life are Certain....
NRO MF94 Famm 5: Homersfield, will of Thomas Breese, 1709
NRO MF441 Roger 38: Homersfield, will of John Moor[e], 1763
NRO MF490 Traxton 289: Homersfield, will of Edward Cooper, 1841

Chapter 10 – The Three Rs
NRO MEA 8/2: Deepening of the Waveney from Homersfield Mill to Ditchingham Mill, 1756–60
SRO(L) 128/A1/8: Homersfield, bills and receipts, appointment of parish surveyor, 1854
SRO(L) 128/A1/15: Homersfield, bills and receipts, Thomas Smith, constable, 1864
SRO(L) 128/G7/2: Homersfield, Footpaths Notice, 1832
SRO(L) 128/H1/1: Homersfield, Highway Surveyor's Account Book, 1837–46

Chapter 11 – A Victorian Perambulation
Census returns, 1841–1901 inclusive
NRO WKC 1/491: Deed to declare uses of a fine between Vincent Freeman and William Ireland, Homersfield, 1679
SRO(L) 128/A1/7: Homersfield, bills and receipts, Swan Inn, 1853–54
SRO(L) 128/A1/10: Homersfield, bills and receipts, Homersfield Mill, 1857
SRO(L) 128/A1/15: Homersfield, bills and receipts, H.E. Debenham, 1902
SRO(L) 128/G2/1: Homersfield, Poor Rates, 1833
SRO(L) 947/A/10/1: Homersfield, Apportionment, 1839
SRO(L) 947/A/10/2: Homersfield, Tithe Map, 1839
SRO(L) HA12/B1/1/7: Flixton Hall estate papers, Homersfield, ale-house recognisance, 1610
SRO(L) HA12/B4/21/2: Flixton Hall estate papers, Homersfield, Abstract of Title for the Swan, 1828
SRO(L) HA12/G4/2: Flixton Hall Estate Book, 1883
SRO(L) HA12/6864/1: Flixton Hall Estate Book, 1851
SRO(L) HA12/6864/11: Pocket Companion of the Flixton Estate, 1856

Subscribers

Keith Alexander, Denton

The Alexander family, Homersfield

Graham Baldry, formerly Glebe Cotts, Homersfield

Mrs Jennifer Baldry, formerly of Homersfield, Suffolk

Tim Bedborough, Norfolk

Harry Bedborough, Derbyshire

Andy Belcher, Homersfield

D.H. and R. Bird, The Green, Homersfield, Norfolk

Andrew Blakesley, Harleston, Norfolk

Joan Boothby (née Hudson), Earsham

Sandra Buck, Ditchingham

Clive Chenery, Bungay, Suffolk

J.G. Debenahm, Earsham

Ms Debenham, Wortwell

Peter and Rosemary Dingley, Napier, New Zealand

The Dove Restaurant, Homersfield

Durrant, Alburgh, Norfolk

Samuel Earl, Homersfield

Francesca Elizabeth Eaves, The Black Swan

Nicole Samantha Eaves, The Black Swan

Harry and Cath Eaves, The Black Swan

Mrs Ann Fairhead (née Pointer), Bungay, Suffolk

Katherine W. Flint, Harleston, Norfolk

Kevin and Jacqueline Gibbons, 1 Sawmills, Flixton Hall Estate

Cecil Hadingham, Mendham, Suffolk

Audrey R. Hadingham, South Elmham, St James, Suffolk

Lawrie Hammond, Homersfield, Suffolk

Richard Hand, Hockley, Essex

S. Harris, Dereham, Norfolk

Anne Hawley, Michigan, USA

Lilian A. Hinsley, Flixton, Suffolk

Mrs Sheila Holmes, Holly Tree House, Mendham, Suffolk

Mr Peter R. Honywood

Shirley A. Howard (Blakesley), Diss, Norfolk

Mr and Mrs John Howell, Mendham, Suffolk

R.C. Howell, Mettingham

John and Julia Hunt, Heath Farmhouse

Robert E. Hunter, Fressingfield, Suffolk

Mr and Mrs G. Jaye, Barnfield Cottages, Homersfield

Richard W. Jones, Kelsale, Suffolk

Eric King, Bungay, Suffolk

Edward Leggett, Bungay, Suffolk

Harold, Brenda, Alec, Ted, Neville and Brian Leggett, formerly of The Green, Homersfield

R. Limebear, Church Lane, Homersfield, Norfolk

Sir Laurie and Lady Magnus, Bungay, Suffolk

Brenda Meachen (née Wallace), Leigh-on-Sea, Essex

John and Jean Neale, Rumburgh, Suffolk

Mrs I.L. Palmer, Essex

Mr and Mrs F.K. Palmer, Essex

Mrs Ivy Parsons, Flixton, Suffolk

Lloyd and Janet Phillips, Waveney Cottage, Homersfield

Stephen M. Plumb, Beccles, Suffolk

Keston M. Plumb, Beccles, Suffolk

Malcolm M. Plumb, Beccles, Suffolk

E. Plumb, Homersfield, Suffolk

Mr Roy Pointer, Bungay, Suffolk

Mr and Mrs T. Pointer, Homersfield

Diane and Sarah Poppy, Stoke Ash, Suffolk

James Pulford, Harleston, Norfolk

Mary M. Rackham, Leicester

Helen Raynor, Eastwood Junior School

Maurice A. Reeve, Lowestoft (Homersfield 1940-1948)

Captain and Mrs David Rice, Sunset House, Flixton Hall Estate

Mr and Mrs C.H. Richards

Hilda Poppy Rowe, Kelsale, Suffolk

Charmian Smy, Hacheston, Suffolk

Deborah Snook, Leigh-on-Sea, Essex

Stable Cottage, Homersfield

Mr and Mrs R.H.F. Stanton, Bungay, Suffolk

Stephanie Starck (née Mackie), Homersfield

Elizabeth Starling, Swaffham, Norfolk

Joan Stevens, Leigh-on-Sea, Essex

Jill Stevens, Cratfield, Suffolk

Mrs J Stone, Barnfield Cottages, Homersfield, Norfolk

Thomas family of Denton and Wortwell

F.J. Thompson, Yoxford, Suffolk

Rev. Richard Thornburgh (Rector)

John Thurston, Homersfield, Suffolk

Judith M. Turner, Emsworth, Hants

Bernard J.W. Wallace, Thundersley, Essex

John F.W. Walling, Newton Abbot, Devon

John and Jo Westgate, Homersfield, Suffolk

Robin and Karin Whalley, Cwm Oergwm, Breconshire

Charles C. Whipps